ADDICTION

FROM BIOLOGY TO DRUG POLICY

ADDICTION

FROM BIOLOGY TO DRUG POLICY

AVRAM GOLDSTEIN, M.D.

W. H. FREEMAN AND COMPANY
NEW YORK

Library of Congress Cataloging-in-Publication Data

Goldstein, Avram.
  Addiction: from biology to drug policy / Avram Goldstein.
      p.   cm.
  Includes bibliographical references and index.
  ISBN 0-7167-2384-0
  1. Drug abuse—Physiological aspects.   2. Drug abuse—Social
aspects.   I. Title.
  RC564.G66 1994
  616.86—dc20   93-14243
                                                                CIP

Printed in the United States of America

1 2 3 4 5 6 7 8 9 0 VB 9 9 8 7 6 5 4 3

To

Vincent P. Dole
John T. Edsall
Hans W. Kosterlitz

For Their Influence in Shaping My Career

Contents

Contents

CONTENTS

CONTENTS

Preface

This book grew out of my experiences during 25 years of laboratory and clinical research and teaching about the addictive drugs. The more I learned, and the more drug addiction became a subject of national concern, the more I realized how great was the gap between our growing scientific knowledge and the ever more heated debates about drug policy. A book directed primarily at intelligent nonexperts might close this gap by translating what scientists have discovered about drug addiction into easily understood concepts. I believe it will be of interest, too, to students and practitioners of medicine, psychiatry, nursing, pharmacy, and other health professions, who deal with addicts as part of their daily work. Finally, it will provide teachers with solid factual information to help educate a new generation about this much-neglected societal problem.

The subject of drug addiction can be divided into three broad areas—how the drugs act on the brain, how each drug causes the medical disorder we call addiction, and what impact the addictive drugs have on society. Accordingly, the book is divided into three parts. I attempt to explain what we know about drug addiction in each of these three areas, how we know what we know, and what we can (and can not) do about the drug problem.

I present the uncertainties of our present knowledge as well as the surely established facts. I avoid technical jargon; but where a technical term is essential, I define it at first use and also provide a reference to that definition in the Index. I try to make the biomedical science interesting to the nonexpert by speaking whenever possible from my own point of view as experimenter and by attempting to convey the spirit of adventure as the scientist experiences it. When I write auto-biographically, therefore, it is not to claim undue credit for research advances to which so many others, the world over, have contributed. And when I describe how the experiments are actually done, it is to help the reader follow the logic of the conclusions.

Many people and institutions contributed to this book. Stipend support for the writing was provided by the former Board of Directors of the Addiction Research Foundation of Palo Alto: Jean Kuhn Doyle, Herbert Dwight, Henry Organ, Martin Packard, Charles Schulz, and Brooks Walker, Jr.; I am deeply indebted to them all. With the help of Robert J. Glaser a grant was obtained from the Henry J. Kaiser Family Foundation to defray research expenses. The Albuquerque heroin addiction follow-up study described in Chapter 11 was made possible through the generosity of the Carnegie Corporation of New York and its president, David A. Hamburg.

I owe a special debt of gratitude to Harold Kalant, who has been a valuable colleague over the years, who contributed much to my ideas on the pharmacology and sociology of the addictive drugs, and who offered helpful advice about the manuscript. Robert L. Campos has been an important source of information and assistance from the days of my first involvement in the treatment of heroin addicts. And for lively disagreements that helped sharpen my thinking about drug policy issues I am indebted to Ethan Nadelmann.

My scientific associates at the Addiction Research Foundation of Palo Alto who participated in most of my own investigations described here include Brian M. Cox, Priscilla Grevert, Barbara Judson, and Louise I. Lowney. Abbie Freiley was the skillful administrator of all the Foundation's efforts.

I am indebted to many people in Albuquerque. At the University of New Mexico are James Herrera, David Broudy, Marcia Starr, Walter Winslow, Al Vogel, Philip J. May, and Patricia McFeeley. Indispensable help in tracking subjects at the clinics and in the community was provided by Angie Barchus, Abigail Brooks, Steven R. Campos, Frank Fernandez, the late Paul Garcia, Ted Hicks, Marion Saxton, and Joseph Tartaglia. Special thanks are due Robert Kahn for arranging access to the Monroe Clinic.

For their generous assistance and hospitality during my study visit in the U.K. I thank especially Griffith Edwards, Martin Mitcheson, Michael Russell, and John Shanks; for similar help in the Netherlands,

Eddy Engelsman (who also commented on a draft of Chapter 17), Charles Kaplan, and Govert van de Wijngaart; and in Zurich, Aurelio Pasi. Several others who were helpful are mentioned by name in Chapter 17.

Finally, I thank my colleagues Dora B. Goldstein, Mary Jeanne Kreek, and Roger E. Meyer for their helpful comments on an earlier draft of the manuscript; and my publishers, W. H. Freeman and Company, especially senior editor Jonathan Cobb, project editor Janet Tannenbaum, and copy editor Denis Cullinan, for criticism, suggestions, and expert assistance in bringing the book to publication.

AVRAM GOLDSTEIN, M.D.
Stanford, California
August 1993

ADDICTION

FROM BIOLOGY TO DRUG POLICY

CHAPTER 1

Introduction

A 50-year-old man lies in a hospital bed, desperately ill. Emphysema has destroyed his lungs, and the pitiful sound of his labored breathing fills the room. Watch him! Incredible as it seems, he begs his wife to bring him some cigarettes. Cigarettes put him here, cigarettes will surely finish him off. Why doesn't he quit? Why didn't he quit 25 years ago, when the first Surgeon General's report on smoking, widely publicized, had already made it clear what his future would be if he continued his pack-a-day habit?

This introduction could have started differently.

A 50-year-old man gets off the bus in a seedy downtown neighborhood. Just hours before, he was released after serving a two-year sentence for burglary, his third time in prison. His regular income as a grocery clerk had barely been enough to support his wife and child, so burglary seemed the only way to raise the large sums he needed for his heroin habit. Watch him! Only a block from the bus terminal, he makes his "connection," buys a syringe and needle and some white powder. Heroin put him in prison three times, heroin will surely finish him off. Why doesn't he quit? Why didn't he quit 25 years ago, when he could see clearly enough what his future would be if he continued using heroin?

TRUTHS AND FALSEHOODS
ABOUT ADDICTION

Why did I choose to begin with an opening paragraph about nicotine addiction rather than about heroin addiction? Our society makes artificial distinctions among addictive drugs, fostering the false impression that because nicotine and alcohol are legal, they must somehow be less dangerous and less addictive than the illicit drugs. Even the way we use (or don't use) the term *addiction* compounds this error. Addicts, we are accustomed to thinking, belong to an underclass; the word brings to mind street people, "junkies," ethnic minorities in the inner cities. For white middle-class folk in the suburbs, we are accustomed to using soft words to describe their "habits," not their addictions. We call them "heavy smokers," not nicotine addicts; "heavy drinkers" or perhaps "alcoholics," not alcohol addicts; "heavy coffee drinkers," not caffeine addicts. And even though many heroin and cocaine users are middle-class professionals, that image seldom comes to mind when we think about heroin or cocaine addiction.*

Curiously, nicotine and alcohol and caffeine, in common parlance and political rhetoric, are often not even called "drugs" and they are rarely included in the recurring "war on drugs." The frequent use of phrases like "alcohol *and* drugs" or "tobacco *and* drugs" reinforces this idea. The objection to these phrases is not a matter of mere semantics; incorrect use of language shapes and reinforces incorrect ways of thinking. There is in fact no basis in biomedical science for setting aside the legal addictive drugs as different from the others.

A *drug* is any chemical agent that affects biologic function. Drugs are typically used to treat or prevent disease. Some drugs act in the brain, some in other organs, and some in several parts of the body at the same time. A *psychotropic drug* is one that acts in the brain to alter mood, thought processes, or behavior. Nothing about drugs as such, even psychotropic drugs, makes people like them or try to secure them. On the contrary, when physicians prescribe drugs, a major difficulty is getting patients to take them regularly. This so-called "com-

---

* *Addiction* is not a term officially accepted by the psychiatric community (see DSM-III-R and ICD-10 under Suggestions for Further Reading). I find it appropriate for this book, nonetheless, because it is well established in the language and its meaning is clear.

pliance problem" is just as troublesome with many psychotropic drugs (such as those used to treat mental illnesses) as with drugs of other kinds. Among all psychotropic drugs, however, there is something special about a very few. These *addictive drugs* are defined by the fact that they typically are *self-administered*, without medical prescription—repeatedly, compulsively, even self-destructively.

Once regarded with sympathy as an unfortunate disease, drug addiction in the United States was seen increasingly during the present century as a morally reprehensible sort of behavior, which addicts could control if only they made the effort. This book argues that drug addiction—although it is often associated with crime—is primarily a public-health problem. Addictive drugs pose dangers to the health of users, and they threaten nonusers as well. Like all public-health problems, addiction is a complex one, with multiple causes, multiple prevention strategies, and multiple cures.

THE SEVEN DRUG FAMILIES

To speak of "the drug problem" is to miss the point. The addictive drugs fall into seven families, which differ from one another in chemistry, in effects on behavior, in long-term toxicity, and in the likelihood of a compulsive use pattern developing. Each affects brain chemistry differently. Some drugs—alcohol is an example—disturb behavior in a way that threatens the safety of others, even when used occasionally and nonaddictively. Other drugs—nicotine in tobacco smoke is an example—are primarily dangerous to the health of the user, but have no adverse effect on the user's behavior. Still other drugs—heroin is an example—are dangerous mainly for their powerful addictive quality, while their direct behavioral effects are largely limited to quieting and calming the users themselves. Thus, the features that distinguish the seven drug families have obvious implications for prevention, for treatment, and for social policy. To think rationally about drug policy, we need to understand the characteristic effects of various drugs by learning everything we can about how each modifies brain function and how each contributes to the public-health problem we call drug addiction.

1. *Nicotine.* The active principle in the tobacco leaf, this drug may be taken into the body not only by smoking (typically

cigarettes) but also by absorption through the membranes of the mouth or nose when tobacco is chewed or used as snuff.

2. Alcohol and related drugs. In addition to beer, wine, and the distilled liquors, the alcohol family also includes the barbiturates and benzodiazepines (e.g., Valium), which have legitimate uses in medicine—barbiturates for surgical anesthesia and the treatment of epilepsy, benzodiazepines for relief of anxiety and sometimes of insomnia. In the alcohol family, too, because their pharmacology is similar, are the volatile solvents, which are taken by inhalation, illicitly, as in glue sniffing.

3. The Opiates. This family contains the products of opium poppies, principally crude opium, morphine, and codeine. Heroin (the overwhelming favorite) is prepared from morphine by chemical treatment. Codeine and several synthetic opiate painkillers (e.g., Dilaudid, Demerol) are used by some opiate addicts. Heroin is typically administered by vein; but, like crude opium, it may also be smoked. The other opiates are usually taken by mouth. Many opiates are legitimately prescribed as strong pain-relieving medications, but heroin is prohibited in the United States.

4. Cocaine and Amphetamines. Cocaine is the active principle of the coca leaf. There are two chemical forms of cocaine, called *hydrochloride salt* and *free base.* ("Free base" means a compound that has not been neutralized by an acid to make a salt.) The hydrochloride salt dissolves in water and can be taken by vein or in the nose ("snorted"). The free base ("crack") is smoked. Amphetamines are made in the laboratory. Their salts, like cocaine hydrochloride, dissolve readily and can be taken by vein or by mouth. A pure form of one amphetamine (methamphetamine, or "ice") is not destroyed by heat, so it can be smoked. The biologic effects of cocaine and the amphetamines are very similar. Both have certain approved uses in medicine (cocaine, for example, is a very effective local anesthetic agent for the eyes, nasal passages, mouth, or throat), but otherwise their use is illegal.

5. Cannabis (marijuana, hashish, THC). Marijuana is the leaf of the hemp (cannabis) plant; hashish is a concentrated cannabis resin. THC (tetrahydrocannabinol) is the pure active principle in cannabis and is responsible for its biologic effects. Marijuana and hashish are smoked, sometimes taken by mouth. THC is almost exclusively a research tool. Cannabis products are not legally available, but there is a limited exception for experimental medical treatment of glaucoma and of nausea associated with chemotherapy.

6. Caffeine. Caffeine is the active principle in coffee beans and tea leaves. It is also present as an additive in soft drinks and some over-the-counter medications.

7. The Hallucinogens. This is a diverse family that includes many naturally occurring and synthetic compounds with similar mind-altering effects. Among the natural products are various "magic mushrooms" (containing psilocybin and other active principles), cactus (containing mescaline), and a variety of exotic substances used ceremonially in native cultures throughout the world. Among the synthetics are LSD (lysergic acid diethylamide), MDMA ("ecstasy"), and PCP (phencyclidine, or "angel dust"). These substances are all typically taken by mouth. There was a time, in the sixties, when hallucinogens were used experimentally by some psychiatrists, but they are no longer legally available.

ADDICTION AS A PUBLIC HEALTH PROBLEM

The extent of the use of addictive drugs is illustrated in Figure 1.1, which shows the number of people who used each of them at least weekly* (heroin at least once in the past year) in the United States in

---

* The purpose of adopting the "at least weekly" criterion is to exclude casual users, who contribute only insignificantly (if at all) to the problem. Daily use might seem an even better indicator of problem use, but this depends on the specific drug. For example, daily use of heroin is certainly an indication of serious addiction, but daily use of alcohol will include a large number of casual users who may only take a beer or a glass of wine every day in a social context. Problem use of alcohol would be better indicated by amount consumed weekly, not shown in these data. Thus, Figure 1.1, which compares all the addictive drugs, can only give an approximate picture, which may be misleading unless interpreted in the light of what we know about use patterns for each drug.

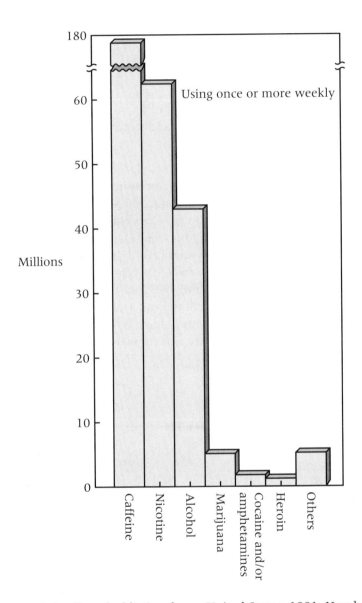

FIGURE 1.1 Use of addictive drugs, United States, 1991. Numbers of people, in millions, who used each drug at least weekly (heroin use at least once in past year). "Others" includes inhalants and hallucinogens. [Data from *National Household Survey on Drug Abuse*, U.S. Department of Health and Human Services, Public Health Service, Alcohol, Drug Abuse, and Mental Health Administration, DHHS Publication No. (ADM) 92-1887, Washington DC, 1992.]

1991. The estimates are based on the *National Household Survey on Drug Abuse*—a study of a random sample of people in all kinds of residential circumstances, representing a total population of 203 million over the age of 11.

An amazing number of difficulties interfere with obtaining good estimates of the extent of the drug problem. Omitted from the survey, for example, are homeless people not in shelters, whose number (the subject of uncertainty and controversy) is at least 300,000 and possibly much greater; many of these transients are known to be drug addicts. Another uncertainty is whether all householders—no matter how skilled were the interviewers—would have been likely to reveal all the facts, especially about the illicit drugs.

At the left of Figure 1.1 we see that caffeine use is nearly universal; furthermore, although the data relate to a frequency of use of at least once a week, nearly the same number of people use it daily as weekly. Moderate intake of caffeine, as far as our present knowledge indicates, is probably not harmful to adults. However, even very young children consume caffeine in soft drinks, and this is giving rise to concern among some medical authorities in view of our lack of information about possible effects of prolonged high caffeine intake on brain development.

Nicotine and alcohol are the next most widely used addictive drugs. Unlike caffeine, these two substances cause enormous harm, as measured by death and disability. The number shown for nicotine includes both smoked and smokeless tobacco. The nature of nicotine addiction is such that almost all tobacco users are daily users. Among those who use alcohol weekly, however, are many truly casual users, who are not addicts at all; nevertheless, even occasional use of alcohol can cause serious problems for society on account of intoxication. Of the 43 million users indicated here it is estimated variously that between 10 and 15 million are truly addicted, with their lives seriously disrupted by alcohol.* We can see at a glance that the total number who use nicotine or alcohol regularly is far greater than the number

---

* C. Everett Koop, as Surgeon General, gave an even higher figure: "An estimated 18 million adult Americans have medical, social and personal problems directly related to the use of alcohol, as do several million adolescents for whom alcohol is an illegal drug."

who use marijuana, cocaine (and/or amphetamines), heroin, and "all others" (including volatile solvents and hallucinogens) combined. To point out this fact is not to minimize the importance of the illicit drugs, but to set all the drugs, licit as well as illicit, in a public-health context.

Not included in the illustration is the number who used "any illicit drug in the past week"—13 million people, three-quarters of whom used marijuana. Each of the principal illicit drugs—cannabis, heroin, cocaine and amphetamines, and hallucinogens—has an added impact on the user's health and on society because of the combination of illicit status and intensity of addiction. This is seen most strikingly with cocaine, amphetamines, and heroin; addicts to these drugs may often place their uncontrollable desire for the drug above all other needs. They may neglect nutrition and gainful employment while they devote inordinate amounts of time to criminal activity related to drug-seeking behavior.

To understand the public-health implications of the use of addictive drugs one needs to know more than just the number of users. One wants to know how many of them were harmed by the drugs. Systematic collection of data from hospital emergency rooms all over the United States (the Drug Abuse Warning Network, "DAWN") yields information about the most serious harmful effects of addictive drugs, but of course not all who suffer adverse effects come to an emergency room. The most useful information about the extent of harmful effects can be gleaned from data collected by the National Institute of Mental Health (see Table 1.1). Thousands of people were sampled randomly in five communities—Epidemiologic Catchment Areas (ECA)—from 1980 to 1984. The questionnaires included items about a broad range of mental-health disorders including drug addiction. A "substance abuse disorder" is a diagnostic category that reveals not only that a drug was used, but also whether that use led to significant harm: the table shows what fraction of the total population had ever suffered from such a disorder. Although there are some differences, the numbers tell the same story on the whole as Figure 1.1. Nicotine and alcohol remain the principal problems by a large margin. The exceptionally small number for cocaine is in doubt because the diagnostic criteria at the time did not include the concept of cocaine dependence, and also because the present epidemic of cocaine use (including crack) was just getting under way.

TABLE 1.1 Lifetime prevalence of drug abuse/dependence disorders in total population (1980–1984), Epidemiologic Catchment Areas (ECA) sample of 19,417 persons.

Nicotine	36.0%
Alcohol	13.8%
Any other drug	6.2%
Marijuana	4.4%
Cocaine	0.2%
Amphetamines and other stimulants	1.7%
Opiates	0.7%
Hallucinogens	0.4%
Sedatives	1.2%

[Adapted from Table 4 in D. B. Kandel: "Edipemiological Trends and Implications for Understanding the Nature of Addiction," Chapter 2 in C. P. O'Brien and J. H. Jaffe, eds. *Addictive States*, Vol. 70 (Research Publications, Association for Research in Nervous and Mental Disease, Raven Press, New York, 1992]

ADDICTION AS AN INFECTIOUS DISEASE

The drug addictions are in many ways like infectious diseases. A virus or bacterium infects some people but not everyone; there are differing degrees of relative immunity. Susceptibility (as for instance to tuberculosis) depends typically on a complex set of genetic and environmental factors, among them ethnicity, degree of crowding and lack of sanitation, status of the immune system, and adequacy of nutrition. People carrying an infectious agent can transmit the disease to susceptible uninfected people. An infectious disease is spread most readily by people who have just caught it, and so it is with drug addiction; it is primarily new users who transmit the behavior to their peers.

Through public-health measures, enforced by law, we try to eradicate infectious agents; this is analogous to attempts to control drug supply. At the same time we provide for education about the kinds of behavior and lifestyles that expose people to infection or that reduce their immunity. We try to improve people's resistance in many ways, for example by vaccination. Finally, we offer treatment to all who are infected, not only to alleviate the illness (or cure it if possible), but also to reduce the total pool of infection in order to limit the spread of the epidemic.

Some will object that the analogy to infectious disease is false because people are passive victims of infectious disease, whereas they actively seek out addictive drugs. But this distinction breaks down when one looks at specifics. In both situations human behavior is responsible, at least in part. There are risk takers who recklessly drink unsterilized water in areas where hepatitis or cholera or water-borne parasites are endemic. There are people who fail to use mosquito netting or other forms of protection against insects where malaria or encephalitis are prevalent. There are individuals who contribute to the AIDS epidemic by having promiscuous sexual contacts without taking elementary precautions. Are those behaviors, which contribute to the spread of infectious diseases, really different in principle from that of pack-a-day cigarette smokers who will not try to quit, despite all the evidence of physical harm to themselves and their families?

Each infectious disease is different. The unique characteristics of each one have to be understood before methods of prevention or treatment can be implemented. In every case, policy must rest on a firm basis in biomedical science. Likewise, each addictive drug has its own characteristics, its own mode of action in the brain, its own pattern of biologic effects—severity of the addiction, changes in behavior affecting the user and others, harmfulness to health, long-term toxicity.

Many simplistic solutions to our drug addiction problem have been put forward. At one extreme are those who want to step up the "war on drugs." They argue for stronger law enforcement to try to eliminate all the illicit drugs. This position typically sees only that small part of the drug problem that concerns the illicit drugs. At the other extreme is a libertarian stance, held by those who would legalize all drugs, claiming that the drug problem is due primarily to the prohibitions rather than to the drugs themselves. A moderate position seeks policies that balance the harm caused by the drugs against the harm caused by their regulation. To formulate that position in specific detail is the purpose of this book. It requires a thorough analysis of their properties, drug by drug—how each one acts, and what harm it does to users and to society.

The misery suffered by addicts and their families is incalculable. The costs to society are also enormous, due to loss of productivity, additional requirements for medical care, dangers of drug-induced behaviors, and burden on the criminal-justice system. If we set aside political bombast, media sensationalism, and ill-informed calls for quick fixes, we can try, calmly and dispassionately, to examine what the various scientific disciplines can teach us about addictive drugs and addictive behavior.

WHAT DOES THE AUTHOR KNOW, AND HOW DOES HE KNOW IT?

The reader of a book that claims to impart authoritative information is entitled to know something about the author's qualifications. I am a pharmacologist, a neurobiologist, and a physician. *Pharmacology* is the scientific study of drugs and their uses in medicine; it should not be confused with pharmacy, the preparation and dispensing of drugs. In an academic career spanning 45 years, mostly at Stanford University, I studied, carried out experimental research on, and taught about addictive drugs. I focused especially on the opiates (morphine, heroin, methadone) and on nicotine and caffeine. My interest in opiate addiction led me to fundamental laboratory research on the brain receptors that are responsible for the drugs' effects. In the course of that research my colleagues and I discovered the dynorphins—one of the three families of naturally occurring morphinelike peptides, which are commonly called endorphins.

I organized the first major methadone program in California, and I supervised the treatment of more than a thousand heroin addicts in San Jose and other communities in Santa Clara County. By means of rigorously controlled clinical trials, my colleagues and I were able to learn and publish a great deal about the most effective methods of treatment and rehabilitation. I founded and directed the Addiction Research Foundation in Palo Alto, where I gathered a staff of talented investigators for basic neurobiology research at the laboratory bench, for research with normal human volunteers, and for clinical treatment research with heroin addicts.

In Part One of this book (Addictive Drugs and the Brain), I explain what we know about the biology of the drug addictions, and how we know it. How do the addictive drugs act on the brain, and how do they affect behavior? What is there about this particular group of drugs that makes them so powerfully seductive?

In Part Two (The Drugs and the Addicts), I discuss the medical and psychologic features of each drug addiction. How do people fall into the addiction trap? What effects, positive as well as harmful, does each family of addictive drugs have on the people who use them, and what dangers do they pose for society? What special hazards (such as the transmission of AIDS and other infections) arise from intravenous drug use? Are there long-term consequences of drug addiction, such as brain damage? What are the special dangers to the unborn? What treatments are available, and how successful are they? Can addicts ever really put their addiction behind them?

In Part Three (Drugs and Society), I consider some of the history, sociology, and politics of the drug problem. The use of drugs to alter mood and behavior is not unique to our times; it may be as old as human civilization. But is it more widespread or more severe today than in the past? Is there really a "drug epidemic," or are the news media creating an exaggerated impression? With what success have some other countries dealt with their drug problems? What methods of prevention education have been tried, and how effective have they been? How do harsh control measures (as have been employed often in some countries and occasionally in our own) compare with gentler ones? Finally, I present my own thoughts about drug policy for the nation—about how to reduce the harm caused by addictive drugs to people and society, while at the same time keeping to a minimum the harm caused by governmental intrusions and punitive sanctions.

If you know that a certain addictive drug may give you temporary pleasure but will, in the long run, kill you, damage your health seriously, cause harm to others, and bring you into conflict with the law, the rational response would be to avoid that drug. Why, then, do we have a drug addiction problem at all? In our information-rich society, no addict can claim ignorance of the consequences. Is it just perverse risk-taking, then, that makes some people ignore the hazards and use addictive drugs? Or have our efforts at education been inadequate to inform people sufficiently about the dangers? Is there an "addictive personality," which makes certain people especially vulnerable, while others can use the same drugs without losing control?

Drug addiction starts with the brain's being exposed to a particular substance belonging to one of the seven families of addictive drugs. To understand how that exposure affects behavior and why it leads to compulsive use, we first need to learn something about brain chemistry and how it is altered by each of the addictive drugs. That is the subject of the next three chapters.

PART ONE

Addictive Drugs and the Brain

CHAPTER 2

The Brain's Own Drugs

Roger Whitcomb* is absent from the office this afternoon. Unable to wait until evening, he has quit work and rushed home, the craving nagging at him relentlessly. He is missing important business, but no business is as important to him as what he is about to do. Sitting on a soft easy chair, he places a pellet of crack cocaine in the bowl of a little pipe. He trembles with anticipation as he lights it and inhales deeply. A few seconds later he feels it "hit." An overwhelming sense of alertness, of power, of deep satisfaction sweeps over him.

How can a chemical in smoke transform a person's behavior so dramatically? How can it become so important to Roger and people like him? What does the cocaine do to his brain? As we shall see, not only cocaine but every addictive drug works by mimicking or blocking one of the substances that *neurons* (nerve cells) in the brain use to communicate with each other. These substances, called *neurotransmitters*, are key to understanding how addictive drugs can produce such powerful effects.

Recalling that a *drug* is any chemical agent that affects biologic function, we may say that our bodies make drugs of their own. For

---

* Names associated with case histories in this book are fictitious.

example, insulin is produced by the pancreas and stimulates cell metabolism in other tissues; insulin can also be administered as a therapeutic agent when the natural supply is deficient. In this same category are other hormones such as growth hormone, thyroid hormone, sex steroids, and substances like interferon and the interleukins, which regulate the immune system. In this category, too, are the neurotransmitters, which are released from neurons to act on other neurons or on muscles or glands. When you walk, for example, nerves in your leg tell each muscle when to contract by releasing a neurotransmitter, acetylcholine, directly onto that muscle. The acetylcholine is a chemical trigger which activates the machinery that causes the muscle fibers to shorten, thus exerting the force that moves your leg. When you are frightened, your adrenal gland releases a hormone, epinephrine (adrenaline), which circulates in the blood and acts on your heart to make it beat faster. When you salivate in anticipation of tasty food, it is because nerves release neurotransmitters onto your salivary glands.

All human behavior has a biologic basis in the workings of the brain. The "hardware" of the brain consists of the thousand billion neurons with their amazingly complex network of interconnections, the neurotransmitters they manufacture, and the specialized apparatus on which each of those neurotransmitters acts. All this hardware develops according to the genetic blueprints in the DNA of our genes. The "software" consists of the memories, learning, and conditioning that reflect life's experiences from birth to death. Behavior is the traditional field of psychologists and psychiatrists, who once viewed drug addiction as purely a maladaptation to life's stresses. However, because the brain is a chemical organ, the software, as well as the hardware, operates through brain chemistry. Thus, even psychologic disorders must arise, ultimately, through chemical changes. It is not a question of psychology *versus* biology; on the contrary, in the final analysis (but our present knowledge falls far short) psychology *is* biology.

CHEMICAL TRANSMISSION

The origins of our modern understanding of chemical transmission in the brain can be traced to the middle of the last century, to France. Explorers had brought back from South America an arrow poison called *curare*, which natives smeared on their blow-gun darts to paralyze prey. Claude Bernard, who is today regarded as the father of pharmacology, used frogs to study how curare paralyzes. When he applied a mild electric shock to a nerve in the frog's leg, the leg muscle contracted; but if he had first injected the frog with curare, it did not. Either the electrical signal was not reaching the muscle, or the muscle itself was not responding to it. Which alternative was true? Bernard soaked the nerve in a curare solution, without exposing the muscle to the poison. No paralysis resulted, so it seemed that curare must paralyze muscle directly. To his great surprise, however, when he reversed the conditions, soaking the muscle (but not the nerve) in curare, and then shocked the muscle directly (not through the nerve), it contracted normally, even though it would not respond to nerve stimulation. Bernard was forced to conclude that curare acted neither on nerve nor on muscle but somehow at the place where nerve endings contacted muscle tissue (see Figure 2.1A). Today we know there is actually a specialized structure there, the *neuromuscular junction* (shown as a shaded area in the figure).

In 1909, at the University of Cambridge, England, J. N. Langley discovered that nicotine, applied directly to the neuromuscular junction, made the muscle contract; remarkably, this action of nicotine could be prevented by curare. No nerves were needed; even if they were destroyed, nicotine made the muscle contract, and curare prevented the nicotine action (Figure 2.1B). The fact that curare could

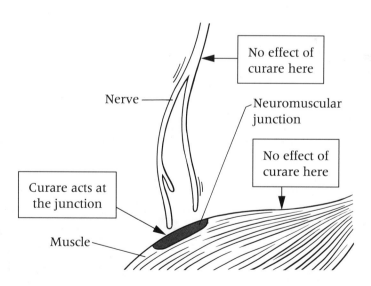

No effect of curare here

Nerve

Neuromuscular junction

No effect of curare here

Curare acts at the junction

Muscle

FIGURE 2.1A Historic experiments on neurotransmitters and receptors. Bernard's experiment.

block both nerve impulses and nicotine suggested to Langley that a nerve might normally stimulate muscle by releasing a chemical like nicotine, which would act on the neuromuscular junction and cause the muscle to contract. Since various other substances did not cause muscle contraction, he also had to suppose that the neuromuscular junction contained some kind of specialized material upon which nicotine, as well as the substance released by nerves—but not other substances—would act. Langley called this hypothetical material *receptive substance*, a name later shortened to *receptor*. So nicotine was said to act on a *nicotinic receptor* (Figure 2.1C).

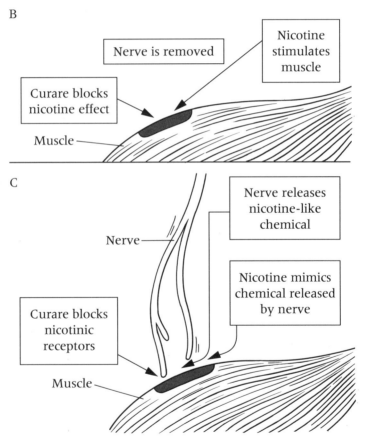

FIGURE 2.1 B, C Historic experiments on neurotransmitters and receptors. (B) Langley's experiment; (C) Langley's conclusion.

Shortly thereafter, in London, H. H. Dale discovered that visceral smooth muscles (as found, for example, in the intestine, the bladder, or the pupil of the eye) behaved very differently from the skeletal muscles studied by Bernard and Langley. Nicotine did not stimulate them to contract, but a mushroom poison called *muscarine* did. Curare did not prevent the action of muscarine, but a plant poison called *atropine* did. Thus, the novel receptors on smooth muscle, which responded to muscarine and were blocked by atropine, were called *muscarinic receptors.* Dale's experiments first showed clearly how very specific the receptors could be; nicotine and curare acted only on nicotinic receptors, muscarine and atropine only on muscarinic receptors.

What were the supposed substances, released from nerve endings by nerve impulses, which caused these different types of muscle to contract? Not until the 1930s was it proved, in a famous experiment conducted by the Austrian pharmacologist Otto Loewi, that nerves actually did transmit their messages by means of neurotransmitters released from the nerve endings (see Figure 2.1D). A frog heart, placed in a small container of salt solution with its nerve intact (the heart on the left in the figure), continues to beat; and a record of the heartbeat can be written by a pen on a slowly turning drum. The nerve is immersed, as shown, to keep it moist. Loewi collected the fluid in which this heart was bathed, and added it to another heart in a different container. The second heart continued to beat as usual. However, if he slowed the first heart by stimulating its nerve electrically, and then transferred the bath fluid to the second heart, that heart—which was not otherwise stimu-

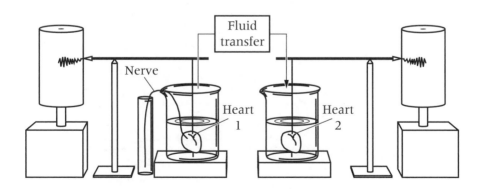

FIGURE 2.1D Historic experiments on neurotransmitters and receptors. Loewi's experiment.

lated—also slowed. This proved conclusively that some substance released by the nerve onto the first heart had slowed it; and that the same substance could be transferred with the bath fluid to the second heart, slowing it, too. (Dale and Loewi shared a Nobel Prize in 1936 for these fundamental discoveries about neurotransmission.)

A few years later the chemicals released by neurons in Loewi's and Dale's experiments were discovered to be one and the same substance—*acetylcholine*—the first of many neurotransmitters to be recognized. It is released by the nerves that impinge on the heart, and also by nerves supplying visceral and skeletal muscle. Thus, Dale's nicotinic and muscarinic receptors were actually two types of acetylcholine receptor—a nicotinic acetylcholine receptor on skeletal muscle, and a muscarinic acetylcholine receptor on visceral smooth muscle and heart.

Acetylcholine turned out to be an important neurotransmitter, not only between nerve and muscle, but also between nerve and nerve, as in the brain (Figure 2.1E). The junction (called a *synapse*), where the ending of one nerve contacts another, is—like the neuromuscular junction—a microscopically tiny gap. A neurotransmitter released into this gap from the ending of one neuron can cross over to one of the many processes (called *dendrites*) on another neuron and stimulate a specific receptor on the other side. Thus a "message" is transmitted to the second neuron.

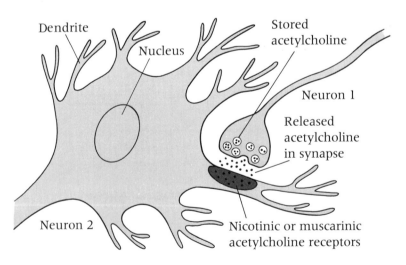

FIGURE 2.1E Acetylcholine receptors in brain.

Nicotinic and muscarinic acetylcholine receptors are found in various regions of the brain, and acetylcholine is one of the brain's most abundant neurotransmitters. Nicotine, when delivered to the brain in a smoker's blood, combines with the nicotinic receptors at synapses, and thus it mimics the actions of acetylcholine that is normally released there. The action of nicotine in *binding* (attaching) to a neurotransmitter receptor is typical of addictive drugs in general; each one, by binding to a receptor, affects the action of a specific neurotransmitter in the brain.

THE NEUROTRANSMITTERS

There are two kinds of neurotransmitters, each of which plays a role in one form of addiction or another. The first to be identified were, like acetylcholine, compact molecules composed of only 25 or so atoms. Most of them—though not acetylcholine itself—are related to one or another of the 20 amino acids that are the building blocks of all the proteins in the body. Especially important for understanding addiction are dopamine, serotonin (5-HT), glutamate, and gamma-amino-butyrate (GABA). Another compact neurotransmitter of importance is adenosine, which is not related to the amino acids but is one of the four building blocks of the nucleic acids DNA and RNA.

The other group of neurotransmitters are *peptides*. A peptide is a linear string of amino acids, like a string of different colored beads. Peptides typically consist of between two and about 30 amino acids. Proteins are longer strings; insulin, for instance, is a small protein containing 51 amino acids. Thus, a peptide neurotransmitter is really a very small protein, but considerably larger than the compact neurotransmitters. Dozens of peptide neurotransmitters are already recognized, and we have no idea how many more there may be. The number of possible arrangements of the 20 naturally occurring amino acids in a string (i.e., the number of different sequences), is incredibly large.* The enormous diversity of peptides and proteins in the body

---

* How large? Consider a very short peptide, only five amino acids long. For each of the 20 possibilities at the first position there are 20 possibilities at the second, thus 20 times 20. So with five positions we have 20 raised to the fifth power, or 3.2 million. For a protein several hundred amino acids long, the number of possibilities is truly astronomical.

represents only a small fraction of what is possible, selected by evolution to serve all the structural and functional needs of our bodies.

Although the peptide neurotransmitters are bigger than the compact ones, they usually do not lie stretched out like a string of beads, but fold into a more compact shape. Thus, many of them are able to fit into receptor pockets very much like those that accommodate the compact neurotransmitters. For the same reason, compact molecules can fit receptors to which peptides ordinarily bind. The addictive drugs are all compact molecules, and each one is able to combine with (or otherwise affect) a particular neurotransmitter receptor. The result is either to mimic the effect of whatever neurotransmitter normally activates that receptor, or to prevent that neurotransmitter from acting by interfering with its binding to the receptor. For example, nicotine mimics acetylcholine by acting on the nicotinic acetylcholine receptor; caffeine blocks adenosine by binding to the adenosine receptor without producing any effect of its own.

THE ENDOGENOUS OPIOIDS

The early discoveries that curare, nicotine, and muscarine bind to acetylcholine receptors should have raised the question of whether every substance of plant origin that acts on the brain is actually a mimic or a blocker of some neurotransmitter. And that logic should have led to a deliberate search for an unknown neurotransmitter as the counterpart of each psychotropic plant product.

The ground has to be fertile, however, before an idea can sprout. As long ago as 1903, for example, a French researcher, M. Mavrojannis, observed that when rats were given high doses of morphine, they became immobile, and they would hold any bizarre position into which they were placed. This strange kind of plastic immobility reminded Mavrojannis of similar states—catatonia, catalepsy—seen sometimes in schizophrenic patients. Making an intuitive leap of creative imagination, he wrote:

> If one supposes that the organism normally produces narcotic substances, one can imagine that in certain cases, at least, cataleptic phenomena are due either to an excessive production of these narcotic substances or to a defect in their elimination.

This remarkable insight and suggestion had no effect whatsoever.

It did not stimulate a search for "narcotic substances" in the brain. Conditions were not ripe, technology was not adequate, peptides (as the endogenous opioids turned out to be) were not even known—indeed, the amino acids had not yet been discovered. When, 72 years later, the substances postulated by Mavrojannis were finally identified, his own paper had been lost in the obscurity of forgotten archives, and had to be rediscovered.

The eventual discovery of the *endogenous* (i.e., intrinsic to the organism) opioid peptides has had a great impact on the way scientists view drug addiction. At a time when the great diversity and importance of brain peptides were just beginning to be appreciated, these peptide neurotransmitters seemed very likely to play an important role in opiate addiction. They are called *opioid* (meaning "opiatelike") because their biologic actions resemble those of morphine and other opiates. (The family of opioids includes true opiates like morphine from the opium poppy and synthetic compounds related to morphine, as well as the opioid peptides.)

By the late 1960s, a very large number of compounds related to morphine had been synthesized in the search for a painkiller as strong as morphine but not addictive. It was evident, from the way very small chemical changes made very big differences in the potency of these trial compounds, that a highly specific receptor had to be responsible for the pain relief. The following question arose: Is it sensible to suppose that such highly specific receptors developed, over the long course of evolution, only to combine with morphine, which is a product of the opium poppy? Was it not more likely that there were natural morphinelike neurotransmitters in the brain, and that these receptors had evolved to accommodate them?

My colleagues and I decided, in 1972, that endogenous morphinelike molecules were worth searching for. It would be easy enough to make extracts from animal brains and other tissues; but how would we go about finding a completely unknown substance? The term "morphinelike" provides the answer. We needed some reliable and easy way to detect a biologic action like that of morphine. Fortunately, a leading opiate researcher, Hans W. Kosterlitz, in Aberdeen, Scotland, had perfected just such a method, a simple laboratory technique. The time-honored procedure for determining whether a new compound was a good painkiller had been to administer it to a live rat or rabbit or monkey in a pain test. This was extremely laborious and costly, as are all animal experiments. Because individual animals vary so much in their sensitivity to drugs, even to obtain a single reliable result with a single dose of a pain-relieving drug required repeated trials with many animals. But Kosterlitz, as we shall see presently, found that the behavior of a small piece of tissue immersed in about a teaspoonful of solution containing salts and sugar in a little container could predict with great accuracy whether a compound would have a morphinelike pain-relieving effect in experimental animals or humans.

A tiny strip of muscle from the guinea-pig small intestine is fastened at one end to a hook in the bottom of the little tissue bath, in an arrangement much like that shown in Figure 2.1D. The other end of the muscle strip is attached by a thread to an electrical device—a strain gauge—that signals the pull whenever the muscle contracts. Regular electric shocks, one every ten seconds, make the muscle contract, pulling on the thread, and thus make a pen deflect on a moving strip of paper. Anything that weakens the muscle contraction writes a clear record of its effect.

The electric shocks activate nerves in the muscle, making them release acetylcholine. The released acetylcholine, as in Bernard's frog experiments, activates the muscle, causing it to contract. Morphine blocks the muscle contraction.* However, many other compounds do the same. For example, since the strip is a typical smooth visceral muscle, it contains the muscarinic type of acetylcholine receptor, and so atropine blocks the contraction. Consequently, the method, as described so far, would be nearly useless for identifying a morphinelike substance. Something more was needed.

That "something more" is a compound very much like morphine in chemical structure which attaches to the same site on the opioid receptor but has no effect of its own. It is called *naloxone*. Biologically active compounds like morphine are called *agonists*. Biologically inactive compounds like naloxone, which—by occupying a receptor without triggering any effect—exclude agonists, are called *antagonists*. (Both agonists and antagonists are used in treating drug addictions. An agonist would mimic the effect of the addictive drug but be preferable in some way, as when a nicotine patch substitutes for cigarettes. An antagonist would block the effect of the addictive drug, as when naltrexone prevents relapse to heroin use. These and other therapeutic applications are described in Part Two.)

---

* It does so by activating opioid receptors on the nerve endings; this activation prevents the release of acetylcholine by the electric shocks.

Returning now to the search—naloxone is a highly specific antagonist, binding to opioid receptors but to no other receptors. If naloxone itself is added to the tissue bath, it does not disturb the electrically stimulated muscle contraction, because it does not bind to muscarinic acetylcholine receptors. However, morphine no longer has any effect in the presence of naloxone. Naloxone, like many antagonists, not only prevents an agonist from binding to its receptor; it even replaces an agonist that is already acting. Thus, if morphine is added first, and has already reduced the strength of the muscle contraction, adding naloxone will promptly reverse the morphine effect.

A typical record of naloxone reversal, obtained in my laboratory, is shown in Figure 2.2. Starting at the left we see the muscle contractions every 10 seconds, caused by the electric shocks. At the first arrow, an opiate is added to the tissue bath, causing an immediate weakening of the contractions. As long as the opiate remains, the muscle will not recover. When naloxone is added, however, at the second arrow, the contractions promptly return to normal even though the opiate agonist is still present.

The characteristic and specific naloxone blockade makes possible a search for a morphinelike substance, namely, a substance that inhibits the muscle contraction and is antagonized by naloxone. This method paid off. In 1975, Kosterlitz and his colleague John Hughes, in Aberdeen, after laboriously purifying material from thousands of pig brains, were able to isolate two active substances that behaved just like morphine. The big surprise was that the chemical structure of these substances was nothing like that of the compact morphine molecule; they were peptides, five amino acids long. They were named *enkephalins*.

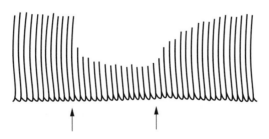

FIGURE 2.2 Bioassay of an opioid. Actual record of electrically stimulated contractions (every 10 seconds) of guinea-pig intestinal muscle. Opiate added at first arrow; naloxone added at second arrow. (Experiment from the author's laboratory.)

Immediately, by searching through a database of all known amino-acid sequences, the Aberdeen scientists recognized a much longer opioid peptide that contained the five amino acids of an enkephalin. Obtained years earlier from the pituitary gland, and 31 amino acids long, its opioid character had not been suspected. Now it was given the name *beta-endorphin* by its original discoverer, the renowned hormone chemist C. H. Li in San Francisco. Interestingly, this peptide is made in the body as part of an even longer one that includes the pituitary hormone ACTH (corticotropin), which stimulates the adrenal gland in response to stress.

DISCOVERING DYNORPHIN

Meanwhile, my colleagues and I were using the guinea-pig intestinal muscle to test the idea that one of the known hormones might be the sought-after endogenous morphinelike compound. After all, no hormone had been examined by this procedure. Systematically, therefore, we tested many hormones, but without success. Then, one day in March 1975, there was a great commotion in the lab. I hurried over to one of the little tissue baths, where my colleagues were watching with excitement as the pen wrote its record. A crude sample of the pituitary hormone ACTH was being tested. The record showed clearly that the muscle contraction was reduced by the ACTH preparation, and then, that naloxone brought it back to normal. Obviously, either ACTH itself was morphinelike in its action, or else the impure ACTH sample contained a morphinelike impurity. Which was it?

Not far away, in San Francisco, C. H. Li had purified ACTH, and he generously gave us a small amount for testing. Li's totally pure ACTH had no effect at all on the muscle strip. So our ACTH sample, made commercially from pig pituitary glands, obviously contained a morphinelike impurity. When our crude ACTH was exposed to an enzyme that destroys peptides, the biologic activity was lost, indicating that the morphinelike impurity was a peptide. Our task was cut out for us—to isolate that impurity and find out what it was. We turned to the Armour Company, which makes huge amounts of pituitary hormones in their meat packing business. Fortunately, a biochemist there, J. D. Fisher, had had the foresight to realize that the by-products, which would ordinarily be thrown away, might contain valuable substances, as yet undiscovered; so he had saved all such materials from the production process. Thus, we were able to obtain from him many pounds of crude pig pituitary powder, the leftovers after preparing ACTH for the pharmaceutical market. We found, right away, that a soup made from this powder had typical naloxone-reversible morphinelike activity on the muscle strip.

In May 1975, we reported on this finding at an international meeting, and we also heard progress reports from the Aberdeen group, who had not yet determined the structure of the enkephalins. When, later that year, they published the amino-acid sequences of the two enkephalins, we were hard at work trying to purify our pituitary opioid peptide.

The method is truly laborious. It is a question of separating the crude soup into its components (a process called *fractionation*), testing each fraction, throwing away what has no activity, and then further purifying the active fractions. As an illustration, one can separate molecules according to size into, say, a dozen fractions from the size of small peptides containing only a few amino acids to the size of large proteins containing hundreds. Testing revealed that all the biologic activity was in a fraction corresponding to a length of around 15–20 amino acids. All the other fractions were thrown away. The active fraction was then separated further according to a different criterion, electrical charge. With a dozen or so fractions in hand having different electrical charges, from strongly negative to strongly positive, we could again identify the active fraction (strongly positive), and discard the rest. We found some major differences between the biologic effect of our material and that of either the enkephalins or beta-endorphin, so we knew we were onto something novel. It took us four years of persistent hard work to obtain two micrograms (less than a millionth of an ounce!) of a pure peptide with morphinelike activity.

Which amino acids did our peptide contain, and what was their sequence in the chain? Leroy Hood, the leading expert in the technology of peptide sequence determination, worked at Caltech, in Pasadena. With Shinro Tachibana, a postdoctoral fellow from Japan who had done much of the work in my laboratory, I flew to Pasadena, carrying our precious but nearly invisible speck of material in a little test tube. I shall never forget the telephone call a few days later from Mike Hunkapiller, Hood's associate. "Here's the sequence," he said, and began reading the abbreviated names of amino acids, "Tyr, Gly, Gly, Phe, Leu, Arg, Arg, Ile, Arg ...." I knew at once that we had discovered a completely novel opioid peptide. The first five amino acids were the familiar sequence of one of the enkephalins, but everything after that was different.

The thrill of discovery is the major reward of scientific research. And knowing something about nature that no else in the world has ever known before is a wondrous experience, hard to convey in words. Here was this peptide, 17 amino acids long, the blueprint for which had been hidden in the genes for millions of years—and we had cracked the secret! Moreover, we had not only discovered a new opioid peptide; as we soon realized, we had found one that was hundreds of times more potent than morphine or any opioid peptide known at that time. I named it *dynorphin*, from the Greek prefix meaning *power* (as in *dynamic*), and the suffix *-orphin*, which was already standard for many opiates.

The opioid peptides have many important functions, and they play a significant role in opiate and other drug addictions, as will be discussed in later chapters. There are three families of opioid peptides that contain the enkephalin sequence, and each family includes several closely related peptides. The enkephalins, endorphins, and dynorphins are encoded by three different genes, which, because of their similarities, are thought to have evolved from a common ancestral opioid peptide gene. Representatives of all three families are found throughout the animal kingdom, and not only in brain but in other tissues throughout the body. Dynorphins, for example, are present in the brain, spinal cord, intestinal tract, heart, and testicles, as well as in the pituitary gland, where they were first discovered.

The logic that led to the discovery of the endogenous opioid peptides was based on the assumption that morphine is found only in the plant kingdom, and therefore that the opioid receptors in animal tissues must be there to accommodate some endogenous substance other than morphine. As happens so often in science, the logic was fruitful, and it led to important discoveries, but it may have been wrong. Research by Sidney Spector and in my own laboratory by Charles J. Weitz has proved irrefutably that morphine itself is present in animal brain. And not only morphine, but at least two other compact molecules very close to morphine in chemical structure. What is not so clear yet is how they get there. They could be endogenous, made in the animal body and having a function in the brain, especially since dopamine, which is so abundant a neurotransmitter in the brain, is also the starting material for morphine synthesis in the opium poppy. But proof of an endogenous origin of brain morphine is not yet conclusive; though unlikely, it is possible that the morphine we detect in the brain comes from a dietary source or is made by bacteria in the intestine.

As noted earlier, the story of the endogenous opioids has wider implications. The presence of an addictive substance, morphine, in opium poppies led to the discovery of neurotransmitters with similar actions in the brain. This encouraged scientists to look for other novel neurotransmitters in the brain which might be counterparts of other plant substances with psychotropic actions. One stunning success of this strategy is the recent identification of an endogenous substance that acts like THC, the active principle in cannabis (see Chapter 12). Finding a neurotransmitter that mimics or blocks the effects of an addictive drug is a necessary first step in understanding the biologic basis of the addiction, the mechanisms whereby the disease process disturbs normal brain function. The next step, described in Chapter 3, is to learn about the receptors on which the addictive drugs act in the brain.

CHAPTER 3

Locks for the Addictive Keys

To Bernard, Langley, Dale, and Loewi, receptors were more a concept than a physical reality. Whatever receptors might actually be, they were obviously highly specific. The lock-and-key analogy served to describe this specificity very early. The nicotine "key," for example, activated the nicotinic receptor "lock" but did not fit the muscarinic receptor. Similarly, the muscarine "key" did not fit the nicotinic receptor "lock." If not for the brain receptors, with their amazing specificity, all the addictive drugs would have the same biologic actions (or more likely, none at all). It is the different receptors and their special locations in the brain that account for the differences—one drug a stimulant, another a depressant; one causing vivid hallucinations, another paranoid psychosis; one powerfully addictive, another only weakly so.

As additional compact molecules like muscarine and nicotine were studied, it became clear that the slightest alterations could have drastic effects. Adding or taking away a single carbon atom, for example, could make a substance hundreds of times more or less potent; codeine, for example, has just one carbon atom more than morphine, yet it is very much weaker as a painkiller. The most striking finding about specificity concerned chemically identical molecules of different "handedness." Our two hands have the same structure (thumb and four fingers, palm side and knuckle side), yet they are not actually identical in three-dimensional space. A glove can fit one hand but not the other. In the same way, some molecules can be "right-handed" or "left-handed." A left-handed molecule, for example, might be highly potent, whereas its right-handed twin would be inert. Thus, a typical receptor must have an irregular, asymmetric, glovelike pocket, which accommodates only molecules with precisely the correct three-dimensional shape.

As noted in Chapter 2, each neurotransmitter acts on its own receptor. And each addictive drug mimics or blocks a particular neurotransmitter by combining with the corresponding receptor. Thus, the next step in understanding what addictive drugs do in the brain is to learn where the receptors are located, how they are constructed, how they function, and how that function is altered by drugs.

BINDING

In the past twenty-five years, the study of receptors has been transformed. The story begins in 1958, when Rosalyn Yalow and Solomon Berson invented the method of *radioimmunoassay* to measure tiny amounts of a hormone (for example, insulin) by its ability to combine with a specific antibody. This method opened the way to studying how hormones, neurotransmitters, and addictive drugs combine with receptors. Here is how radioimmunoassay works. First, a rabbit is injected with insulin from some other animal species. After a few weeks the rabbit's immune system reacts to the foreign protein by making antibodies. These anti-insulin antibodies circulate in the animal's blood, from which they can be extracted for use in the assay. Insulin is then *radiolabeled* by attaching a radioactive atom to it. Now, in the test tube, the radiolabeled insulin attaches avidly to the antibody molecules, which have glovelike cavities that exactly match the shape of insulin. This perfect fit is represented by the binding of the black triangle to the triangular cavity in Figure 3.1A. It is then a simple matter to separate the antibody with its bound radioactive insulin from any free (unbound) insulin, and to measure its radioactivity.

Now if ordinary unlabeled insulin is also present in the same test tube, it competes for the antibody, as in Figure 3.1B. Less radiolabeled insulin can combine with the limited amount of antibody because the

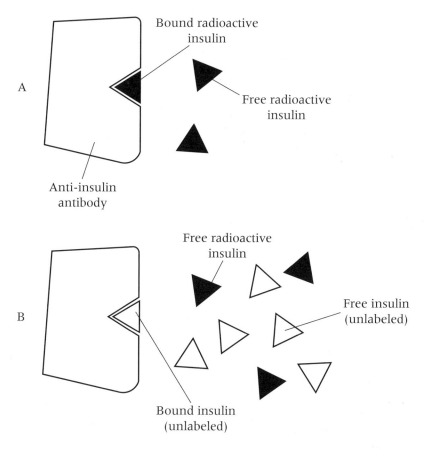

FIGURE 3.1 The principle of radioimmunoassay. (A) Radiolabeled insulin alone (black triangles); (B) competition by unlabeled insulin (white triangles).

ordinary insulin occupies the binding sites. The extent to which bound radioactivity is reduced tells how much competing insulin is present—the more competing insulin in the test tube, the less radiolabeled insulin can be bound. The method proved to be extraordinarily sensitive, and it quickly became the preferred way to measure all sorts of substances (including neurotransmitters) that are present in minute amounts in blood, brain, and other tissues. Yalow received the Nobel Prize in 1977 (after Berson's death) for this accomplishment.

When the immune system is challenged by a substance like insulin, the antibodies it makes are quite specific for that substance; an antibody to insulin, for example, will not react with other hormones. This property of antibodies makes them useful for localizing neurotransmitters and mapping their distribution in brain tissue by a method called *immunocytochemistry*. A certain antibody is labeled by attaching a fluorescent chemical to it; the anibody is then applied to a thin slice of brain tissue. Then, under the microscope, ultraviolet light makes the fluorescent chemical glow; and one can actually see the fluorescent clusters in the endings of the neurons, representing packages of a particular neurotransmitter that is stored there.

Beginning around 1965 scientists realized that the binding method introduced by Yalow and Berson could be extended to receptors. After all, a receptor, like an antibody, has a specific pocket in which a radio-labeled molecule can bind. Sex-hormone receptors and insulin receptors were the first to be studied by this technique, and shortly thereafter, my own initial research on opiates involved the development of a binding technique for brain opioid receptors. Binding made it possible to study receptors as physical realities, no longer just conceptual inferences.

A compound that binds to a receptor is called a *ligand*. Ligand binding is of key importance for our attempts to understand drug addictions. As a result of refinements in binding technique, recent decades have seen astonishing progress in our understanding of the detailed structure of receptors, how they are made in the body, how their production is regulated, how they bind the substances with which they interact, and—most interesting of all—how they mediate the biologic effects of hormones, neurotransmitters, and drugs. I shall illustrate by reference to the opioid receptors, which I and my colleagues have studied for many years.

For investigating opioid receptors by ligand binding, the brain of a rat, mouse, or guinea pig is removed and homogenized (as in a food blender) to break open all the neurons. The receptors are in the cell membranes that are the outer sheath of the neurons. Test tubes containing the homogenate are rotated at high speed in a centrifuge so that centrifugal force packs down the cell membranes. After pouring off the watery "soup," we stir up the membranes in a fresh salt water rinse, then pack them down again; in this way they are washed repeatedly in the centrifuge. Next, we add an opioid ligand, like morphine, which has been radiolabeled. The more radiolabeled ligand is added, the more is bound to the receptors in the membranes, but only until the limited number of receptor binding sites are filled. If a nonradioactive opioid is added, less radioactive ligand can be bound—the same competition principle as in radioimmunoassay. This competition step proves that the radiolabeled opioid is really bound in a limited number of binding sites, not merely stuck to the surface of the membranes. Substances that are not opioids fail to compete, proving that the binding is *specific*, that we are really dealing with opioid receptors. Furthermore, although left-handed opiates compete for the binding sites, right-handed opiates do not, showing that the binding is *stereospecific*; this is consistent with the fact that only left-handed opiates produce the typical biologic effects, such as relief of pain.

Ligand binding gives us two important numbers. First, we can learn how many receptors are on the neurons in brain tissue. In one test tube containing some membranes we measure the binding with a very small amount of radiolabeled ligand. Then, in other test tubes containing the same amount of membranes, we measure the binding of gradually increasing amounts of the radiolabeled ligand, until no more can be bound. This maximum amount of radiolabeled ligand that will bind specifically is a measure of the total number of receptors. Locations in the brain with many receptors are very sensitive to the addictive ligand, and changing the number of receptors is one of the ways the brain reacts after repeated exposure to an addictive ligand.

Second, ligand binding tells us, from the same set of test tubes, the *affinity* of the ligand for the receptor, how tightly it binds. The more avidly a ligand is bound (the higher its affinity), the lower the concentration that is needed to occupy the receptors. A high-affinity receptor ligand might typically be effective at a concentration of about 1 nanomole per liter. (A concentration that tiny is hard to comprehend: it corresponds to a single grain of salt dissolved in a 250-gallon tank of water.) Differences in binding affinity are largely responsible for the fact that LSD—as an example—is active in extraordinarily tiny amounts, whereas the biologic activity of a drug like caffeine requires hundreds of times higher dosage.

There are two quite different ways of studying receptors. The ligand-binding assay lets us characterize any receptor according to what ligands it will or will not bind, and with what affinities. We say that a receptor is *selective* for a particular ligand if it binds that ligand with higher affinity than other ligands. Binding assays give direct information about ligand affinities but can not distinguish readily between agonists and antagonists (defined in Chapter 2), since both bind. The other approach looks at receptor function rather than at ligand binding by measuring some biologic consequence of the binding. For example, one might measure the response of the electrically stimulated intestine preparation to an opioid, as described in Chapter 2.

Functional assays give information about the biologic *potency* of an agonist or antagonist. Potency is a measure of the agonist concentration needed to produce the biologic effect or the antagonist concentration needed to block it. Potency, of course, is related to binding affinity, but it is not necessarily the same thing. For example, a full biologic effect might result from an agonist occupying only a small fraction of the receptors; such an agonist would be very potent even though it might have only modest affinity for the receptors. Functional biologic assays and ligand binding assays complement each other nicely.

The two kinds of acetylcholine receptors exemplify a general principle—that virtually all receptors come in families, with *subtypes* having strong similarities but also important differences. An apt analogy might be the breeds of dogs, all easily recognized as dogs, but with distinct differences among them. All subtypes can bind all ligands in a set of closely related chemical structures, but with very different relative affinities. In the case of the opioid receptors, for example, one subtype (designated by Greek letter *mu*) is selective for morphine and beta-endorphin, another (*delta*) prefers enkephalins, and yet another (*kappa*) has greatest affinity for dynorphins. There are even subtypes of subtypes (like *kappa-1* and *kappa-2*), with yet others undoubtedly waiting to be discovered. Living systems always prove more complicated than we expect; the purpose of receptor subtypes may be to fine-tune the control of biologic processes more precisely than if there were fewer kinds of receptors.

To learn where an addictive drug acts in the brain, and to get further information about how it acts there, we need to know in what parts of the brain the specific receptors for that drug are located. Instead of homogenizing a tissue, we can carry out the same binding procedure with thin tissue slices, which are then pressed against photographic film, a technique known as *receptor autoradiography*. The radioactivity, bound selectively to the receptor sites in the tissue sample, exposes the film and makes a pretty picture of the receptor distribution. The combination of ligand binding assays and receptor autoradiography tells us much of what we know today about where the various kinds of receptors are located in the brain.

Neurobiologists are now beginning to locate receptors in the living human brain by a method called *positron emission tomography (PET scan)*, in which the radioactivity of a labeled compound can be detected through the bony skull. In a ligand PET scan, the binding of a radiolabeled ligand depicts the receptor distribution directly. Another kind of PET scan measures the uptake of a radiolabeled sugar by neurons.

Sugar is taken up most rapidly by neurons that are most active, as they need sugar for energy. If an addictive drug stimulates a particular group of neurons in the brain, the inrush of labeled sugar there will take its own picture (so to speak) on the PET scan. This method has been used to show, for example, that nicotine stimulates certain highly localized areas in the brain, while the ligand PET scan confirms that these are areas dense in nicotinic acetylcholine receptors.

RECEPTOR STRUCTURE

To learn about how addictive drugs act in the brain it is not enough to know where the receptors are located and how they bind ligands. We really want to learn the detailed structure of the receptors in order to understand what happens next, after a ligand binds. A receptor is a complicated miniature machine. The binding site for the ligand is like the ignition lock in a car; the key turns on the engine, but taking apart the lock would not tell us much about how the car runs. We want to know how the receptors are constructed, and how their machinery works. Revolutionary advances of the last decade or so produced a major leap forward toward that goal.

Receptors are large proteins, chains of hundreds of amino acids. Which amino acids are present in the chain, and the sequence in which they are strung together, determines how the chain is folded, and therefore accounts for the distinctive three-dimensional structure. To *sequence* a protein means to dissect such a chain in order to learn the order in which the amino-acid building blocks are arranged. One method starts by purifying the chain exhaustively in order to obtain a tiny amount of the absolutely pure receptor protein. The method is much like that described for our little dynorphin peptide in Chapter 2. The numerous proteins in brain tissue can be fractionated according to size, electric charge, and so on, but now the protein we want is traced by its ability to bind a ligand. When purification is complete, so that the only protein remaining is the receptor, its amino-acid sequence can be determined. Because the protein chain is so long, it is usually first cut into overlapping fragments; then each fragment is sequenced by starting at one end and removing and identifying each amino acid in turn.

Modern biotechnology has simplified this task by providing alternative ways to learn the sequence of amino acids in a receptor. But before examining these methods, let us review briefly some fundamentals of molecular biology.

Since every protein is built according to the blueprint in the DNA of the genes, it is often possible to analyze the gene sequence directly, or that of the messenger RNA (mRNA) that is copied from the DNA. A gene is said to be *expressed* when it is copied into mRNA, which in turn directs the assembly of amino acids into a protein.

There are four different building blocks (called *nucleotides*) that make up the linear sequences of DNA and mRNA. In DNA these are abbreviated A, T, C, and G. Their chemical properties are such that A can bind tightly to T in another strand, and C to G. Such pairs of nucleotides are the glue that hold together the two complementary strands of DNA—"complementary" because all the way along the gene every A is opposite a T, every C is opposite a G. Four very similar nucleotides make up the long strands of mRNA (except that a modified form of T is present, called U, which also binds to A).

The mechanism of gene expression is like reading out the linear information on a magnetic tape. Here the linear sequence of nucleotides on one strand of the DNA (called the *coding strand*) directs the assembly of a complementary strand of mRNA. The nucleotide sequence in mRNA then directs the assembly of amino acids in a growing protein chain according to a set of rules known as the *genetic code*. This means that if the nucleotide sequence in DNA or mRNA is known, the amino acid sequence of the corresponding neurotransmitter or receptor can be deduced.

Now, an important advance made possible by the pairing principle is the localization of specific mRNA molecules in brain tissue. This method, called *in situ hybridization*, is analogous to the way antibodies are used to localize neurotransmitters, or the way ligand autoradiography can be used to map receptor distribution. If we know the sequence of the mRNA that encodes a certain neuropeptide or receptor, we can expose thin slices of brain to the appropriate radiolabeled probe. Then wherever mRNA containing that sequence occurs in the tissue, it will bind the probe, as in Figure 3.2. The resulting radioactivity in a brain slice can take its own picture (by autoradiography), producing a dark image on a photographic film. The specific mRNA is present only where the neuropeptide or receptor of interest is in the process of being assembled—not necessarily the same place it is stored and released.

Determining how much neurotransmitter or how many receptors are present paints a valuable but static picture. Measuring the mRNA by in situ hybridization provides a dynamic picture, which can give insight into how addictive drugs disturb regulatory processes in the

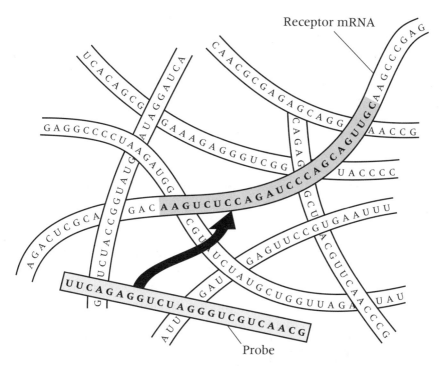

FIGURE 3.2 A probe for finding the mRNA that encodes a receptor. The figure represents a mixture of mRNA molecules in a tissue. Black arrow indicates where a radiolabeled probe will hybridize to a portion of one receptor mRNA molecule. See text for explanation.

brain. One major regulatory mechanism enables an organism to compensate for a stress imposed on its normal state. This is *negative feedback*, about which we have learned a great deal from studies on hormones. For example, if a person or animal is treated for a long time with cortisol (a product of the adrenal cortex), the normal production of ACTH (a necessary stimulant of the adrenal cortex) by the pituitary gland is suppressed, as though to compensate for the high cortisol level. With neurotransmitters and receptors, too, addictive drugs can cause suppression or stimulation of gene expression. Thus, by studying specific mRNA we can investigate such questions as whether chronic exposure of an animal to an opiate will shut down the production of the endogenous opioid peptides, the opioid receptors, or related proteins—effects that might lead to a state of tolerance and dependence (see Chapter 6).

ADDICTIVE DRUGS AND RECEPTORS

With sequence information in hand, and knowing the locations of a given receptor in the brain, scientists can begin dissecting the machinery to understand how an addictive drug affects it. The first receptor to be sequenced, in 1982, was the nicotinic acetylcholine receptor at the neuromuscular junction, the same one that Claude Bernard first identified by means of curare, the same one activated by nicotine. It turned out to be a channel composed of five different protein subunits. Each of these subunits crosses the cell membrane four times, and thus the whole structure is an array of 20 parallel segments that form a cylindrical structure spanning the cell membrane. Figure 3.3A shows how the five subunits surround a pore that runs down the middle. This kind of receptor is called a *ligand-gated ion channel* because it is designed to open and allow certain ions (electrically charged atoms) to pass when a specific ligand binds at the mouth of the channel. The cell membrane is depicted as an elongated box, the outside surface on top, the inside of the cell at bottom. The channel is normally closed. When acetylcholine (or nicotine) binds, the five subunits move apart slightly, opening the channel momentarily. Positively charged sodium ions rush into the cell, reducing its internal negative electric charge (*depolarizing* it) and thus initiating an electrical signal. In muscle, this

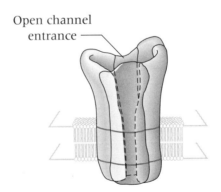

Open channel entrance

FIGURE 3.3 A Typical ligand-gated ion channel (nicotinic acetylcholine receptor). [Adapted from J.-P. Changeux et al., *Quarterly Review of Biophysics* 25: 395, 1992.]

signal is propagated along the fibers, causing them to contract. In the brain, acetylcholine is released from the ending of one neuron, crosses a synapse, and binds to the receptor on another neuron. The resulting electrical signal is then propagated down that second neuron. Nicotine mimics this process. Muscarinic acetylcholine receptors in the brain belong to an entirely different family (see below).

The GABA receptor in brain is also an ion channel. When the neurotransmitter GABA is released from a nearby nerve ending, it binds to this receptor, opening the channel to allow passage of negatively charged chloride ions. This increases the negative electrical charge inside the neuron, making it more refractory to the neurotransmitters that ordinarily stimulate it. For this reason GABA is called an *inhibitory neurotransmitter*, whereas acetylcholine is an *excitatory neurotransmitter*. The GABA receptor has a special binding site for the psychotropic and addictive benzodiazepine drugs (like Valium), and yet another binding site for the psychotropic and addictive barbiturates. It is also a good candidate for the site at which alcohol and volatile solvents exert their main effects. All these drugs, when they bind, loosen the channel structure, make it easier to open, and thus enhance the inhibitory effects of GABA.

Another ion channel that is relevant to addictive drugs is called the *NMDA receptor*, which is normally activated by the abundant excitatory neurotransmitter glutamate. Glutamate opens the channel, allowing sodium, potassium, and calcium ions to flow into the neuron, thus exciting it. Calcium ions play a special role inside neurons by triggering the release of stored neurotransmitters. Alcohol may interfere with the opening of this ion channel. As the GABA and NMDA receptors have opposite functions—one inhibitory, the other excitatory—alcohol produces similar effects by enhancing the inhibition by GABA and opposing the activation by glutamate. Phencyclidine (PCP) has its own unique binding site on one of the NMDA receptor subunits (see Chapter 14).

A different architectural motif is represented by a very large group of receptors—the *seven-helix family*. These include muscarinic acetylcholine receptors and the receptors for dopamine (Chapter 4), THC (Chapter 12), adenosine (Chapter 13), and serotonin (Chapter 14). Also in this family are several neuropeptide receptors, including the opioid receptors (Chapter 10), the structures of which were first discovered in 1992 and 1993. The common design of a seven-helix receptor, illustrated in Figure 3.3B, is a single protein chain of about 450 amino acids (represented by small beads), which threads back and forth across the cell membrane seven times, forming loops and tails of

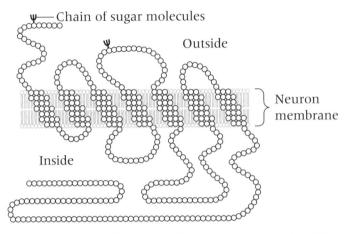

FIGURE 3.3 B Typical seven-helix receptor (dopamine D1 receptor). [From D. R. Sibley and F. J. Monsma, Jr., *Trends in Pharmacological Sciences* 13: 64, 1992.]

different sizes. The diagram shows the seven membrane-spanning segments side by side, but in reality—in three dimensions—they are thought to form a cylindrical barrel, something like the ion-channel receptors but without a central pore. Instead, the mouth of the barrel is exposed on the outer surface of the cell membrane, forming a pocket that accommodates the specific ligands.

When a ligand binds to the outer part of a seven-helix receptor, the helixes move in such a way as to cause a special protein (called *G-protein*), which is bound to the part of the receptor that extends into the inside of the neuron, to be released and to activate other functional proteins within the cell. Often a G-protein regulates the open or closed state of some ion channel and thus affects the activity of the neuron. The mechanism whereby the binding of an agonist ligand on the outside of a cell membrane transmits a signal across the membrane to influence biochemical events inside the cell is called *signal transduction*. The study of signal transduction is a very active field of current research because it addresses the key questions about how receptors for the addictive drugs actually work—for example, how the binding of an agonist causes a biologic effect but the binding of an antagonist does not.

Finally, a third family of receptors of interest comprise the transport proteins (*transporters*), which are embedded in the cell membrane and are specialized for carrying a specific ligand across into the cell. Many essential molecules—for instance, sugars and amino acids—are unable to penetrate the oily cell membranes because they are too soluble in water, and "oil and water don't mix." Without transporters, cells could not survive, for they require many water-soluble nutrients. Transporters remove some neurotransmitters from synapses after their release; this reuptake process not only terminates their action but also conserves them for subsequent use. The transporters for several neurotransmitters, such as GABA, serotonin, and dopamine, share a similar architecture. Of special interest for drug addiction is the dopamine transporter in brain (Figure 3.3C). This protein chain crosses the cell membrane 12 times, leaving two long tails inside the cell and loops of different sizes outside. Four chains of sugar molecules are attached to the largest loop on the outside of the cell. How such a structure actually moves a neurotransmitter like dopamine across the neuronal cell membrane and into the inside of the neuron is still a complete mystery. Cocaine binds to this transporter and blocks its function, causing dopamine to accumulate to excessive levels in the synapses.

Some receptors—opioid receptors are a good example—are located on the endings of certain neurons, where those neurons release some neurotransmitter into the synapse. As the design of the synapse is unidirectional, the neuron endings that release the neurotransmitter are called *presynaptic*, while the sites that receive the neurotransmitter

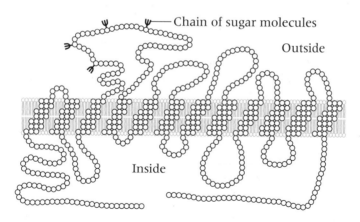

FIGURE 3.3 C An example of a transporter protein (cocaine-sensitive dopamine transporter). [From S. Shimada et al., *Science* 254: 576, 1991.]

are called *postsynaptic*. Presynaptic receptors control the release of neurotransmitters into the synapse. For instance, when activated by an opioid agonist, the presynaptic opioid receptors on the endings of acetylcholine neurons in the intestine (Chapter 2) affect ion channels in such a way that acetylcholine release is impeded.

Postsynaptic receptors are activated by neurotransmitters that are released into the synapse. Examples are the nicotinic and muscarinic acetylcholine receptors in the brain, which are positioned strategically just across the synapses from the ends of acetylcholine neurons. Both presynaptic and postsynaptic receptors form parts of regulatory feedback loops. Excessive stimulation by agonists—for example by addictive drugs—generally leads to a reduction in the number of receptors, and insufficient stimulation results in an increase. Likewise, the production and release of neurotransmitters are regulated by the degree of stimulation of the receptors—too much stimulation calls for less neurotransmitter, too little calls for more. With respect to both receptor regulation and neurotransmitter regulation, the brain behaves as though trying to maintain all its operating systems on an even keel. In general, the addictive drugs behave as though they were trying to upset the normal balance.

The preceding account will have made it apparent that scientific knowledge about brain receptors is still very incomplete. The knowledge gained already has helped pinpoint sites of action of addictive drugs in the brain and has implicated specific receptors and neurotransmitters. The research has opened the way for understanding how addictive drugs alter brain chemistry and how those chemical changes cause drug tolerance and dependence. Especially important is the possibility, now, of understanding how each addictive drug affects the dopamine receptors and dopamine transporters in the natural reward systems of the brain, to be described in the next chapter.

CHAPTER 4

Addictive Behavior

Neurotransmitters and receptors are the basic neurochemical units on which the addictive drugs act, and we have learned about them in the previous chapters. The ultimate aim, however, is to understand how the neurochemical effects of the drugs result in changes of mood and behavior. This chapter describes three different experimental approaches to the study of behavior. It presents evidence obtained in animals and in humans that bears on the following three questions:

- How is each drug recognized by the distinctive feeling it produces, so it can be discriminated from other drugs, and so be preferred for self-administration?

- What are the principles and patterns underlying compulsive drug-seeking and drug-using behavior?

- What are the brain circuits and mechanisms that are responsible for the addictive properties of the seven drug families?

Answering these questions requires direct experiments because simple observation, anecdotal evidence, and historical study of human societies do not allow definite interpretations to be made. Moreover, controlled experiments are needed if unambiguous conclusions are to be reached. Many of the necessary human experiments would require administering addictive drugs to people (even children or adolescents) who have had no prior drug experience, and that would be unethical. However, ethical human research—always, of course, with the informed consent of the subject—is often carried out with addicts, especially in testing alternative treatments. Much information has also come from studies in which an addictive drug is administered to an ex-addict; but this raises ethical questions if the subject is trying to remain abstinent. Thus, though human research is very difficult, it is necessary, feasible, and informative. Yet many of the fundamental biologic questions can be investigated only in experimental animals.

HOW RATS TELL ONE DRUG FROM ANOTHER

People who seek out a particular drug will know when they have found it because they will recognize how it feels, provided they have had it before. This subjective recognition is called *drug discrimination*. It is that certain feeling, different for each kind of psychotropic drug, that users seek. Without it, there would be no possibility of repeatedly seeking out and using a particular drug, and therefore there could be no drug addiction.

Drug discrimination can be demonstrated in animals as well as in humans. I illustrate by experiments carried out in my own laboratory. The aim was to see if rats could discriminate the subjective feelings caused by nicotine from those caused by other drugs or by a *placebo* (an inert substance). It might seem ridiculous to expect a rat to tell us what it feels when we give it nicotine. But a clever method invented by Donald Overton allows this to be done quite precisely. A T-maze, a diagram of which is shown in Figure 4.1, has a central alleyway (the stem of the T) with a grid floor that is constantly electrified. A rat placed on the central alleyway will receive a continuous mild but unpleasant footshock. The rat runs along the stem of the T, looking for a way to escape, and finds it can go into the right or left arm of the T. Around a corner, at each end of the cross-arm, is a safe haven with a gate that can be open or closed according to the experimenter's design.

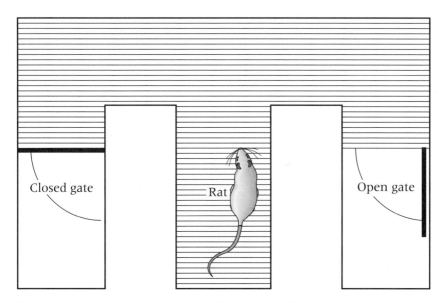

FIGURE 4.1   Overton T-maze. Electrified grid floor is shown, with controlled access to safe havens on each side.

Neither gate can be seen from the cross-bar of the T. In trying to escape the foot shock, the rat runs the whole length of either cross-bar, and then, if that gate is closed, it has to retrace its steps and try the other arm of the T.

To train a rat in this apparatus, we first take the animal out of its home cage and give it an injection of an inert salt solution, a placebo. A few minutes later we place the rat in the central alleyway of the T, leaving the right gate open, the left gate closed, as in the diagram. Either by good luck or after trying the wrong side, the rat finds the safe haven, escapes the shock, and is then removed and replaced in its home cage. The same procedure is repeated day after day. The rat learns that as soon as it is placed in the maze it must run straight ahead, make a fast turn to the right, run to the end, turn the corner, and scurry through the open gate into the safe haven.

Once the rat has learned this lesson, we inject a dose of nicotine instead of placebo, and this time we close the right gate and open the left gate. Of course, the rat applies what it has learned, and turns right. When it finds the gate closed, it is astonished and confused (if we may impute human emotions). Realizing its error, so to speak, it desperately seeks another way to escape the uncomfortable footshock. Sooner or later it discovers the safe haven on the left.

We make an injection every day, sometimes placebo, sometimes nicotine. Whenever it is placebo, we open the right gate; whenever it is nicotine, we open the left gate. Sooner or later the rat begins to adopt a strategy that works. It behaves as though it were reasoning, Aha! When I feel my normal self, I can escape to the right, but when I have that odd unusual feeling, I have to turn to the left. After about a month of daily trials, most rats learn the lesson perfectly.

Of course, we balance the experiment so that with half the rats we reverse the pattern, leaving the left gate open for placebo, the right one for nicotine. This is to avoid being misled by any natural left- or right-turning preference of the animals.

The procedure has now trained the rats to "tell" us if they have had nicotine or not, and we are ready for a test session. We inject something, leave both gates open, and see which way a rat turns. If we make this test with placebo or with nicotine—and we know what the correct behavior should be for either of these—we find almost perfect discrimination; a rat rarely makes an error, and since we never depend on only a single rat, we can be virtually certain of not getting a wrong answer.

What happens, then, if we give a drug that is chemically related to nicotine, one that might or might not act like nicotine in the brain? The trained rats can classify such a drug for us as "like nicotine" or "not like nicotine" by simply turning one way or the other after a test injection.

In the same way, we can train rats to distinguish other psychotropic drugs such as morphine, cocaine, or diazepam (Valium) from a placebo. But suppose a rat has been trained to recognize nicotine, and then, at the test session, it is given one of these other drugs. What does such a rat do? A reasonable guess would be that since the animal was trained to discriminate nicotine from placebo, it will recognize morphine or cocaine or diazepam as "not placebo"; feeling "drugged"—we would guess—it will respond as it did to nicotine.

We would be wrong. Apparently it is we, not the rat, who interpret the animal's behavior as discriminating "drugged" from "normal." Actually, what the rat seems to do is discriminate "nicotine" from "not nicotine"; in other words, the discrimination is highly drug-specific. This behavior is not really too surprising if we think about human responses to addictive drugs. These, too, are drug-specific. For instance, an experienced drug user knows very well the difference between feeling drunk on alcohol, "stoned" on marijuana, or "high" on cocaine.

The same method can be used to test antagonists, which block the effects of active drugs. First we give a drug that we think might be an antagonist to nicotine. Will it block nicotine discrimination? A few minutes after injecting such a drug, we give nicotine, in the usual manner, and place the rat in the T-maze. If the rat was trained as described above, it can tell us "I feel nicotine" by turning to the left, or "I don't feel nicotine" by turning to the right. If the supposed antagonist is effective, a rat will no longer respond to nicotine by turning in the "nicotine direction." Trained rats are tested with different antagonist doses; when the dose is small enough, the responsiveness to nicotine will be seen again. In this way we can see how the biologic effect varies with the drug dosage; thus, we can not only decide that the new drug is an effective antagonist, we can estimate its potency in blocking the nicotine discrimination.

Our experiments showed that nicotine discrimination is highly specific, depending on receptors in the brain. Very small changes in the chemical structure of nicotine made big differences in the dose required to make a rat say, "Yes, it's nicotine." By studying the pattern of activities of various agonists and antagonists, we found a parallelism with pharmacologic effects that are known to be mediated by nicotinic acetylcholine receptors.

CAN PEOPLE DO
AS WELL AS RATS?

An interesting human experiment in drug discrimination was carried out with volunteers who were former heroin addicts. These young people were experienced users who knew exactly what they liked about heroin. They could even put a price on a heroin injection according to its strength. The aim of the experiment was to test the effectiveness of the heroin antagonist *naltrexone* (a drug that is closely related to naloxone), which was being considered for use as a means of preventing relapse to heroin use in former addicts. A dose of naltrexone was given by mouth, followed by a standard effective dose of heroin intravenously. The subject was then asked, "How much would you have been willing to pay for that injection?" On different days and with different subjects, various doses of naltrexone were tested, the subjects being unaware of what dose, if any, they were getting. The result was remarkably unambiguous, especially in view of the crude measurement technique. After a zero dose of naltrexone (i.e., a placebo) the heroin injection was rated, on the average, as worth 18 dollars, but after a sufficient dose of naltrexone, the same dose of heroin was rated as worthless. The theory behind the therapeutic use of naltrexone is that if people take this antagonist regularly, they will not continue buying heroin, because they know that heroin will be worthless to them. In Chapter 10 we shall see how this works out in practice as a means of preventing relapse to heroin use.

Most drug testing in humans requires *double-blind design*. This means that neither the subject nor the experimenters know whether a drug or a placebo is administered, or—in studies of dosage—what dose is given. The purpose is to exclude subjective biases, especially when the drug effect has a significant psychologic component. But the ability to discriminate psychotropic drugs can make double-blind design in human experiments difficult. We could even find ourselves in the absurd situation that the subjects would easily be able to discriminate drug from placebo by the way it felt, while only the experimenters were left in the dark! This is not to say double-blind design should be abandoned, only that the investigator has to be aware of the problem and devise clever ways of getting around it.

TAKING A DRUG, AGAIN AND AGAIN

If a person self-administers a drug repeatedly without a medical reason, we conclude that there must be something satisfying about it, that the user is seeking a desirable sensation or mood state produced by the drug. Experimental animal psychology, chiefly through the work of B. F. Skinner, has taught us that behaviors are often determined by their consequences. This means that if a particular behavior results in a desirable consequence, such as access to food or water for a hungry or thirsty animal, the probability will increase for that behavior to be repeated.

In the classic Skinner-box experiment, a hungry rat (or pigeon, mouse, monkey, or other animal) can operate a lever to obtain food. The animal does not know this at the outset, and merely explores the cage, eventually pressing the lever by accident. Food appears at once, and the animal eats it. If we keep a continuous record of the lever-pressing activity, we see that a pattern soon emerges, as the animal learns how to bring about the desirable consequence. We say that the food is a *reinforcer* because it strengthens the probability that the appropriate *operant* (active, self-initiated, working) behavior—in this case lever pressing—will occur again.

Human behavior, of course, is subject to many complex influences, but the same rules often apply. An apt analogy to the Skinner-box experiment is a person working one of those gambling machines called a "one-armed bandit." If it never paid off, people would soon stop putting in their coins. The money it delivers is the reinforcer, while putting in coins and pulling the handle is the operant behavior that is being reinforced. In gambling devices, as in laboratory experiments, various schedules of reinforcement are possible. In a *fixed-ratio schedule*, a certain number of lever presses produces a reinforcement. The *fixed-interval schedule* provides no reinforcement until a minimum time-out has elapsed since the previous reinforcement, and then the very next lever press is effective. In a *variable-ratio schedule*, the average number of lever presses required to get the reward is set by the experimenter, but the actual number required for each pay-off varies in an unpredictable manner. It is interesting that for laboratory animals, as for people at Las Vegas, the strongest incentives are provided by variable schedules of reinforcement, the very system on which the "one-armed bandit" operates.

In order to study self-administration of a drug by an animal we implant a thin flexible tubing into the jugular vein in such a way that the animal can still move about freely. Now, instead of food, a certain number of lever presses will deliver a small dose of an addictive drug like heroin. The animal sooner or later discovers that pressing a lever produces a drug injection, and soon it will be taking the drug on a regular schedule. Clearly, in this case the drug itself is the reinforcer. Which drugs act as reinforcers in animals? In general, the same ones that are addictive in people, and that are recognized in drug discrimination experiments.*

Animals will sometimes work amazingly hard to get a drug. If every lever press results in the injection of a small but effective dose (a 1:1 fixed-ratio schedule), an animal will press the lever only occasionally, evidently allowing one dose to wear off before taking another. But what if we change the rules and require 10 lever presses to get a single injection? The animal will quickly adapt to the new arrange-

------

* Cannabis and many of the hallucinogens are exceptional among the addictive drugs in not being self-administered readily by laboratory animals. However, such drugs are distinguished well from inert substances, so that discrimination by animals serves as a good predictor of self-administration by humans.

ment, giving itself the same amount of drug as before, but now work-ing 10 times harder to get it. How hard an animal is willing to work for a drug is one measure of the drug's addictiveness. By this criterion cocaine is the most addictive drug of all; a monkey will self-administer it to exhaustion, not eating, not drinking, and ignoring opportunities for sexual activity. Eventually, such a monkey will die taking cocaine—of starvation or dehydration or sudden heart stoppage due to the drug excess in the body.

An interesting feature of self-administration behavior is the way an animal will tend to maintain a certain effective dosage. This is called *self-titration*. If the program is unaltered with respect to the number of lever presses required, but the dose delivered at each lever press is changed, the animal responds appropriately. Make each single dose bigger, the animal presses less frequently; decrease each single dose, the animal presses more frequently. If the dose is suddenly reduced to zero, there is usually a burst of pressing (as though expressing frustra-tion?) before the animal gives up. Again the slot machine offers an analogy; would not the gambler behave the same way (probably shak-ing the machine, too!) if the rules suddenly changed, if pay-offs in-explicably stopped?

In much the same way that the drug discrimination procedure allows us to test various active drugs and antagonists, similar kinds of experiments can be done with self-administration. Suppose a rat is working on a regular schedule for heroin injections, and it is then given a small dose of naltrexone. As the antagonist spreads through the body and reaches the brain, the rat discovers that the heroin in-jections produced by lever pressing seem suddenly to have become weaker, just as in the naltrexone discrimination experiment with hu-man subjects. The rat responds, accordingly, by working harder, taking more heroin to overcome (if possible) the antagonist. Sooner or later, however, if lever pressing yields no reward, the animal quits (see Chapter 10 for the human counterpart), and the behavior is said to be "extinguished." Thus, an animal's self-administration record can give us information about whether a novel drug is an antagonist, and if so, how potent it is.

For drugs that are effective by mouth, the self-administration pro-cedure can be as simple as presenting a choice between two water bottles, one of which contains the drug and the other a placebo solu-tion made to taste like the drug. This free-access drinking choice ar-rangement is less artificial than the lever pressing. Rats and mice can be housed socially, can have opportunities for exercise, and can have places to explore and toys to play with. Then one can test how the choice between drug and placebo is affected by environmental influences. One such experiment showed that the preference of rats for morphine over plain water was greater under conditions of isolation than in a more normal social setting. With people, too, the generally accepted wisdom is that the use of addictive drugs is influenced by social circumstances and by the availability of alternative activities and sources of satisfaction.

An interesting experiment in human self-administration was carried out to see if smokers titrate their intake of nicotine. Would they adjust their rate of smoking in order to obtain a certain desired amount of drug? Addicted cigarette smokers were gathered in a room, ostensibly to be tested on problem-solving ability. Paper-and-pencil tasks kept them busy. Each subject was given an ash tray and told to feel free to smoke. Hospital-style intravenous drip systems were set up, into which injections could be made, but out of the subjects' sight. Some subjects were randomly chosen to receive nicotine injections, others to receive placebo. At completion of the experiment a few hours later, the ash trays were collected, and the cigarette butts were counted and weighed. The result was clear. The more nicotine had been injected—without the subject's knowledge—the fewer cigarettes were smoked. Experiments like this one answered an old question—do smokers smoke primarily for oral gratification, for the visual pleasure of watching the smoke, or for the nicotine? Here it was evident that they smoked primarily for the nicotine, unconsciously adjusting their smoking behavior to maintain a certain nicotine level in their brains.

FEELS SO GOOD!

About 25 years ago James Olds invented a technique called *intracranial self-stimulation* (ICSS). He implanted a thin wire electrode in a rat's brain and arranged things so that by pressing a lever the animal could give itself a small electric shock. Many different locations of the electrode tip were tried. Olds found that although most placements did not encourage lever pressing, some did, quite consistently. In other words, at those specific brain sites the animals "liked" the electrical stimulation: it was reinforcing. Later the neurosurgeon Robert Heath repeated the procedure in human patients, incidentally to an attempt to find a surgical cure for epilepsy. He found that people, too, performed ICSS, reporting that it produced an intensely pleasurable and satisfying feeling, provided the electrode was correctly positioned in certain specific locations in the brain.

Mapping the whole rat brain by trying all sorts of electrode placements, Olds found that a site especially favorable to ICSS was a nerve pathway known as the *medial forebrain bundle*. Figure 4.2A shows the corresponding region of the human brain in its normal position in the skull, cut open lengthwise through the middle. Many of the neurons in this bundle originate in the midbrain, in the *ventral tegmental area* (VTA). This important nerve tract, in the so-called limbic system of the midbrain, is known as the *mesolimbic dopaminergic pathway*. It carries messages to several clusters of nerve cells in more forward parts of the brain, including the *nucleus accumbens* (NA) and *frontal cortex* (FC).

Figure 4.2B is an exploded view of the oval area in Figure 4.2A, presented as a cartoon. The neurons in this pathway are called *dopaminergic* because they manufacture the neurotransmitter dopamine, which is transported down their whole length, then packaged and stored at the nerve endings, ready for release into the synapses. When electrical signals (whether initiated normally in the brain or by ICSS) arrive at the nerve endings of this pathway, dopamine is released, and dopamine receptors on nearby neurons in the nucleus accumbens are stimulated. As explained later, opiates (and endogenous opioid neurotransmitters) inhibit the release of GABA at the VTA, freeing the dopamine neurons to fire more actively. Cocaine and amphetamines block the reuptake of dopamine at the nerve endings; amphetamines also cause increased dopamine release there.

This nerve tract is called a *reward pathway* because animals will work (press a lever) to stimulate it with electric shocks, just as they

FIGURE 4.2 *(Right)*   The mesolimbic dopaminergic reward pathway. (A) Human brain sliced open lengthwise, showing the relevant midbrain and forebrain area, outlined by an oval, with ventral tegmental area (VTA), nucleus accumbens (NA), and frontal cortex (FC) labeled; (B) Cartoon diagram of the area outlined in (A) and described fully in text. Symbols: Heavy dots represent stored neurotransmitter at nerve endings; + represents excitatory (– represents inhibitory) neurotransmitter released into synapse.

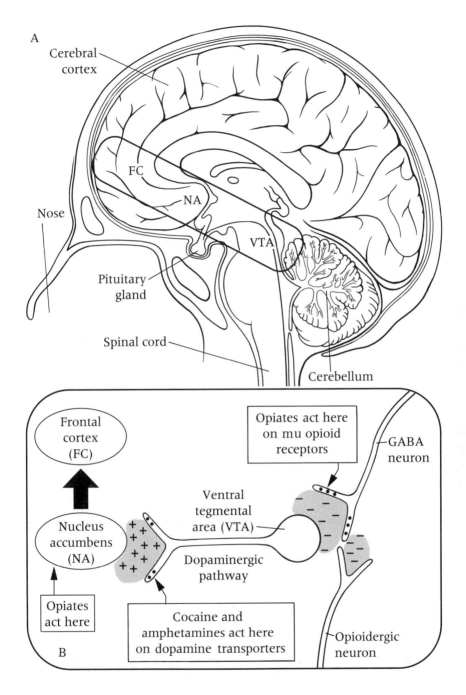

work to get a food reward if they are hungry, or a water reward if they are thirsty—and just as they work to get an injection of a drug that is a reinforcer. Here dopamine, released by ICSS, is the reinforcer.

Is this one of the same pathways that is responsible for the rewarding effects of addictive drugs? Although the techniques are tricky, it has indeed been shown that animals will work to inject tiny amounts of certain addictive drugs into discrete locations in their own brains. As we shall see, these reward sites are at the beginning and the end of the medial forebrain bundle—the VTA, the nucleus accumbens, and the frontal cortex.

HOW RATS LEARN WHERE TO GET THEIR "FIX"

In order to study the reinforcing properties of drugs and to localize drug reinforcement in the brain, Roy Wise and his student Michael Bozarth developed a novel procedure with several advantages over self-administration. This is an elegant technique called *conditioned place preference* (CPP). A special kind of shuttle box is used, into which a rat can be placed. The two sides of the box are made distinctive in various ways (such as different textures of flooring) to help a rat distinguish one side from the other. The animal can move freely within the box, shuttling as it wishes between the two sides. First, a rat is placed in the box every day, and the time it spends in each side is carefully recorded. Then one day the animal is placed in the nonpreferred side, injected with a drug (perhaps heroin or cocaine) or a placebo, prevented for a while from returning to the preferred side, and then returned to its home cage. The procedure is repeated daily for a week or two.

After this period of conditioning, the rat is simply placed in the box without any injection. What does it do? If the daily injections were placebo or if they were drugs known not to be reinforcers in other tests, the animal's behavior is unaltered; it chooses to be on the side of the box it preferred at the outset. On the other hand, if a reinforcing drug was injected during the conditioning period, the rat will have learned to associate the rewarding effect of the drug with the place where the injections were given (thus the name of the procedure), and it will linger on that side of the box as though waiting for its drug "fix."

This experiment showed plainly that the procedure could distinguish drugs that are rewarding from drugs that are not. The next step was to find where in the brain reinforcing drugs act to produce reward.

Under surgical anesthesia, a very fine injection needle was implanted into a selected site in a rat's brain. This microsurgery has no discernible effect on the animal's behavior; and we know from neurosurgical procedures in people that such fine needle implantations are harmless. Then place conditioning was carried out, as before; but now the daily drug injections (of tiny amounts of drug) were made into the discrete area of brain surrounding the needle tip instead of into a vein or under the skin. Different groups of rats were used for each brain site tested— a truly laborious experiment.

The results were remarkable. Drug injections into most parts of the brain did not modify the animal's behavior at all. But two locations were very effective in producing CPP, depending on which drug was being tested. Morphine and other opiates were effective at both ends of the dopaminergic reward pathway—at the VTA and the nucleus accumbens (Figure 4.2B). Cocaine produced CPP only at the nucleus accumbens. Thus, these two reinforcing and addictive drugs do seem to stimulate one of the very same pathways that animals self-stimulate with electric shocks in the ICSS procedure. It appears that some action of dopamine in the nucleus accumbens (and probably the frontal cortex) is the rewarding event in both cases. Apparently, anything that causes dopamine to be released there, or that enhances its action there, whether by electrical stimulation or by drug stimulation, is rewarding.

Reward Pathways

How does cocaine or amphetamine act at the nucleus accumbens? There, in the endings of the dopaminergic neurons, the stored neurotransmitter awaits the arrival of a nerve impulse (Figure 4.2B). Immediately upon its release into the synapses, dopamine combines with a dopamine receptor on another neuron. Then it is quickly taken up again (sponged up, one might say) by the same neurons that released it, and that is how its action in the synapses is terminated. The special transporter protein (described in Chapter 3) that is responsible for dopamine reuptake was recently identified, and its function was shown to be blocked by cocaine (to a lesser extent by amphetamines). When the transporter is blocked, more dopamine accumulates in the synapses, and thus its effects are greatly enhanced. Amphetamines act directly on the dopaminergic nerve endings to cause excessive release of dopamine into the synapses. A long-term effect of both drugs is to shut down dopamine production by a feedback mechanism, the normal regulatory controls reacting as though too much dopamine was being made and released.

How do opiates produce their rewarding effects? We know that opioid receptors on nerve endings suppress the release of neurotransmitters, but how can that result in stimulation of the reward pathway? The following example, first worked out in Floyd Bloom's laboratory, illustrates an important principle about the brain—that stimulation can result from disinhibition. Morphine provokes intense electrical activity in a part of the brain known as the hippocampus; it may actually cause seizures. But the excitation is produced in a curious way. Large neurons here are held continuously in check by smaller neurons releasing GABA. Presynaptic opioid receptors are deployed on the ends of the GABA neurons. When morphine activates these opioid receptors, GABA release is impeded, the braking action of the GABA is greatly diminished and the large hippocampal neurons become more active. Thus, the excitation caused by morphine is actually due to disinhibition—that is, inhibition of the release of the inhibitory neurotransmitter GABA. As one might expect, the opioid receptors on which morphine acts are normally activated by enkephalin, which is released from nearby *opioidergic* neurons (neurons that contain and release an opioid peptide) as part of the regulation of hippocampal activity.

In the same way, the neurons in the VTA are thought to be held in check by GABA, as indicated by minus signs at the GABA-releasing neuron in Figure 4.2B. By inhibiting GABA release (indicated by minus signs at the opioidergic neuron), opiates diminish the braking action of GABA on the dopaminergic neurons that originate in the VTA; so they fire more frequently, releasing more dopamine from the endings of those same neurons in the nucleus accumbens (indicated by plus signs). A similar disinhibitory effect of opiates presumably accounts for their stimulatory action when applied directly to the nucleus accumbens.

It now appears that dopamine effects in a reward pathway are enhanced not only by cocaine, amphetamines, and opiates, but also by nicotine and alcohol. As the evidence accumulates, many researchers are coming to the view that this common mechanism of reinforcement is shared by all the addictive drugs—in other words, that stimulation of such a pathway is what makes a drug addictive. The account given here, it should be understood, is oversimplified and probably very incomplete, and there are likely to be more reward pathways than the one described. Moreover, we have no idea how dopamine stimulation in the nucleus accumbens actually produces the reward phenomenon.

A crude way of putting this uncertainty is to ask: But where in the brain is the feeling of pleasure and satisfaction localized? Is the nucleus accumbens only a way-station, a relay in a much more complex network of neurons? The question may not even make sense; perhaps a mood state is not localized at all, but is spread over many parts of the brain. Nevertheless, despite all the uncertainties, the studies described here have opened the way for deeper understanding. Most important, there seems to be no reason to think that the biologic mechanisms of drug reward in the human brain are fundamentally different from those uncovered by these landmark experiments in rats.

REWARDING AND AVERSIVE OPIOIDS

Opioidergic neurons containing enkephalins, beta-endorphin, and dynorphins are found normally in the VTA. Not surprisingly, an enkephalin or beta-endorphin, if injected directly into the VTA, acts like an addictive opiate, evidently activating mu opioid receptors there. But the dynorphin peptides, which act preferentially on kappa opioid receptors, have an opposite effect; they activate a system that mediates aversion (delivers punishment rather than reward). Evidence for such a system was obtained recently in pioneering investigations by Albert Herz and his colleagues at the Max-Planck Institute for Psychiatry near Munich. It was already known that animals would not self-administer kappa agonists. Using the CPP procedure, the Munich scientists now discovered that these drugs condition a rat to avoid rather than to prefer the side of the shuttle box where they are administered.

What about people? The same investigators gave human volunteers a synthetic opiate agonist that is selective for kappa receptors. It was expected that the subjects would find the drug unpleasant, as animals seemed to. What actually happened was dramatic and totally unexpected. The kappa agonist was more than unpleasant—it produced a frightening psychotic state, with weird distortions of time and space, a terrifying feeling of impending death, and hallucinations. How could the experimenters be sure that these bizarre drug effects were due to activation of kappa opioid receptors and not to some nonspecific toxic disturbance of brain function? First, the kappa agonist they used was available in both left- and right-handed forms, as described earlier for other opioid ligands, and only one of the two was active. Such a distinction between identical opioids that differ only in three-dimensional shape typically signifies interaction with an opioid receptor. Second, and most convincing—and to the great relief of experimenters and subjects alike—the mental state of the subjects reverted to normal instantly when the opiate antagonist naltrexone was injected.

In summary, a natural opioid system exists for signaling both reward (probably by beta-endorphin) and punishment (by dynorphins). Thus, the balance of these opposing opioid peptides may regulate many aspects of our normal state of mind. We can speculate that reward systems drive adaptive behavior in the following way. They signal "good" when food is found and eaten by a hungry animal, when water is found and drunk by a thirsty animal, when sexual activity is promised and consummated, when a threatening situation is averted. They signal "bad" when harmful behavior is engaged in or when pain is experienced. These signals become associated with the situations in which they are generated, and they are remembered. Thus, the conditioning observed in the CPP procedure seems to represent the necessary process by which an animal learns to seek what is beneficial and avoid what is harmful.

That addictive drugs "feel good" must be understood in this evolutionary context, for in a sense they are not even foreign to the body; they merely mimic or block the neurotransmitters that function normally to signal reward. However, they activate the pathways artificially—short-circuiting the natural process, one might say—and thus they disturb the mechanisms that keep people on an even keel. This delicately regulated system was perfected by evolution over millions of years to serve the survival of all species, and to let us humans experience pleasure and satisfaction from the biologically appropriate behaviors and situations of daily life. No prudent person would try to beef up the performance of a personal computer by jolting it with high voltage electric shocks. It always astonishes me, therefore, to hear users of addictive drugs and apologists for their use—some of whom are sensible people in other respects—defend what is really a reckless chemical attack on the human brain. The more we learn about addictive drugs and brain chemistry, the more clear it becomes that the brain is far too delicate to tamper with, too complex an organ to risk damaging its intricate regulatory controls. So the big question is: Why do some people nevertheless engage in risky drug-using behavior, and why do some of them fall victim to addiction?

CHAPTER 5

Pain and Pleasure

In the Cornaro Chapel in Rome a brilliant shaft of sunlight illuminates the masterwork of the great seventeenth-century sculptor Bernini. A marble statue of Saint Teresa, it depicts the moment of her famous ecstasy, when an angel with a flaming golden arrow pierced her heart repeatedly. In her own words:

> The pain was so great that I screamed aloud, but simultaneously felt such infinite sweetness that I wished the pain to last eternally. It was the sweetest caressing of the soul by God.

Saint Teresa's experience reflects the familiar yet mysterious psychologic relationship between pain and pleasure. Pain relieved leaves not merely a normal pain-free state, but a special kind of pleasure and satisfaction in its absence. Pain unrelieved can activate endogenous mechanisms that not only suppress the pain but also produce pleasure in their own right. And though the response is considered an abnormal reaction, some people derive a masochistic pleasure from pain itself.

It is interesting, therefore, that this pleasure-pain connection is grounded in neurochemistry; the endogenous opioids are responsible both for suppressing pain and for producing pleasure through the reward systems. The same duality seems to apply to the behavior of opiate addicts—they use heroin for pleasure, certainly, but also for relief of physical and emotional pain. This chapter focuses on the endogenous opioids because we know most about their relationship to pain, pleasure, and addiction. It may well turn out, however, that there is a general principle here, namely, that suppression of pain and enhancement of pleasure are mediated by common neural circuitry. Indeed, there is evidence that addictive drugs other than opiates—for example, caffeine, alcohol, and cannabis—have pain-relieving qualities, too, but working out the details will require a great deal more research.

SUPPRESSION OF PAIN BY ENDOGENOUS OPIOIDS

Opioid receptors and opioid peptides are found in the dopamine reward pathways of the midbrain, as described in Chapter 4. They are also distributed widely throughout the entire nervous system—in the brain and spinal cord; and in the nerves that supply the extremities, the skin, the blood vessels, and most of the internal organs of the body. Nerves that conduct pain enter the spinal cord, where they impinge on other neurons. Those synaptic connections constitute the first of several relays in the pain pathway. Within the spinal cord successive sets of neurons carry the pain message higher, to further relay stations in the lowest part of the brain, and finally to higher centers that handle emotional and intellectual functions. Opiates act at several of the synaptic relays, at progressively higher levels of the pain pathway, to block transmission of the pain message. The sensory nerves that are activated by a painful stimulus in the skin or an internal organ release, at the first spinal cord relay, a special peptide neurotransmitter called a *neurokinin*, which stimulates the next neurons at that synapse. Opioid receptors located on the endings of the neurokinin-containing neuron are able to suppress neurokinin release. Morphine, given for pain relief, activates these receptors and thus interrupts the pain pathway. The most dramatic effect of morphine, however, occurs in the brain, where it disconnects the perception of pain from the usual emotional response to pain. As some patients put it, "I know the pain is still there, but I don't mind it any more."

Because the seemingly magical property of abolishing both emotional and physical pain underlies the addictive use of heroin (and of some other addictive drugs), we need to understand how our natural system for suppressing pain works. Is that system turned on by painful and stressful stimuli? How might we obtain direct experimental evidence about this? Suppose, for example, that the opioid peptide beta-endorphin were a neurotransmitter in such a system; then we would want to measure its release inside brain and spinal cord in response to pain. In humans we can easily take a blood sample but not a sample of brain or spinal cord. Consequently many measurements have been made on blood after pain and other stressful stimuli. The most popular version of this approach sought to relate the "runner's high" to increased beta-endorphin blood levels. Unfortunately, such measurements are based on radioimmunoassays, which can not distinguish between opioid-active beta-endorphin itself and peptides that are chemically related to beta-endorphin but have no opioid activity. Most of this "beta-endorphin" consists of these other peptides, which are released from the pituitary gland (not the brain) along with the stress hormone ACTH. It is therefore misleading to suggest that the ups and downs of this immunoreactivity in blood have anything to do with pain regulation or emotional states that originate in the brain or spinal cord.

We can measure endogenous opioids in animal brains. However, even in animals, it is not too useful to know how much beta-endorphin or enkephalin or dynorphin is present, stored in nerve endings, waiting to be released. The real question is: Does pain provoke their release? After all, it is the dynamic release process that matters. If you wanted to analyze the operation of a water wheel on a river, you would have to measure the flow of water running down the river, not the height of water behind the dam in an upstream reservoir.

A method long in use for measuring neurotransmitter release is to take small samples of cerebrospinal fluid from the spinal canal or base of the brain and determine by immunoassay how the amount of some neuropeptide varies under different conditions. There is a major problem, however, in that it takes many minutes for a substance released deep inside the brain to appear in the spinal fluid, and during that time a peptide is very likely to be destroyed. One needs to measure release at the site of release. Scientists are developing new techniques for doing just that. Figure 5.1A illustrates one of these, the operation of a *push-pull cannula* inserted deep into the spinal cord of a live rat under anesthesia. The cannula is an extremely fine double-barreled glass tubing filled with a salt solution. A tiny stream of fluid is pushed into the tissue through one barrel of the cannula, and withdrawn continuously through the other, thus bathing the synapses that surround the cannula tip. The amount of such substances as beta-endorphin in the withdrawn fluid is measured by immunoassay. By this procedure it has been shown that extreme stress and pain, as well as electroacupuncture (see below), actually do release opioid peptides at several levels of the pain pathway, not only within the spinal cord but also in various parts of the brain.

Another technique is based on the principle of competition for receptor binding. A thin slice of rat hippocampus can be maintained in a functional state in a shallow tissue bath under a microscope. Here it is exposed to a radiolabeled ligand, so that binding to receptors can be measured (as described in Chapter 3), and an autoradiograph shows the location of those receptors in the slice. The following experiment, carried out by Charles Chavkin, used a radiolabeled ligand that is highly selective for kappa opioid receptors. One of the neural pathways that is known to contain dynorphins was stimulated electrically before the slice was exposed to the radiolabeled ligand. The subsequent autoradiograph showed a reduction in radioactivity compared with unstimulated tissue used as a control. In other words, a dynorphin peptide released by the stimulation occupied the kappa binding sites, excluding the radiolabeled ligand. This method is being used to establish which opioid ligands are released, and with which opioid receptor subtypes they combine, when known nerve pathways are stimulated. Researchers are beginning to apply similar methods to the VTA, the nucleus accumbens, and other parts of the reward pathways implicated in addiction.

A novel method—also based on the competition principle—uses a fine needle coated with an antibody that is specific for a particular peptide neurotransmitter. Figure 5.1B illustrates the technique as used to measure release of the neurokinin that delivers pain messages to the spinal cord. The needle, coated with an antibody to the neurokinin, is inserted into a rat's spinal cord, and the animal is subjected to pain by pinching a paw. After a suitable time the needle is removed and immersed in a solution of radiolabeled neurokinin. Binding to the antibody occurs everywhere along the needle except where neurokinin

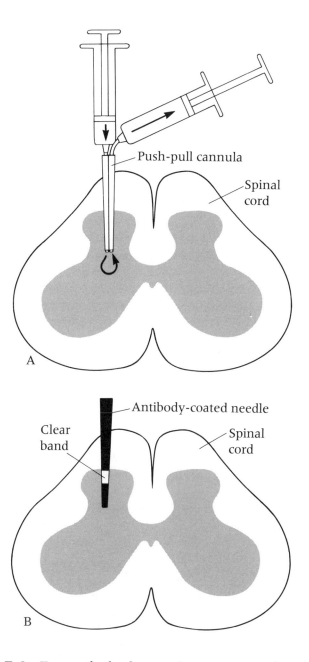

FIGURE 5.1 Two methods of measuring neurotransmitter release. (A) Push-pull cannula, fluid flow indicated by arrows; (B) antibody-coated needle. See text for explanation.

released in the spinal cord (and not radioactive, of course) had bound, filling the antibody binding sites. Finally, the needle is placed on a photographic film. In the illustration the image of the needle is shown positioned exactly as it had been in the living spinal cord; but of course, no actual image is obtained until after the needle is removed. Then, where the needle was radioactive, the image of the needle is black, but where neurokinin was released, a clear band is seen where the radiolabeled neurokinin was excluded. This experiment proved that painful stimulation released neurokinin at precisely the site in the spinal cord where the endings of the incoming neurokinin-releasing neurons that carry pain messages are known to be—the same site where opioids suppress neurokinin release.

HOW ANTAGONISTS REVEAL ONGOING OPIOID ACTIVITY

The opiate antagonists naloxone and naltrexone can shed light on which brain functions require participation of an endogenous opioid. The logic is simply that if any function is altered by one of these antagonists, that function is probably mediated by opioid receptors. If low doses suffice, the *mu* receptor, for which naloxone and naltrexone have highest affinity, is most likely responsible. As no opiate agonists are administered in this type of experiment, we can conclude that an endogenous opioid is responsible.

A good illustration of this approach is the effect of naloxone on the circulating sex hormone gonadotropin (also called LH) in sexually mature male rats. LH stimulates the testicles to produce testosterone, which is responsible for many male sexual characteristics and behaviors. LH is secreted into the blood by specialized cells in the pituitary gland, cells that in turn require for their functioning a brain hormone called gonadotropin-releasing hormone (GnRH). Giving naloxone causes a huge increase in circulating LH, as shown in Figure 5.2, because of increased release of GnRH in the brain. Most interesting here is the contrast between the striking effect in 60-day-old sexually mature rats (upper curve) and the lack of effect in 30-day-old immature rats (lower curve). The conclusion to be drawn is that once this hormonal system develops, at puberty, one of the endogenous opioid peptides acts as a continuous brake on GnRH release—a brake that is removed when naloxone blocks the opioid receptors. This system of inhibition through opioid receptors is analogous to opioid action in the

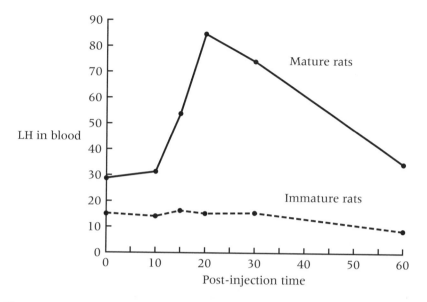

FIGURE 5.2 An opioid antagonist reverses ongoing inhibition of hormone release. Actual record of naloxone stimulating LH release in rats. Blood levels of LH are shown at various times after naloxone injection. Lower record, immature rats, 30 days old; upper record, mature rats, 60 days old. [From T. J. Cicero et al., *Journal of Pharmacology and Experimental Therapeutics* 246: 14–20, 1988.]

hippocampus and the VTA, as described earlier. Morphine (whether derived in the body from injected heroin or administered itself) and other opiates have the same effect in humans, acting in an unregulated and excessive manner to shut down sexual function in men and to suppress the menstrual cycle in women—problems that characteristically afflict heroin addicts.

To test whether an endogenous opioid suppresses pain my colleague Priscilla Grevert carried out a naloxone experiment, modelled on earlier studies by a French colleague, Joseph Jacob. When a mouse is placed on a hot plate, warm enough to be uncomfortable but not hot enough to burn the feet, the mouse reacts by lifting a paw or jumping within a few seconds. The greater the discomfort, the sooner the mouse reacts, so the delay in jumping (called the *latency*) is a measure of the intensity of the pain. If groups of animals are injected with morphine before being placed on the hot plate, the average latency is greatly prolonged, as though the animals experience less pain. If naloxone is given first, and then morphine, the morphine effect is prevented, the latency being the same as if no morphine had been given. These preliminary tests tell us that the method works, that suppression of pain by an administered opiate can be measured as increased latency on the hot plate, and that naloxone blocks that effect. Now, if pain is being to some extent suppressed by an endogenous opioid, we would expect naloxone itself to make it worse. Using fresh mice, and without giving any morphine, we injected naloxone alone. The latency was reduced, the mice jumped sooner than normal, as though the pain had been intensified. We concluded that an endogenous opioid system was, indeed, suppressing pain in these animals; and by blocking that system, naloxone made the pain worse.

A useful feature of naloxone and naltrexone is that they are harmless enough to use in humans. Priscilla Grevert and I carried out experiments with many volunteers. Knowing the result of the mouse hot-plate experiment, we expected naloxone to intensify pain. We produced pain by a standard procedure that involves shutting off the circulation to the forearm by inflating a blood pressure cuff to a very high pressure. The subject exercises the hand for a few minutes and then relaxes. I can say, from my own experience as a subject, that without any blood flow to carry away the products of muscular activity, severe throbbing pain develops—tolerable, but only barely so. The subject reports the increasing severity of pain on a numerical scale. The procedure can be terminated by the subject at any time, but otherwise it lasts 10 minutes. To our great surprise we found that naloxone had no effect whatsoever.

Now we know why. Under the artificial conditions of the testing laboratory, with so many reassurances by the investigators, subjects remain calm and relaxed; the procedure, although painful, is not stressful. Other investigators have shown that if pain is experienced while under stress, naloxone does indeed make it worse. For example, actual clinical pain (always stressful)—as after tooth extraction or other kinds of surgery—is indeed intensified by naloxone. So stressful pain in humans can activate the endogenous opioid system. We know now, in fact, that severe stress alone, even without pain, activates the endogenous opioids so that noxious stimuli become less painful than they otherwise would be.

In animal experiments stressful procedures reveal this mechanism. For example, we can place a rat in cold water so that it has to swim to a distant platform—a stressful task. Then we test it for pain sensitivity by applying heat to the tail and measuring how many seconds pass before the animal reacts. Such an animal displays a much more sluggish reaction to the painful stimulus after the cold-water swim than before, and this pain reduction is abolished by naloxone.

A common response of animals to an overwhelming threat or to extreme pain is total immobility, giving the impression of paralysis or indifference. This reaction may be mediated by endogenous opioid release, as in a few instances it has been shown to be prevented by naloxone. In the rat, morphine causes an immobile state (described in Chapter 2) which is reversed by naloxone. We do not know if such reactions in humans are also mediated by endogenous opioids, but it would not be surprising if they were. An extraordinary documented case is the description by the famous explorer David Livingstone of being attacked by a lion:

> He caught my shoulder as he sprang ... he shook me as a terrier does a rat. The shock produced a stupor similar to that which seems to be felt by a mouse after the first shake of the cat. It caused a sort of dreaminess in which there was no sense of pain nor feeling of terror, though [I was] quite conscious of all that was happening. ... This peculiar state is probably produced in all animals killed by the carnivora; and if so, is a merciful provision by our benevolent creator for lessening the pain of death.

Lawrence Durrell, in his *Alexandria Quartet*, describes something similar; but it is not clear whether this passage is based on fact or whether it is pure fiction:

> The camels of Narouz were being cut up for the feast. Poor things, they knelt there peacefully with their forelegs folded under them like cats while a horde of men attacked them with axes in the moonlight. ... The animals made no move to avoid the blows, uttered no cries as they were dismembered. ... Whole members were being hacked off, as painlessly, it seemed, as when a tree is pruned.

Speaking of camels brings to mind an amusing story that illustrates how a scientific myth can take hold, based on premises that may sound logical but later turn out to be completely wrong. Chapter 2 recounted how beta-endorphin is produced in the body as part of a long precursor peptide. As long as it is part of the longer peptide, beta-endorphin has no biologic activity and does not relieve pain; the long precursor peptide has to be cleaved first to release free beta-endorphin. The chemist C. H. Li had obtained the long peptide from pig pituitary glands. When an Iraqi postdoctoral fellow finished his work with Li, it was proposed that on his return home he should isolate the precursor peptide from camel pituitary glands to see how it differed from the pig peptide. Remarkably, he could find no precursor peptide at all; only free beta-endorphin was found—and in extraordinarily large amounts. Li explained at scientific meetings: "Now we know why camels are so insensitive to pain; they have a huge amount of free beta-endorphin." Subsequently, when an Israeli scientist tried to repeat this work, he found the precursor peptide but almost no free beta-endorphin. Were Israeli camels really different from Iraqi camels? Not at all. The explanation lay, very simply, in a difference of refrigeration; without adequate freezing, the enzymes in the pituitary glands of Iraqi camels cleaved the precursor peptide after death, releasing free beta-endorphin. Live camels did not have a large amount of beta-endorphin after all. Then what about the pain sensitivity of camels? To this day—despite Lawrence Durrell's account—there is no evidence to suggest that camels are less sensitive to pain than are other species of mammals.

PAIN SUPPRESSION BY ACUPUNCTURE

The ancient Chinese procedure of acupuncture employs fine needles, which pierce the skin at specified spots and are rotated or heated to stimulate the local nerves. Largely because acupuncture had been claimed, over the centuries, to cure every imaginable disease, Western medicine tended to discount the whole thing as superstition. Only in the late 1970s, when Western scientists could again visit China freely, did we learn that acupuncture produces real pain relief—in surgical operations on animals as well as on humans.

Extensive experiments over many years by J. S. Han at Beijing Medical University have demonstrated that electroacupuncture (stimulating an acupuncture point by a mild electric shock) reliably produces pain relief, not only in humans, but in laboratory animals as well. I recall Professor Han's first visit to my laboratory, in 1978. "The problem for science," he told me, referring to acupuncture, "is to sort out the superstition from the reality." He had wisely decided to concentrate on the pain-relieving effect of acupuncture, putting aside all the other supposed benefits of the technique. He used laboratory animals, applied electric shocks of known strength and frequency through the needles, used standardized pain stimuli, measured pain by response latency (as described above), and employed the whole array of modern neurobiology techniques to get at the mechanism. He established beyond doubt that pain relief by electroacupuncture is a reality, and he soon found that it is blocked by naloxone. Moreover, he showed that the suppression of pain is accompanied by measurable release of opioid peptides within the spinal cord and brain at several sites along the known pain pathways. These pioneering studies established acupuncture as a valid technique for relieving pain, and they have since been extended to humans. They have also added to the evidence that pain relief by endogenous opioids, as by administered morphine, occurs at the first relay in the spinal cord, in lower parts of the brain, and also at many of the higher centers where pain is perceived and elicits emotional responses.

ENDOGENOUS OPIOIDS AND THE EMOTIONS

The discoveries of reward pathways, and the feelings of satisfaction evoked by heroin and morphine, suggested that certain kinds of emotional satisfaction might be caused by endogenous opioids released onto opioid receptors within the brain, perhaps in the mesolimbic dopaminergic reward pathway. The so-called "runner's high" may be an example. It is a state of intense emotional satisfaction after maximum stressful physical effort.

I looked for a way to bring about an emotional response under experimental control in the laboratory. A "thrill" accompanies emotionally arousing experiences in many people. It is a pleasant tingling vibration that starts at the back of the neck and travels down the spine, often also sweeping over the arms and down the legs. It may be accompanied by tears, sighs, a "catch" in the throat, and even gooseflesh on the arms or chest. The word "thrill" is interesting for its double meaning, long established in our language; according to the dictionary a thrill is both a vibratory sensation (the common meaning in medicine) and an emotionally arousing experience. Thrilling experiences are described frequently as "raising the hackles" (i.e., gooseflesh that causes hairs to rise at the back of the neck) or as making "chills run up and down the spine." Thrills are evoked by many kinds of moving experiences. Some people have them when they hear certain passages of music. Opera fans are familiar with the intensity of these emotional reactions, typically experienced after a superb performance of one of the great operatic arias.

Musical thrills are easily studied in music-loving volunteers. I reasoned that if the thrills were mediated by the release of endogenous brain opioids, they should be blocked by naloxone. All of my volunteer subjects knew, from experience, what musical passages gave them thrills. One by one, they listened to such a passage in the laboratory, and they reported the occurrence and intensity of the thrills. Then they were given an injection—double-blind, with all the injections coded, so neither I nor the subjects knew which was naloxone, which was placebo. After an injection, they listened again, and rated the thrills once more. Altogether, there were 10 subjects and 10 sessions for each, spaced a week apart. Whether there was no intervening injection or a placebo injection was given, repeating the same musical passage yielded the same pattern and intensity of thrills. But—at least in some subjects—if an injection of naloxone was given, the drug clearly blocked the thrills. This was only a small-scale experiment; it ought to be repeated with more subjects and with higher doses of naloxone (the doses I used are now known to be only marginally effective). Nevertheless, although it remains speculative, the outcome did suggest that endogenous opioids play a role in purely emotional responses, possibly through one of the reward pathways.

The hallmark of opiate action is suppression of the anxiety and distress associated with pain. And opiates relieve emotional pain, even in the absence of physical pain. Finally, opiates produce emotional satisfaction and pleasure. This unique mixture of biologic effects goes a long way toward explaining why these powerful painkillers are also powerfully addictive, especially when emotional suffering results from intolerable conditions of life. A quick "fix" offers immediate satisfaction, immediate pleasure, immediate escape from misery.

CHAPTER 6

Tolerance
and Dependence

If you take an addictive drug repeatedly, over a long period of time, the drug becomes less and less effective, so that more is needed to produce the same effect as before. That is called *tolerance*. Typically, addicts who have become tolerant self-administer many times their original drug dosage. At the same time, a state develops in which stopping the drug actually causes illness. That is called *dependence*. Stopping suddenly ("cold turkey") results in a withdrawal sickness, which is dramatically relieved by another dose of the same drug. Tolerance and dependence result from biochemical changes in the brain. To understand these changes, and possibly learn how to prevent them, is a major aim of current research.

TOLERANCE

If a drug is injected into a vein, it is carried quickly in the blood to all parts of the body including the brain. If the drug is smoked, it passes directly into the bloodstream at the lungs, and it reaches the brain within a few seconds. Taken by mouth, a drug has to be absorbed into the blood that is passing through the stomach or intestine, whence it is carried to the liver; there some or most of it may be destroyed, and only what remains reaches the other body organs. Some drugs pass from the blood into body fat, leaving less for the brain. Some drugs are destroyed by enzymes in the bloodstream.

Alcohol, for example, is metabolized in the following way. It is converted by a liver enzyme, alcohol dehydrogenase, to a very toxic product, acetaldehyde. A second liver enzyme, acetaldehyde dehydrogenase, destroys the acetaldehyde as fast as it is formed, so that very little accumulates. Were it not for this second enzyme, alcohol would be too poisonous to drink. In Chapter 9 we shall see that one way of discouraging alcohol addicts from drinking is to block their acetaldehyde dehydrogenase so that even a single drink will make them severely ill.

Sometimes metabolism activates an inert substance. Heroin, for example, is not biologically active because its two acetic acid groups, which confer the property of rapid passage from the blood into the brain, also prevent its binding to opioid receptors. In the brain the acetic acid groups are removed, yielding biologically active morphine. Morphine itself is then inactivated by a liver enzyme that attaches a sugar molecule to it. So here we have one enzyme that converts a "pro-drug" to an active drug, and another that destroys the drug's biologic activity.

Cocaine is destroyed very rapidly, both in the blood and in the liver, by enzymes that cleave the molecule into two inert parts. And some drugs—THC is an example—are metabolized slowly or not at all, but are stored for a very long time in body fat, trickling out into the bloodstream and being excreted in the urine for days or even weeks after a single dose.

These complex patterns of metabolism differ greatly among people, so that people differ widely in their sensitivity to any given drug and therefore in the necessary dosage of that drug. The effective dose of any psychotropic drug is whatever is necessary to establish an effective concentration in the brain. That will depend on the affinity of the particular drug for its receptors, and also on drug metabolism and distribution. Not surprisingly, average doses vary widely among different drugs. We express dosage in grams, milligrams, and micrograms; a gram is one twenty-eighth of an ounce, a milligram is one thousandth of a gram, and a microgram is one thousandth of a milligram. An effective dose of morphine or heroin, injected directly into a vein, is a few milligrams; of nicotine a fraction of a milligram; of cocaine or amphetamine about 20 milligrams; of LSD about 20 micrograms; of caffeine about 100 milligrams. Alcohol is the least potent of all; about 10 grams by mouth is required (one-third of an ounce of 200-proof pure alcohol) to produce a noticeable effect on behavior.

A psychotropic drug takes effect as soon as enough of it reaches the brain, where it acts on its receptors; and the effect wears off as the drug concentration there declines. How long a single dose lasts is different for each drug, depending on how fast the drug is removed from the blood by the metabolic processes and by excretion in the urine. As the drug level falls in the blood bathing the brain, the drug concentration at the brain receptors drops below an effective level, and the effects of the initial dose wear off.

In *metabolic tolerance,* the body (primarily the liver) adapts to a drug by developing an increased capacity to destroy it. Then a dose that was effective initially becomes less so. Each repetition of the initial dose provides less and less drug for shorter and shorter times at the sites of action in the brain so that progressively higher doses are needed to produce the desired psychotropic effect. Metabolic tolerance develops if a drug causes increased production of the very enzyme that destroys it. An example is pentobarbital, a short-acting barbiturate that was once widely prescribed as a sleeping pill. A dose sufficient to cause sleep remains in the blood for a few hours, but with repeated dosage the drug is destroyed more and more rapidly and thus becomes some-what less effective.

Cellular tolerance results from fundamental changes in the brain itself. In contrast to metabolic tolerance, which rarely is extreme, this adaptation by the brain itself is responsible for the extreme degree of tolerance that can develop to such drugs as morphine and heroin. The neurons adapt to the drug, becoming less sensitive to it with continued exposure. Even at the moment the first dose wears off, repeating that dose will produce a somewhat smaller effect than before, and the dosage will have to be increased somewhat to fully obtain the original intensity of drug action again. As the neurons continue to adapt to higher and higher drug doses, their function remains seemingly normal despite their being bathed in the drug. In this state, when the psychotropic effect of a dose has just worn off, a considerable drug concentration remains—enough to have caused an extreme behavioral effect (possibly even death) originally. The apparent normality of brain function masks an underlying neurochemical change that only becomes manifest if the drug is withdrawn. The brain has become dependent on the drug.

The development of cellular tolerance has a time course all its own, one that can be studied experimentally. For a given drug, there is a *critical interval* between doses, the shortest interval of time that must elapse before repetition of the dose will produce the same effect as the one before. With any shorter interval, tolerance (and dependence) will build up, so that successive doses have to be increased in order to obtain the original drug effect. The critical interval for heroin in humans can be recognized by the typical experience of addicts when they first begin using the drug. They inject it into a vein and experience the "high." A week or two later they take another "fix," and again they get the desired effect. If they continue using the drug at an interval of a week or so, the dose requirement does not escalate, and some people manage to control their use in this manner for months or even years. Most, however, once they have started, are unable to resist the temptation to experience the heroin effect more often, and they start to use it more frequently. When the interval becomes shorter than a day or two, the initial dosage starts to be less effective. With use several times a day, the required dosage escalates sharply. Cocaine has a shorter pharmacologic action than heroin (measured in minutes instead of hours), and also a much shorter critical interval, so that the need for higher dosage develops very quickly, even during a single "run" of cocaine use. During a typical cocaine binge, the addict injects (or smokes) again and again, increasing the dosage, until the entire supply of drug is exhausted.

Experiments with ex-addict volunteers, closely monitored in a closed hospital ward, showed that when heroin or morphine was made freely available, the maximum permissible doses were eventually taken—amounts that greatly exceeded what would have been an effective dose at the outset. In one famous experiment, a subject built his dose of morphine up to ten thousand times the initial effective dose—and still demanded more. Furthermore, it was shown by Roger E. Meyer, in experiments with heroin in human volunteers, that allowing frequent access and dosage escalation did not satisfy the addict's desire for heroin. On the contrary, it became increasingly difficult for the addicts to obtain rewarding effects comparable to those produced by the initial, lower dosages. Eventually, a negative mood state developed, with increasing irritability, hostility, and paranoia. A similar picture is seen with escalating dosages of cocaine or amphetamines. These observations argue strongly against the simplistic idea, sometimes advanced, that if only we let addicts have all the heroin or cocaine they want, the problems associated with their addiction would be solved.

The ultimate degree of tolerance that can develop is different for each drug and also probably varies among users. Opiates represent one extreme: there seems to be virtually no ceiling on tolerance. Nicotine addicts, on the other hand, rarely smoke more than three packs of cigarettes daily; and although this amount of nicotine would be lethal to the nonsmoker, the peak nicotine concentration in blood and brain is not more than about 10 times the nontolerant level. Likewise, when tolerance develops to alcohol, quite large daily amounts may be consumed; but the amount taken at a single sitting is rarely more than a few times the initially effective dosage. Caffeine intake by tolerant coffee drinkers may be as great as 10–20 times the usual single dose (of one cup of coffee) in the course of a day.

Tolerance makes life difficult, especially for heroin and cocaine addicts, because as they increase their dosage, expenditures for the drug become ever more difficult to afford. Ordinary, legitimate sources of income soon prove insufficient for all but the wealthiest addicts; and then robbery, burglary, theft, embezzlement, and other property crimes, as well as prostitution, are seen as practical ways to obtain the necessary wherewithal. Thus, tolerance is important because of the problems it creates for the addict, but from the standpoint of biology it is not fundamental: it is not a cause of addiction but a consequence of addiction. To be addictive, a psychotropic drug must be reinforcing, must stimulate a reward system, but it need not necessarily lead to tolerance. Finally, one might well ask: If addicts get into trouble because of the dosage escalation, why don't they just stop using the drug, and let the tolerance (which is fully reversible) dissipate? Why, indeed? We do not have a good answer, but the question speaks directly to the compulsive quality of all the drug addictions.

DEPENDENCE

Dependence (sometimes called *physical dependence*), which typically accompanies tolerance, is not a drug effect in the usual sense, for it can only be observed in the absence of the drug that caused it. When an addictive drug is administered repeatedly at an interval that produces tolerance, the brain adapts to the presence of the drug. Then, even with repeated high dosage, which establishes a high drug concentration at the sites of action in the brain, the psychotropic effects may be minimal or absent. Only when drug administration is suddenly stopped do brain disorders ensue, known collectively as a *withdrawal syndrome* (also called *abstinence syndrome*).

Remarkably, despite their dramatic features, the withdrawal syndromes seen after chronic use of opiates or alcohol were only first recognized as such during the 1930s, 1940s, and 1950s. Before that, physicians and law-enforcement personnel believed that the vociferous complaints of opiate addicts deprived of their drug were manipulative behaviors designed to secure an opiate. And many physicians thought that the alcohol withdrawal syndrome was actually due to a persistent direct effect of alcohol itself on the brain. The confusion was finally clarified by controlled clinical studies with human subjects.

In 1938 at the U.S. Public Health Service prison hospital for addicts, at Lexington, Kentucky, C. K. Himmelsbach and his colleagues demonstrated unequivocally that the opiate withdrawal syndrome—nausea, vomiting, sweating, gooseflesh, diarrhea, tremor, chills, and fever—was caused predictably by discontinuing morphine administration in a person who had been maintained on a regular schedule of morphine injections with escalating dosage. The prime necessity in studying anything scientifically is to be able to make measurements—if at all possible—and collect the quantitative data needed to analyze what happens when this or that condition is changed. Himmelsbach's contribution was to develop a method of scoring the intensity of the withdrawal syndrome, placing emphasis on easily recognized objective disturbances of physiology rather than on subjective complaints. At the same time, he trained medical personnel in using the method so that consistent results could be obtained. With the Himmelsbach scale, one could accurately chart how long it took for the withdrawal disturbances to develop after the last dose of morphine (about 48 hours), and how long it took them to dissipate (about 10 days). The scores also showed that the intensity of withdrawal was directly related to the prior daily morphine dosage.

Proof that the alcohol withdrawal syndrome was due to discontinuing alcohol, rather than to alcohol itself, was accomplished by the same group of medical scientists. Alcohol withdrawal, as was first recognized in these experiments, is much more severe and dangerous (potentially fatal) than that due to opiate withdrawal (rarely fatal). As alcohol leaves the body after a period of high intake, a state of agitation develops, with severe tremor, sometimes leading to major seizures like those seen in epilepsy. In some people, bizarre psychiatric abnormalities also occur during alcohol withdrawal, including vivid and lurid hallucinations (*delirium tremens*, "the D.T.s").

Proof that the dramatic opiate and alcohol withdrawal syndromes were consequences of drug dependence led to confusion about psychotropic drugs that did not produce such an obvious constellation of bodily malaise and multiple physiologic abnormalities when withdrawn. For example, it was long held that cocaine is not addictive because stopping its use does not produce a withdrawal syndrome of the opiate or alcohol type. We know now, however, that cocaine is actually intensely addictive, in that an overpowering compulsion develops for the addict to continue using it. And not surprisingly, there is, after all, a cocaine withdrawal syndrome, manifested primarily by psychologic disturbances—for example, severe fatigue and even suicidal depression. Early doubts about the addictiveness of caffeine, nicotine, and marijuana had the same origin; with each of these drugs, as described in later chapters, withdrawal affects mental functions and mood state rather than causing obvious abnormalities of physiology in the body's organ systems.

Each drug has its own characteristic rate of development of dependence, determined by how fast the brain brings into play the mechanisms that counteract the drug effect. Once the dependent state has been established, stopping the drug will lead to a gradual onset of the withdrawal syndrome as the drug leaves the body. Opiate dependence can be studied easily because the opiate withdrawal syndrome can be brought on quickly and intensely (*precipitated withdrawal*) by the opioid antagonist naloxone, which abruptly abolishes all effects of opioid agonists on their receptors. Mice in precipitated withdrawal jump in a bizarre manner reminiscent of popcorn. The pharmacologist E. Leong Way developed a method of scoring this jumping (how many in a group jump, how frequently they jump) in order to establish quantitatively how drug dosage and dosing interval determine the intensity of dependence and withdrawal. The greater the dependence on an opiate (as from higher dosages or more frequent injections), the easier it is to precipitate withdrawal with naloxone—in other words, the lower the naloxone dose that is needed.

In experiments carried out in my laboratory to study opiate dependence in mice, we measured the average dose of naloxone required to make a group of mice jump. By this standard, even the first dose of an opiate was able to produce a small but measurable degree of dependence. Testing a few animals at a time with fairly large doses of naloxone, hour by hour after a single injection of opiate, we found that jumping behavior developed, reached a maximum after about eight hours, and had disappeared entirely after 16 hours.

In people who are not users of opiates, as in normal animals, naloxone is virtually without effect. Therefore naloxone can be used as a diagnostic test for opiate dependence. A tiny dose of naloxone, administered with care, precipitates a very mild set of incipient withdrawal signs, revealing the opiate-dependent state.

Accompanying every withdrawal syndrome is an intense craving for the drug that was withdrawn. The opiate withdrawal syndrome can be terminated instantly by an injection of opiate. The alcohol withdrawal syndrome can be terminated by a drink, or by sedative hypnotic drugs like benzodiazepines or barbiturates, which act like alcohol. The seemingly magical ability of the addictive drug to relieve its own withdrawal syndrome makes it hard for addicts to abstain; they know that the drug will bring immediate relief. With alcohol, a "hangover" is the beginning of a withdrawal syndrome, and alcohol addicts know that the easiest way to suppress it is to take "the hair of the dog that bit you"—namely, another drink. Early-morning headache is the first sign of caffeine withdrawal, and caffeine addicts know how to cure it with that first morning cup of coffee.

Brain Mechanisms of Tolerance and Dependence

It might seem logical to argue that dependence, like tolerance, is a consequence and not a cause of addiction. But it might be both consequence and cause, in that (as noted above) even a single dose of an addictive drug produces a tiny amount of dependence. In my experiments, I only showed that to be true of opiates, but it may well also be true of other addictive drugs. It is conceivable, therefore, that this early and subtle disturbance after a single dose could be a factor producing craving, and driving the user to repeat the dose, just as happens during full-blown withdrawal after chronic use at high dosage. If we understood the biochemical, cellular, and molecular changes in the brain in tolerance and dependence, and if we could then develop pharmacologic means of preventing them, it is possible (though speculative at this time) that we could reduce the tendency for one dose to lead to another. That might be a useful adjunct to treatments that seek to modify addictive behavior.

Unfortunately, the present state of knowledge concerning the brain chemistry underlying tolerance and dependence is rather confusing. Numerous biochemical changes have been demonstrated in specific brain regions (like the nucleus accumbens) of rats made dependent on morphine or cocaine. These include quite dramatic alterations in the *phosphorylation* of certain proteins; such attachment of phosphate groups to (and removal of phosphate groups from) enzymes and other proteins is a mechanism for making them more or less active. Large changes also occur in some of the signal transduction systems (like the G-protein mechanism described in Chapter 3) through which the drugs act. Finally, opiates turn on the transcription of certain genes—again, in some brain regions but not others. During precipitated withdrawal from opiates, most of these biochemical effects are dramatically reversed. All these diverse modifications of brain chemistry are interesting and significant, but a coherent picture has not yet emerged to explain—for opiates or cocaine—either the rewarding effects or the long-term tolerance and dependence.

Without regard to the unknown biochemical details, we can nevertheless consider a plausible conceptual model of tolerance and dependence that helps us to think about the problem. If morphine or heroin is administered to an animal repeatedly, well within the critical interval, tolerance and dependence develop rapidly. However, if naloxone is given at the same time, to prevent all the pharmacologic effects of the opiate, neither tolerance nor dependence will develop. Thus, the mere presence of an addictive drug is not sufficient; the drug must actually produce its effects. Therefore, the brain's adaptation to the drug may be thought of as an opposing process that tends to restore normal brain function despite the presence of the drug—in other words, to neutralize the drug's biologic effects.

Figure 6.1 illustrates this idea with a seesaw analogy. *A* depicts the normal state of the brain. In *B* the drug is like a weight on one end of the seesaw, tilting it downward. In *C* the adaptive mechanism of tolerance opposes this drug action, as represented by a weight on the other end, restoring the balance. Now to obtain a drug effect again requires a higher total dose because it is necessary to override the adaptation, as in *D*. The brain mechanisms—whatever they are—adapt again, as in *E*. Thus, to obtain an effect the drug dose has to be raised progressively as tolerance builds up. In this model, dependence and tolerance go hand in hand, as they do in real life. If all the drug is now suddenly removed (as in *F*)—faster than the adaptive changes can reverse—the unmasking of the opposing adaptation process is manifested as a withdrawal syndrome.

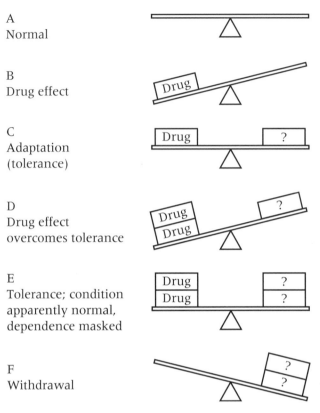

FIGURE 6.1 Tolerance and dependence: The seesaw analogy for adaptation in the brain. See text for explanation.

The model predicts that the signs and symptoms of withdrawal should be opposite to those of the drug itself, and this is, in large measure, true. Withdrawal from stimulants like cocaine and amphetamines causes depression, probably because of dopamine depletion due to repeated overstimulation. Withdrawal from depressant drugs like opiates or alcohol causes excitation. Loss of sensitivity to endogenous opioids could be responsible for the severe aversive (dysphoric) reactions experienced during opiate withdrawal. In the intestine, where endogenous opioids inhibit movement, and where administered morphine causes constipation, loss of sensitivity to endogenous opioids could cause the typical diarrhea of withdrawal. What kinds of neurochemical changes might account for the adaptation that underlies the state of dependence? We do not yet have a complete answer, but we have partial answers:

- There are well-known mechanisms for regulating the number of receptors according to need. If a hormone or neurotransmitter is present in excessive amount, the brain may turn off production of new receptors for it by shutting down the copying of the relevant gene into mRNA. Fewer receptors means reduced sensitivity to a drug—in other words, tolerance. But fewer receptors also means dependence, because when the drug is withdrawn an abnormal state of receptor deficiency will be unmasked.

- Another biologic mechanism for reducing the number of receptors is to stop their transport from inside the cell, where they are made, to the cell membrane in the synapse, where they normally function.

- The production and release of neurotransmitters are also regulated precisely, in order to ensure normal brain function under changing conditions of life. Artificial continuous activation of opioid receptors, for example, as by repeated administration of an opiate, would have the same significance for the regulatory systems as a grossly excessive release of endogenous opioids. As a result the production of endogenous opioid peptides might be suppressed. When the opiate is withdrawn, the unmasked neurotransmitter deficiency would be functionally equivalent to a receptor deficiency. This mechanism is illustrated by the dopamine deficiency associated with cocaine or amphetamine withdrawal.

- Finally, even without any change in the receptors or the neurotransmitters, the signal transduction mechanisms could undergo an adaptive change. It will be recalled from Chapter 3 that signal transduction is the process that mediates the biochemical events inside a neuron when an agonist binds to a receptor. On repeated opiate administration, the G-protein that is coupled to a receptor and that mediates its biologic action could become less efficient, making the receptor less sensitive to—making it tolerant to—endogenous or administered opioid agonists. Again, the result would be functionally equivalent to a receptor deficiency.

Although I have used opiates as a model (chiefly because we know most about them) for discussing possible mechanisms of tolerance and dependence, similar considerations probably apply to all the addictive drugs. All the possible kinds of adaptive changes described here have been demonstrated experimentally, in one system or another, with one addictive drug or another, yielding a confusing abundance of results. We can say that many biochemical changes of the expected kind do occur, but for each addictive drug it will be necessary to learn much more about which specific changes account most satisfactorily for the observed tolerance and dependence.

CHAPTER 7

Are Addicts
Born or Made?

Why is it that of all the people who try an addictive drug only a small fraction use it repeatedly and become addicts? Is it possible that some people are predisposed, are especially vulnerable, to becoming addicted? And if that were so, would a person's vulnerability be restricted to a single addictive drug or would it apply to addictive drugs as a class? Data are still sparse, while speculation is abundant; but new epidemiologic and molecular genetic approaches offer promise of solid information. Thus, genetic predisposition is beginning to emerge as a reality in our approach to understanding drug addiction.

A SPECULATIVE SCENARIO

Psychiatrists have often noted that a common accompaniment of opiate and other addictions is *anhedonia*,* an inability to experience

---

* The word anhedonia is aptly descriptive of a long-lasting profound depression, but it is not an officially accepted diagnostic term.

life's normal pleasures and satisfactions. Is it possible that some addicts may have a chemically defective reward system, for which they try to compensate by using drugs that stimulate that system?

One can imagine many ways in which deficiencies or excesses of hormones, neurotransmitters, or receptors could make a person prone to addiction. Addiction to opiates is a good case for speculation because the corresponding endogenous opioids and their receptors are known, as well as their involvement in a reward pathway. Our genes determine the structure, production, and regulation of every protein in our bodies, and therefore a gene defect can result in an abnormal or missing protein. So there is no doubt that mutated genes could, in principle, be responsible for a defective production of endogenous opioid peptides or their receptors. Think of the days before 1889, when the role of the pancreas and of insulin deficiency in diabetes had not yet been discovered. A young person with diabetes would be ill, and medicine could offer a diagnosis but no remedy. Then imagine a "pusher" offering an illicit drug for injection, prepared from pig pancreas and (as we now know) containing insulin. Most people, if persuaded to try the substance, would experience a drastic fall in their blood sugar; feeling dizzy and weak after an injection, they would refuse to try it again. But our diabetic young friend would feel right and normal for the first time in his life; thereafter he would pay any price, take any risk, for the opportunity to repeat that injection, and he would surely become "addicted." This allegory—fanciful as it may be—implies that once a condition has been diagnosed as a medical one, lifetime dependence on a therapeutic drug is not stigmatized as an addiction.

To apply the analogy to opiate addiction, suppose that some people are born with deficient endogenous opioids or defective opioid receptors. They would, presumably, be unable to achieve normal rewards and satisfactions from normal social interactions and life pursuits. Unlike a person with sickle cell anemia or cystic fibrosis, who would have been diagnosed as suffering from a known genetic disease, they and their families and friends would be unaware of the genetic deficit. One can imagine such people displaying emotional flatness, having difficulty in social relationships, lacking enthusiasm for anything—in short, presenting a classic picture of anhedonia. Then one day during adolescence an acquaintance offers some heroin. Suddenly a feeling of normalcy would be experienced: "Now, for the first time, I feel the way a person should feel. Now I realize what I have been missing all my life."

I have asked many heroin addicts to recall their first experience with heroin. All of them say it was pleasurable; many also say it made them feel "right" for the first time. When I have asked about the circumstances of that first use, the answer is always that a peer group was present; people never begin using intravenous heroin alone—they need instruction. Then I would try to find out what happened to the others in that peer group; did they also become addicts? The answer is that some did, but many did not. Unfortunately, this kind of fuzzy information based on romanticized memories, self-justification, and a desire to tell what the doctor wants to hear, is neither dependable nor decisive; we can hardly take it seriously as an argument for genetic predisposition.

The fact is, everything I have said thus far about a possible genetics of vulnerability to addiction is pure speculation. No defects have been identified in the opioid system—neither inherited nor acquired through chronic use of opiates. Because we are concerned here with peptides and receptors in the brain, making actual measurements presents great difficulty. Scientists are beginning to tackle the problem with promising methods such as the use of PET scans to produce images of receptors and obtain information about neurotransmitter release in the living brain.

GENES AND ENVIRONMENT

The idea that vulnerability to drug addiction can be inherited has been widely misunderstood. It is obvious—indeed, it is a trivial statement—that if a drug were totally unavailable, no one could become addicted to it, regardless of their heredity. In that sense drug addiction differs from clearcut genetic diseases, which do not depend on external factors. The position may be closer to that of diseases with strong hereditary influences, like the common kinds of heart disease or like colon and rectal cancers, in which environmental factors play a major role. An especially clear example was discovered only recently: a kidney cancer in which the ability of chemical carcinogens to produce a cancer is suppressed by a specific gene. If that gene is defective, cancer can develop, but only if there is exposure to carcinogens. If the gene is normal, cancer is unlikely, even with exposure to carcinogens.

When a drug is widely and freely available (alcohol, nicotine, and caffeine are good examples), some people choose not to use it at all, others use it in moderation, and still others use it heavily and become addicted. The strong influence of environmental factors is nowhere more obvious than in nicotine addiction. Only 25 years ago a large majority of young Americans became smokers as they entered the age of adolescence, but today only a small minority (around one-fifth) do. About half of those who ever smoked have been able to quit. Obviously, the genes have not changed in 25 years; the difference must be due to other factors. Unlike the genes, these other factors can be modified to reduce addictive behaviors, as will be discussed in connection with prevention education in Chapter 15 and in the drug policy recommendations of Chapter 19. Here I cite only a few examples, referring specifically to nicotine addiction.

Societal attitudes play a major role in determining the likelihood of a young person's starting to smoke cigarettes. Among a circle of friends we call this peer pressure; in the wider society it may be described as social custom or social acceptability. As an addiction becomes less popular, it becomes less acceptable. This sounds like a meaningless tautology, but it expresses an important fact—that a positive feedback operates. As information about the health dangers of smoking takes hold, fewer people smoke; and as fewer people smoke, the attitudinal change is reinforced. Then prohibitions on where and when smoking is permitted become increasingly acceptable and more willingly complied with. For some people none of this matters, because they have always observed a total prohibition, either on religious grounds (for example, Mormons) or because of strong family rules; and such people never become addicted regardless of their genetic makeup. At the other extreme are a minority who reject the societal consensus and violate the prohibitions; some of that group become addicted, and they constitute a persistent problem.

Socioeconomic class is a strong factor that modifies social acceptance of the addictive behavior, because people are generally more influenced by what their own group does than by the wider culture. Thus, the decline in smoking has been much greater in affluent middle-class circles than in blue-collar society, probably reflecting a difference in educational level as well as in self-confidence about being able to change the circumstances of one's own life. Very likely this class difference in smoking behavior will disappear with time, but change in societal attitudes is typically slow.

The tobacco industry insists that their advertising is not intended to recruit smokers but only to promote one brand over another. Regardless of what is intended, however, advertising unquestionably contributes to the climate of social acceptance of this lethal addiction. That is especially important when athlete heroes and popular music groups—role models for so many young people—are deliberately associated with cigarettes in advertising and other product promotions.

The same environmental influences and the same social patterns apply to illicit drugs, except that the relative importance of the various factors is different. The Vietnam experience sheds light on how strongly social acceptance by a peer group, coupled with easy availability, can influence drug use. American young men were wrenched suddenly from their families and home environment. Placed in a situation that was alternately terrifying and boring, with cheap heroin of high purity readily available, and without serious inhibitions on its use, they became addicted in remarkable numbers. At the height of the epidemic, some 15% of U.S. ground forces were actually using enough heroin to have become dependent on it. However, exhaustive follow-up studies by sociologist Lee Robins found that the great majority, after returning home, put their heroin use behind them and did not seek it out again.

In civilian life, to use an illicit drug in the first place requires a more decisive rejection of societal standards than is needed to use a drug that is sanctioned by the adult society. A rather special psychologic temperament is called for. One has to be more of a risk-taker, more of a sensation seeker, more of a nonconformist, or more influenced by peers. But again we see, as with the legal drugs, that of all those who have the necessary psychologic makeup and actually do try an illicit drug, only a small fraction become addicts. Does genetic predisposition play a role, then, in determining who will belong to that small fraction?

To flatly deny a role to genetics and to argue that only psychologic factors are operative only begs the question, for we know that genetic factors contribute strongly to a person's psychologic makeup—personality, responses to stress, and patterns of behavior. Thus, a genetic predisposition to a drug addiction might take the form of changes in some of the genes that are responsible for the production and regulation of neurotransmitters and receptors in the brain that influence those personality characteristics. Among these could be abnormalities in a reward pathway causing a functional deficit in the feelings that are normally associated with pleasure and satisfaction—a state of anhedonia even before the individual is exposed to any drug.

Unfortunately, detailed information about the psychologic status of addicts is rarely available before they become addicted; and then, after they are addicted, there is no way to determine whether abnormal psychologic traits are consequences of chronic drug use or predated the first exposure to the drug. To gain such understanding, it is necessary to study children and then years later to assess their drug use in adulthood. A few investigators have done this successfully. C. R. Cloninger, for example, recorded personality and behavioral traits of several hundred Swedish 11-year-olds, then found and evaluated the same subjects 16 years later to see which had become alcoholics. Children who displayed character traits of impulsivity, novelty-seeking, and readiness to take risks were far more likely than others to use alcohol excessively as adults. Likewise, long-term studies in the United States by Lee Robins and S. G. Kellam have demonstrated that attention disorders and aggressive behavior, manifested as early as first grade, predict heavy addictive drug use at later ages, especially among males.

Not genes alone, then, nor environment alone, but the interactions of environmental with genetic factors are the true keys to understanding predisposition to addiction. Current research is revealing how neurochemistry is specifically altered by external events. I cite just one example of this exciting development. It has long been known that song birds recognize and respond to songs of their own species and ignore songs of other species. Recordings of same-species and different-species songs as well as pure tones were played for canaries and finches. When the birds' brains were subsequently studied,* a large increase was found in one particular mRNA, representing one gene that plays a regulatory role in turning other genes on or off. To put it bluntly, this gene was turned on by the song. Moreover, the effect was not a general one; it happened only in the brain area known to be involved in song recognition. And most remarkably, it occurred strongly for same-species, but hardly at all for different-species songs, and not at all for pure tones. Here is a concrete example, then, of a specific environmental stimulus interacting with a gene to cause a neurochemical change in the brain. Increasingly, molecular neurobiology is beginning to illuminate the chemical basis of behavior.

PREDISPOSITION TO ADDICTION IN ANIMALS

Animal experiments allow us to study predisposition in a more rigorous manner than is possible with humans. By selective breeding, we

---

* The method used was in situ hybridization, described in Chapter 3.

can obtain animals that will choose and use an addictive drug, and others that will not. Mice, for example, can be offered a free choice of water bottles, one of which contains a drug. Such experiments are difficult to design; an animal may avoid the drug because of its bitter taste, and matching the taste by adding something bitter to the other bottle may not be practical. Moreover, the drug itself might affect thirst and water balance, further confusing the interpretation of how much the animal drinks from each bottle. Nevertheless, by repeatedly selecting and inbreeding animals that prefer a drug and—on the other hand—animals that avoid the drug, high-preferring and low-preferring lines have been obtained. This has been done with several addictive drugs, showing that genetic factors are able to affect the predisposition to prefer a drug.

What is missing in breeding studies is an explanation of the mechanism whereby genetic factors can influence an animal's preference for an addictive drug. As we know that genes control the production of enzymes—and therefore the production of brain chemicals made by enzymes—it is interesting to consider the case of tetrahydropapaveroline (THP). R. D. Myers found that when this substance was administered to mice, it enhanced their preference for alcohol in a free-choice drinking experiment. This finding is provocative not only because it shows that a specific chemical will induce alcohol-seeking behavior, but also because THP is a normal constituent of the brain, derived from dopamine. Moreover, THP was effective in eliciting alcohol preference when it was injected directly into certain specific brain sites—sites rich in dopamine. One of these was the nucleus accumbens, already implicated in the rewarding effects of several addictive drugs. Thus, a possible neurochemical basis for predisposition to alcohol addiction could be postulated—excessive production (or inadequate removal) of THP. Interestingly, animals chronically exposed to alcohol increase their production of THP, suggesting the possibility of a vicious cycle—more drinking, more THP, more drinking. However, no experimental data have yet emerged to link THP decisively to human alcohol addiction.

When mice are given a large enough standard dose of alcohol, they lose their balance, then lose consciousness, lying immobile on their sides as though asleep. By selective breeding, strains of mice have been developed that are sensitive to alcohol ("long-sleep") or relatively resistant to alcohol ("short-sleep"). The obvious question arises: What alcohol-sensitive or alcohol-resistant brain mechanism accounts for the hereditary difference in the behavioral effect of alcohol? Do the GABA receptors of the two strains differ in sensitivity to alcohol? Recent studies by R. A. Harris have demonstrated such a difference, as follows. Tiny membrane fragments were prepared from homogenized brain tissue. Using a method for measuring the passage of radioactive chloride ions through these membranes, it could be shown that GABA opened the chloride channels, just as it does in intact brain tissue. Alcohol enhanced the GABA action, causing more chloride ions to flow through—but only in membranes from alcohol-sensitive mice. Moreover, when mice or rats were selected from a mixed stock according to their sensitivity to alcohol, the result was consistent with the breeding experiments: alcohol enhanced the GABA action more strongly, the more sensitive the living animal had been to alcohol. In addition, membranes from animals made tolerant to alcohol showed increased resistance to the effect of alcohol on GABA receptors.

Modern molecular biology techniques make it possible to study the GABA receptors in a more refined way. Oocytes (egg cells) from toads can be injected with mRNA from any source and will then make proteins according to the sequence of nucleotides in the mRNA—even proteins that are never made otherwise by oocytes. If the mRNA contains a sequence specifying a protein that is an ion channel (like the GABA receptor), that protein will be inserted into the cell membrane of the oocyte, where the appropriate ligand can open it, and the ion flow can be monitored by electrical methods. So, to compare GABA receptors from the two strains of mice, mRNA was extracted from their brains and injected into single oocytes.

When GABA was applied to an ordinary oocyte, nothing happened; the oocyte does not normally have GABA receptors on its surface. However, after injection of mRNA from the brain tissue, GABA caused chloride ions to flow into the cell, showing that GABA receptor ion channels had been made by the oocyte and were active on the cell surface. As expected, alcohol enhanced this GABA effect—but only when the mRNA had come from alcohol-sensitive mice. Moreover, alcohol had no effect on ion channels regulated by a neurotransmitter other than GABA, showing that (at least in this experiment) alcohol was acting specifically on GABA receptors.

These important results show a clear correlation between a functional effect of alcohol and a possible genetic basis for that effect. No similar experiments have yet been carried out with other addictive drugs.

PREDISPOSITION TO ADDICTION IN HUMANS

Before considering evidence of genetically determined vulnerability to addiction in humans, we note an example of an inherited protective factor—in this case protection against alcohol addiction. That is the so-called "Oriental flush." Half of all people of Chinese or Japanese extraction are made ill by alcohol, even in tiny doses. The face flushes, a severe headache develops, and other more serious reactions may occur. The cause is a mutation in the gene that encodes the acetaldehyde dehydrogenase enzyme, which normally destroys acetaldehyde, the toxic product of alcohol metabolism in the body. The defective enzyme allows acetaldehyde to accumulate in the body. Epidemiologic studies show a very low prevalence of alcoholism in China and Japan, but there is controversy about how great a protective role is played by the mutant enzyme. Strong evidence for protection is the fact that only very few Japanese who have become alcoholics are found to have the altered enzyme, compared with 50% in the Japanese population as a whole. On the other hand, studies of various ethnic groups living together—as in Hawaii—show only a weak correlation between the "Oriental flush" and the consumption of alcohol.

The best evidence for predisposition to addiction in humans comes from studies on alcohol. The initial data were from identical and fraternal (nonidentical) twins. Identical twins have identical genes; fraternal twins do not. For any disease, if environment had no influence, identical twins would always be *concordant* (alike) with respect to that disease: both twins of a pair would have it or neither twin would have it. If both genetic and environmental factors contributed, the concordance rate (less than 100%) among pairs of identical twins would reflect the environmental contribution. A lower concordance rate among fraternal twins would reflect the contributions of both factors. Thus, the heritability of a disease can be computed from the differences in concordance rates for sets of fraternal and identical twin pairs. Data from several countries show that identical twins do (or do not) become alcoholics with a significantly higher concordance rate than that of fraternal twins, suggesting a significant heritability of a predisposition to alcohol addiction. In one large study, for instance, 54% of identical twin pairs were concordant, but only 28% of nonidentical pairs were.

But this approach suffers from a serious defect. Identical twins tend to be alike in many ways, for reasons that have nothing to do with genetics. During childhood their parents tend to dress them alike and treat them alike. Growing up to be alike in many respects, they tend to copy each other's behaviors, and this could also apply to the development of drinking patterns. This problem—that identical twins share many environmental factors to a greater extent than do fraternal twins—plagues all twin studies, but especially those concerning behavior, making it difficult to sort out the influences of genetics from those of environment.

The most convincing statistical evidence comes from cross-adoption data obtained by C. R. Cloninger. Sons of alcoholics, adopted at birth and raised in a nonalcoholic family, were found to have a fourfold greater probability of becoming alcoholic than did their stepbrothers. Conversely, sons of nonalcoholic parents, adopted and raised by alcoholic families, did not tend to become alcoholic, even when their stepbrothers did. This result speaks strongly in favor of some kind of inheritance of a predisposition to alcohol addiction. It also tends to discredit the idea that family environment plays the predominant role in the genesis of alcoholism, although it does not rule out a contributory role for environmental factors.

Direct evidence of inherited differences in a response to alcohol has been sought in various studies with sons of alcoholic fathers. The subjects, who were young enough not to have developed immoderate drinking habits, were compared with control subjects from nonalcoholic family backgrounds. All subjects were evaluated on standardized paper-and-pencil tests of mental abilities, memory, and vigilance, after being given a placebo and after receiving a low and a high dose of alcohol. On some of the tests the sons of alcoholic fathers showed significantly less disruption of performance by alcohol than did the matched controls. As none of the subjects had yet become problem drinkers, and as the controls were matched to the sons of alcoholics according to their drinking habits, this result could not be attributed to acquired tolerance; the relative insensitivity to alcohol appeared to be an intrinsic characteristic of the men with alcoholic parentage.

Brain wave patterns have been found, in some studies, to be different in sons of alcoholics, suggesting some innate but subtle abnormality of brain function. A special finding of interest concerns the so-called P300 peak. A subject sits quietly, wearing earphones and listening to a tone, around high C, which sounds every second. Randomly, and about once in 10 times on the average, a higher-pitched "target" tone is presented. The task is to listen expectantly for the higher-pitched tone, and to signal with a forefinger whenever it is heard. At the same time the brain waves are recorded continuously. Almost exactly 300 milliseconds (hence the designation P300)—in other words three-tenths of a second—after the target tone, a prominent peak stands out on the record. This response anticipates the subject's finger signal; obviously, in some way it reflects information processing in the brain. Alcohol reduces the size of the peak. Neither the peak itself nor its reduction by alcohol has anything to do with the high-pitched target tone itself, for the response does not occur unless a subject was first instructed to listen for and respond to that particular tone.

In this test—but all investigators do not agree—sons of alcoholic fathers differed from matched controls in two ways. First, even for the sober condition the peak size was somewhat smaller. Second, a given alcohol dose was less effective than in control subjects in reducing the peak size. Thus, men with an alcoholic family background had a specific abnormality of some kind in information processing, and were also less sensitive to alcohol in the test. What this would really mean, however, and what genetically determined neurochemical abnormalities might underlie the result, is entirely obscure. The task of research now under way is to establish the facts beyond dispute, and then to work out the broader significance.

ADDICTION-PRONE GENES?

Genetic predisposition to a drug addiction is undoubtedly a complex business. It is most unlikely that a single defective gene—like the hemoglobin gene in sickle-cell anemia or the ion-channel gene in cystic fibrosis—is ever the sole culprit. Nevertheless, the extraordinarily rapid advances in our ability to sequence human genes have opened the way to a search for predisposing genes. The massive Human Genome Project, which will construct a complete map of the genes on the twenty-two paired chromosomes and two sex chromosomes (X and Y), will surely hasten the day when vulnerability to each of the drug addictions will be understood in molecular genetic terms.

One promising way to search for a defective gene is to study the *restriction fragment length polymorphism* (RFLP, pronounced "riflip") pattern. This method was spectacularly successful in locating the defective genes in Huntington's disease and cystic fibrosis. Now the method is just beginning to be applied to the drug addictions.

Small differences in DNA sequences (called *polymorphisms*) occur throughout an animal or human population. They often consist of mutations in which one of the nucleotides at a particular position in the sequence is changed to another, such as A to G.

A *restriction enzyme* cuts the DNA chain at certain specific locations. There are many different restriction enzymes, and each one recognizes a particular sequence, typically a palindromic sequence of four to six nucleotides. (A *palindrome* is a sequence of letters that reads the same backward and forward, like the famous 11-letter self-introduction in the Garden of Eden—"Madam I'm Adam.") The result of restriction enzyme action is to break all the DNA into *restriction fragments* of various lengths.

To illustrate the principle by analogy, let's look at a simple sentence: A POT LID IS A POT TOP. Imagine that a certain restriction enzyme cleaves in the middle of the six-letter palindrome POT TOP. The result will be a long fragment A POT LID IS A POT and a very short fragment TOP. Now suppose that because of a typographic error (a mutation), the sentence became A POT LID IS A HOT TOP. Now the critical palindrome no longer occurs anywhere in the sentence, so this restriction enzyme will be unable to cleave at all. The result will be a single long fragment—the whole sentence—instead of the two fragments we had before.

Now, polymorphisms (like the typographic error in the analogy) result in altered patterns of fragment sizes, as illustrated in Figure 7.1. Here we see an example of two RFLP patterns obtained with the same restriction enzyme. The mixture of DNA fragments is applied at the top of a gel slab, which has about the consistency of a gelatin dessert, and the bits of DNA are driven downward by an electric current. The shortest fragments travel fastest and farthest, so different sizes separate readily. If one simply stained all the DNA, it would show up as a blur from top to bottom because fragments of so many different sizes would be present. However, specific radiolabeled probes will only bind to the few fragments that contain a specified sequence (as in the hybridization techniques described in Chapter 3), and therefore discrete bands will be seen. Thus, each band in the figure represents a DNA fragment of a certain length. In the left lane, where the normal full-length sequence was applied after exposure to the restriction enzyme, two fragments, *A* and *B*, were obtained. In the right lane, *C* is the mutated full-length fragment (as in the above example), which was not cleaved by the restriction enzyme. A pattern of DNA fragments of different sizes, from the DNA of all the genes after exposure to several restric-

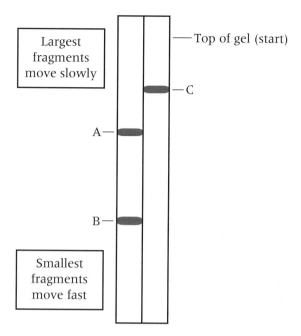

FIGURE 7.1   Restriction fragment length polymorphism. Illustration of the RFLP method. Two lanes are shown on a gel slab to which DNA fragments were applied at the top and driven downward by an electric current. Left lane shows two fragments, *A* and *B*, resulting from cleavage by restriction enzyme; right lane shows only a single large fragment, *C*. See text for explanation.

tion enzymes and to several probes, is a DNA "fingerprint." This is the method used nowadays for unique identifications of individuals in legal proceedings, for no two people (except identical twins) have exactly the same DNA fingerprint pattern.

Now suppose some altered gene has a strong effect in causing predisposition to alcohol addiction. What might one expect to find by RFLP analysis? One would treat the DNA of candidate genes with as many restriction enzymes as possible, looking for a systematic association between a certain RFLP pattern and the predisposition. In other words, such an association should be seen in most alcoholics but not in normal people. Recently the first such apparently positive RFLP result was reported, in the gene that encodes one of the dopamine receptors. Although this discovery, by Kenneth Blum and Ernest P. Noble, is exciting in the prospects it opens, the association with alcohol addiction was less than perfect, so the discovery has been controversial. About half of alcohol addicts did not have the distinctive RFLP pattern, while about a quarter of nonalcoholics did have it. Furthermore, when alcoholic family pedigrees were studied, no strong association was found within families between alcoholism and this unusual form of dopamine receptor gene. It may be, therefore, that the altered gene affects behavior in some general way, which incidentally causes predisposition to alcoholism, but not in all affected people. Alternatively, the altered gene may make alcoholism more severe when it does occur, without affecting predisposition directly. Despite all the uncertainties, this first application of the RFLP method to a drug addiction is exciting, because it opens the prospect of discovering genetic factors that play a role in predisposition to other addictions as well.

The practical significance of such modern genetic research on addictive behavior is threefold:

■ We have learned enough already to suggest that children of alcoholics might be well advised never to touch alcohol; certainly they should be taught the special hazards that heavy drinking holds for them. The same cautionary advice will be appropriate each time a hereditary component of a drug addiction is established. Of course, avoiding a drug entirely is a sure way to avoid becoming addicted!

■ When techniques have been perfected for determining, person by person, who is especially at risk of addiction to a given drug, prevention efforts can be made more efficient by concentrating them on the most vulnerable individuals.

■ Each time a defective gene is discovered that contributes to a drug addiction, we are brought closer to understanding the biochemical basis of that addiction, and thus closer to developing novel strategies for rational prevention and treatment.

PART TWO

The Drugs and the Addicts

CHAPTER 8

Addictive Suicide
Nicotine

As I was driving along the highway recently, my eye was caught by a remarkable billboard advertisement. Nearly filling the field was the weather-beaten face of a man in a cowboy hat, superimposed on what was obviously a product name. Nothing else was on the advertisement. The only part of the product name that was not blocked by the man's face was two letters—"Ma." What a remarkable exploitation of psychologic conditioning! Everyone seeing those two letters and that face could recognize instantly the symbol of Marlboro Country.

The same evening, reading the Sunday *New York Times* magazine section, my eye was caught by a very attractive, well-dressed, sophisticated woman, holding a cigarette delicately between the fingers of her left hand. "Portraits of Pleasure" was the title above the woman's face. Also displayed prominently was the legend "KENT: MORE FLAVOR IN LIGHTS," pictures of three different cigarette packages, and the required Surgeon General's warning: "Smoking Causes Lung Cancer, Heart Disease, Emphysema, And May Complicate Pregnancy." Remarkable is the fact that this typical seductive advertisement, here directed toward an intelligent readership, promotes a product which, when used as directed, causes illness and death. Indeed, it is estimated currently that in the United States alone smoking kills over 400,000 people every year.

Although tobacco has been an article of commerce for hundreds of years, it became a major addictive substance only in the present century. Pipes, cigars, snuff, and chewing tobacco were the principal vehicles for nicotine self-administration from the fifteenth-century importation of tobacco to Europe from America until the second decade of the present century. Several technologic advances opened the way to popularization of the cigarette. First, a new way of curing tobacco made the smoke less irritating to the air passages, so that inhalation became tolerable. Second, the mechanization of cigarette production in the 1880s vastly increased productive capacity, creating an incentive to expand the market. Third, the safety match, invented in the middle of the nineteenth century and first mass-produced toward the end of the century, was a necessary prerequisite to the successful spread of the cigarette. Fourth, new techniques of advertising and mass marketing were being perfected, and these were soon applied to this new commodity. Smoking had not been socially acceptable for women, but the women's suffrage movement and the rapidly changing status of women in society doubled the potential market, and females were recruited to cigarettes in vast numbers. With the rapid increase in cigarette smoking in the United States, illustrated in Figure 8.1, followed by development of the export market, nicotine addiction became a health problem of worldwide scope.

To understand this historic development and to appreciate its relevance to policies concerning the regulation of other addictive drugs, we need first to understand the nature of nicotine addiction. This chapter explains how the technique of deep inhalation, which is characteristic of cigarette smoking, changed the character of the addiction and dramatically altered its health consequences. Finally, some methods of treatment for nicotine addiction are discussed.

THE FAST TRACK
FROM LUNGS TO BRAIN

About 1% of the weight of the tobacco leaf is nicotine. If all the nicotine in a single cigarette were absorbed into the body, it would be very toxic or even lethal. Cigar and pipe smokers typically do not inhale, and nicotine is absorbed through the mucous membranes of

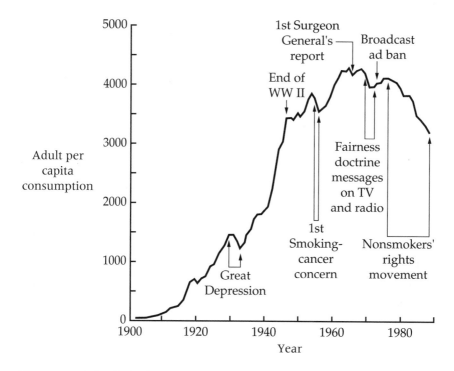

FIGURE 8.1 U.S. cigarette consumption 1900–1985. [From J. Slade, *Journal of Psychoactive Drugs* 21: 281, 1989, Fig. 1.]

their mouths. Cigarette smokers, on the other hand, usually inhale deeply and hold the smoke in their lungs before exhaling.

For a drug to reach the brain receptors by the inhalation route, several key requirements have to be met. The drug must be a gas, or if it is to be smoked it must be carried effectively on the smoke particles without being destroyed at high temperature. After inhalation, it must cross the thin partitions that separate the air sacs in the lung from the blood that passes by, so that it can be carried in the blood to the brain. And finally, it must be able to cross out of the network of fine arteries in the brain and into brain tissue in order to reach the neurons that bear the receptors.

A familiar medical example of this route of delivery is the use of inhalation anesthetics like ether or halothane to put patients to sleep on the operating table. Drugs taken by inhalation act fast because every breath fills the air sacs with a fresh supply of drug, which passes into the blood before that breath is exhaled. A meshwork of fine capillaries surrounds each little air sac. All the blood in the body passes through the lungs—about five quarts every minute. From the lungs all that blood goes directly to the left side of the heart, and from there, as it is pumped out, a certain portion goes to the brain. Consequently, blood that leaves the lungs arrives in the brain carrying drug at full strength, in a few seconds. The brain is swamped by a new inrush of drug immediately after each inhalation. After an intravenous injection, in contrast, the blood carrying the drug is first mixed in the right side of the heart with the large amount of drug-free blood returning from the rest of the body, and thus the drug is diluted before it reaches the brain. And after oral administration absorption is slow, so the drug concentration in the brain builds up slowly.

If a drug is smoked and its effect on the brain is pleasurable, each puff will produce immediate satisfaction in an unmistakable cause-and-effect manner, reinforcing the smoking behavior according to the classic rules of operant conditioning. In this respect, drawing on a cigarette is analogous to pressing a lever in the standard self-administration experiments described in Chapter 4, which demonstrate reinforcement by addictive drugs in animals. To observe this sequence in action, you have only to watch confirmed nicotine addicts draw smoke deeply into the lungs and hold it there; the instant gratification is obvious in their facial expression.

An important feature of the inhalation route is its controllability. Because the drug reaches the brain in small spurts, the smoker can use the psychotropic effect itself to regulate the rate of drug intake. For more effect, the user takes deeper or more frequent puffs. If a toxic concentration in the brain is being approached, the user (feeling dizzy or nauseated) simply stops smoking or slows down. This contrasts to other routes of administration, where a certain total amount of drug is put irretrievably into a vein, under the skin, or into the stomach. Thus, one great advantage of self-administration by smoking is that dangerous overdoses can be avoided; this route is an especially important safeguard with illicit drugs of unknown and variable strength, like cannabis, cocaine, or heroin.

Nicotine is metabolized fairly rapidly, disappearing from the body in a few hours. Therefore the addict starts each day with a very low residual level in blood and brain—in other words, in a state of withdrawal. The first cigarette of the morning has a powerful effect because it brings relief of withdrawal discomfort. Thereafter, each cigarette produces a sharp increase in the nicotine concentration in blood, which is the same as the concentration bathing the brain. Figure 8.2 is

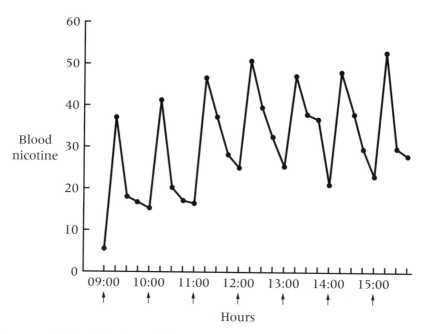

FIGURE 8.2 Nicotine in blood after cigarette smoking. Subject smoked one cigarette every hour (arrows), and blood samples were taken for nicotine determination (in billionths of a gram per milliliter of blood) every 15 minutes. [From M. A. H. Russell and C. Feyerabend, *Drug Metabolism Reviews* 8: 29, 1978.]

an actual record of an experiment in which a subject smoked a cigarette every hour. The peaks and troughs are evident, and also the gradual buildup of the peaks as each cigarette adds nicotine to what still remains in the blood from the previous one.

SMOKING AND HEALTH

Although rapidity of action and controllability make smoking a preferred method of self-administering addictive drugs that are contained in natural products, a major drawback is that something other than the drug has to be burned. Tobacco and marijuana leaves, like any combustible organic matter, produce a host of irritant and carcinogenic products with dangerous effects on the lungs. Lung cancer and emphysema, caused by smoking, are thus not due to nicotine in tobacco or to THC in marijuana, but to combustion products of the leaves.

Before World War I, lung cancer was so rare that medical students flocked excitedly to the autopsy room whenever a patient died of it. Inexplicably to physicians at the time, however, the disease became increasingly common in the years from 1920 to 1950. The study of epidemics is fascinating, and epidemiologists enjoy the mix of clinical medicine, medical research, and detective work that is involved in tracking down the causes. As the epidemic of lung cancer cases seemed to be keeping pace with growth of the big cities, air pollution was blamed at first. When two things are correlated, one is often blamed on the other; this is a classic statistical trap, for the truth may be that both are related to some other, unknown, factor. A somewhat facetious example: There was an excellent correlation, over a period of many years, between the sale of bananas in England and the death rate from cancer; yet bananas do not cause cancer.

Finally, in 1950, it was noted by medical researchers in England and the United States that cigarette smoking among men—but, significantly, not among women—had begun increasing rapidly some years prior to the onset of the lung cancer epidemic. By studying a large number of hospitalized patients with lung cancer and comparing them with patients of the same age who suffered from other diseases, they found a far greater number of cigarette smokers in the lung cancer group. Most impressive was the relationship between lung cancer deaths and the amount smoked, as shown in Figure 8.3. Those data, too, only demonstrated a correlation; they were not proof of cause and effect. However, unlike the banana correlation, this one was corroborated by additional information that pointed to a causal connection—substances generated in burning tobacco were shown to be chemical carcinogens, which produced cancer when painted on the skin of mice.

The most convincing evidence came from a study of British physicians. That occupational group had smoked as heavily as any, but their professional training enabled them to accept very quickly the growing evidence that cigarettes might be dangerous to their health. So while other groups in British society maintained and even increased their cigarette consumption, the physicians reduced theirs. The result was dramatic. While the lung cancer rate continued to climb in the population at large, it began to fall among physicians. Moreover, the chance of death from lung cancer fell steadily the longer a person had stopped

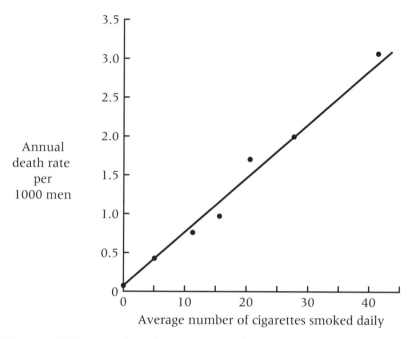

FIGURE 8.3 Number of cigarettes smoked daily and death rate from lung cancer. [From R. Doll and A. B. Hill, *British Medical Journal* 1: 1399–1410, 1964.]

smoking, as shown in Figure 8.4. The evidence from this study was not just correlational but truly showed that cigarette smoking was causing lung cancer. It also demonstrated that the damage caused by smoking is reversible, that it pays to stop, no matter how long the addiction has lasted. As women lagged about 20 years behind men in the extent of their cigarette smoking, it was predicted that the lung cancer rate in women would climb after a similar lag; and that is exactly what happened. Today the number of new cases of lung cancer in women is nearly equal to that in men, and lung cancer now kills more women every year than does breast cancer.

Lung cancer is an especially vicious killer, which ends the lives of more than 100,000 people every year in the United States. This cancer can spread throughout the body before the lung tumor is big enough to cause irritation and coughing. And since smokers usually have a chronic cough anyway, there is a dangerous delay before the victim

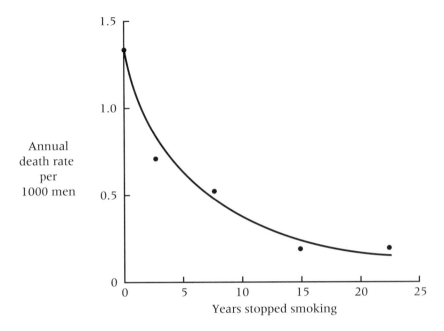

FIGURE 8.4 Death rate from lung cancer falls the longer a cigarette smoker has given up smoking. [From R. Doll and A. B. Hill, *British Medical Journal* 1: 1399–1410, 1964.]

seeks medical attention. By then it may still be possible to eradicate the cancer by removing a lung, but often it is too late.

Bronchitis and emphysema are the two noncancerous lung diseases caused by smoking. Inhaling moves fresh air (and smoke) into finer and finer branches of the bronchial tree until it finally reaches the delicate spongy meshwork of tiny air sacs where oxygen passes into the blood and carbon dioxide passes out of the blood to be exhaled. The bronchial tubes are lined with millions of microscopic hairs called cilia and are coated with a thin layer of mucus. The cilia are in constant movement, beating rhythmically and propelling the mucus layer upward toward the throat, where it is eventually swallowed or expectorated. In this way, dust and other foreign particles are prevented from clogging the system. At the same time, foreign substances are removed by scavenger cells of the immune system, which wander about engulfing particles (especially bacteria) that might otherwise cause infection. Irritants in tobacco smoke paralyze the cilia, the mucus flow stagnates, and the scavenger cells are damaged. More and more foreign matter accumulates, and the stage is set for bronchial infection.

The defective ability of smokers to clear foreign matter out of their lungs was demonstrated in an ingenious experiment. Nonsmoking and heavy-smoking volunteers inhaled a harmless amount of magnetized fine dust particles; then periodically, for a year, a sensitive magnetic detector placed against the chest measured how much of the original dust remained in the lungs. The result was striking. After 11 months, only 10% of the dust remained in the lungs of the nonsmokers but fully 50% remained in the smokers' lungs. Thus, the impaired ability of smokers to clear foreign substances like dust and air pollutants from their lungs poses a significant additional health risk.

Chronic bronchitis becomes emphysema when the thin walls of the air sacs actually break down. This becomes a life-threatening condition when the lungs are so damaged that the necessary transfer of oxygen into the blood and carbon dioxide out of the blood can no longer occur. It is a dreadful disabling disease. The victim feels suffocated, and breathing becomes a terrible effort. In the long run, fatal complications ensue.

Although lung cancer is the most dramatic harmful effect of smoking, the actual numbers of smokers who die of cardiovascular disease caused by their smoking is far greater. Smokers have more heart attacks, more narrowing and hardening of the arteries (arteriosclerosis), more strokes, more aneurysms (ruptures of damaged blood vessels), and more severe high blood pressure than nonsmokers. The risk of dying of lung cancer (an otherwise rare disease) is as much as 25 times greater in heavy smokers than in nonsmokers, but the total number of deaths is relatively small—about 75,000 per year. Cardiovascular disease, on the other hand, is common with advancing age anyway—in nonsmokers as well as smokers—so the difference caused by smoking appears less striking. In fact, however, so many people are affected that the actual number of excess cardiovascular deaths due to smoking—estimated at more than 200,000—is much greater than the total number of lung cancer deaths.

The serious long-term effects of cigarette smoking on the heart and blood vessels are probably due primarily to nicotine itself rather than to other components of the smoke. A consequence of stimulating nicotinic acetylcholine receptors, both in the brain and in the autonomic nervous system, is to cause spasm (narrowing) of the small blood vessels, depriving the tissues of oxygen. Instruments that measure blood flow to the fingers and toes and to the skin elsewhere on the body demonstrate this effect after even a single cigarette. Some think that premature wrinkling of the skin in smokers may result from such reductions in the local blood supply.

Carbon monoxide poisoning is another insidious health hazard of smoking. This toxic gas is a product of incomplete combustion, and its concentration is high in the inhaled smoke. The blood of smokers always contains more carbon monoxide than does the blood of non-smokers, except for garage mechanics and others exposed occupation-ally to automobile exhaust. Carbon monoxide poisons the hemoglobin in the red blood cells so it can deliver less oxygen to the tissues. This results in diminished capacity for exercise or physical work, shortness of breath, dizziness, impairment of mental capacities, and night blind-ness. It also means that at the very time nicotine is reducing the blood supply to the heart muscle and other tissues, carbon monoxide is further reducing the oxygen supply. Thus, carbon monoxide poisoning in conjunction with nicotine is thought to play an important part in damaging the heart and blood vessels of smokers.

All the adverse health effects of smoking a pack of 20 cigarettes daily result in a probability of death from any cause in a given year about twice that of nonsmokers. Death from bronchitis, emphysema, or lung cancer is 10 times more likely in those who smoke a pack a day, and 20 times more likely in those who smoke two packs a day, than in nonsmokers. And as would be expected, the relative risk for the other health hazards is directly related to the amount smoked.

In pregnant women, nicotine affects the blood vessels in the placenta and thus interferes with oxygen supply to the fetus. Moreover, it passes readily from the mother's blood across the placenta, compromising the fetal blood circulation too. Women who smoke during pregnancy have a higher rate of premature delivery and lower birth weight for infants carried to term. There are more birth abnormalities, more sickness and death during infancy, significant damage to the infant's blood vessels, and possibly even retarded mental development. But can we be sure that nicotine is responsible for the adverse effects seen in human preg-nancy? Can we even be certain that smoking is the culprit?

Proof that fetal damage is caused by a certain drug is difficult to come by, not only for smoking but for any drug used during preg-nancy. The problem is that women who are addicted to a particular drug differ in many ways from women who are not. Women who smoke, for example, exhibit higher anxiety levels and more hard-driving ("type A") behavior. Smokers are obviously less concerned about their health than nonsmokers, and this probably leads to less concern about the body during pregnancy, less prenatal care, poorer diet, more use of alcohol and other drugs. Thus, it is difficult, when comparing their offspring with those of nonsmokers, to be sure that observed differences are due to smoking during pregnancy rather than to associated factors or to some innate characteristics of the mother. Female nicotine addicts may even tend to choose different kinds of mates than do nonsmokers, so the paternal contribution to the makeup of the offspring may also be different from that of infants born to nonsmoking mothers.

Administering nicotine to pregnant rodents causes stillbirths, decreased birth weight, and numerous neurologic and behavioral deficits in the offspring. It is true that these effects occur only at dosages that, if corrected for body weight, would correspond in humans to nearly 20 packs of cigarettes daily. Regrettably, too—as with animal toxicity studies in general—there is no sure way to extrapolate dosages to humans. Sometimes, however, when we lack scientific proof, we have to fall back on common sense and the best guesses we can make. Knowing what we do about how easily prenatal development of the human fetus can be disturbed, and knowing the adverse effects of drugs on fetal development in animals, common sense tells us not to expose a fetus to any drug, and certainly not to one like nicotine that has known adverse effects on the blood vessels of the placenta and the fetus.

Finally, it has been established recently that inhaling second-hand smoke is dangerous. Of course, the amount of smoke that actually reaches the lungs of nonsmokers is very much less than what smokers take in directly, so the adverse effects are small compared with those in smokers. Nevertheless, data show that these effects are not entirely negligible. Those exposed to second-hand smoke have detectable nicotine metabolites in their blood, demonstrating that the exposure to nicotine is real. Children of parents who smoke have a distinctly higher incidence of breathing disorders (including asthma) and respiratory infections—several hundred thousand each year in the United States—than do children in homes where neither parent smokes. Altogether, some 3,000 lung cancer deaths each year, in the United States, are attributed to second-hand smoke.

A LOW-KEY HIGH

Nicotine passes from the blood into all parts of the brain, but it only acts where it finds high-affinity nicotinic acetylcholine receptors.

These receptors have been located by the radioreceptor binding technique, using radioactive nicotine. They are concentrated heavily in just a few brain regions. Are these few regions of dense nicotine binding actually the places where nicotine exerts a biologic effect? To find out, experiments were carried out in rats by means of PET scan, using a radioactive sugar as described in Chapter 3. How fast a nerve cell takes up this sugar is a measure of neuronal activity. Nicotine stimulated uptake (and therefore we conclude it stimulated neuronal activity) in just those areas where nicotine was bound with high affinity. Moreover, nicotine antagonists, which occupy the binding sites and prevent nicotine from binding, also prevented the stimulation of sugar uptake by nicotine. This showed that it was, indeed, the binding of nicotine to its receptors on certain neurons that stimulated those neurons. Most interesting, the same results were obtained in experiments with humans, also by the PET scan procedure, using sugar labeled with a positron emitter. What is still missing is an understanding of how the particular brain regions that are stimulated by nicotine cause the psychotropic effects of the drug.

From what we have learned about the dopaminergic reward pathways, we should not be surprised if nicotine caused the release of dopamine, especially at the nucleus accumbens; and that is exactly what has been found in experiments with rats. Thus, nicotine shares with cocaine and opiates the ability to stimulate a reward system through dopamine release.

For many years, it proved extraordinarily difficult to induce animals to self-administer nicotine, and this tended to reinforce the incorrect idea that nicotine was not addictive. Actually, the first exposure to nicotine tends to be so aversive that a rat will not readily repeat the lever-press that delivers the first dose. This initial unpleasant quality is well known to smokers, who can recollect vividly how their first cigarette made them ill—the nausea, heart palpitation, weakness, and even fainting. Young people who are just beginning to smoke become tolerant to these toxic actions by smoking only a little at first, then increasing their dosage very gradually; and the same method worked for getting animals to self-administer nicotine. It is interesting that after a rat has been addicted successfully in that gradual way, the addictive self-administration behavior thereafter is very persistent. Even after a period of forced abstinence, the animal self-administers eagerly when given the opportunity again and readily becomes re-addicted.

The behavioral actions of nicotine in humans are interesting because they are so subtle; indeed, nicotine (and caffeine) cause the least behavioral impairment of all the addictive drugs. As one expert put it: "Nicotine and caffeine are the only addictive drugs about which I can say that it doesn't worry me if my airplane pilot uses them." Without any gross disturbances to measure, animal experiments have not been very helpful in determining the behavioral impact of nicotine. We have to depend on human experimentation, using subjective check-lists for an account of what nicotine does to people. But here we encounter a problem. We would like to know about nicotine effects in smokers, but all we can measure are the added effects of a small dose on top of the nicotine level already circulating in a smoker's blood. On the other hand, if we made them desist from smoking until their nicotine level fell off, we would be dealing with dependent addicts in withdrawal. Of course, nicotine will relieve the withdrawal distress, but that will tell us nothing about the direct effects of the drug. Experiments with former smokers who are long past the discomfort of the withdrawal syndrome have confirmed what smokers themselves say about why they smoke. Double-blind comparisons of nicotine-free (or low-nicotine) with high-nicotine cigarettes implicate the psychotropic drug itself, rather than the oral or visual stimulation of smoking, as the primary reason people smoke. Nicotine alleviates stress and anxiety, reduces frustration, anger, and aggressive feelings, and promotes a pleasurable state of relaxation. Recent evidence suggests it may also relieve a chronic state of depression. How these effects relate to the state of satisfaction produced by other addictive drugs that stimulate dopaminergic reward systems is still unclear. Improvements in attention and in the ability to concentrate are also measurable, but these may well be secondary consequences of stress reduction. Small doses of nicotine produce no adverse effects on mental processes or psychomotor functions, so from the behavioral standpoint alone the addiction does not pose any danger to the individual or to society.

TREATING NICOTINE ADDICTION

If you know any nicotine addicts (maybe you are one yourself), ask them why they don't quit. At one time that would have been regarded as an impolite, intrusive question, and the answer might well have been: "None of your business!" Or more humorously, they might have quoted Mark Twain: "Quitting is easy, I've done it many times." Attitudes have changed, and today addicts are on the defensive. Now you will hear: "I *am* going to quit, tomorrow," or "I'm working on it," or "I've tried so many times, I wish I knew how to make it work."

I hear these same pathetic replies from heroin addicts, too; "tomorrow" is a standard joke about quitting. Nevertheless, there is a certain sincerity about addicts' wish to be abstinent. They really do picture themselves free of the addiction some day, and they like what they see. But getting there is something else again. It is especially hard to break an addiction to a substance that is not only readily available—usually only a few minutes away—and relatively cheap, but also (although to a decreasing extent) socially acceptable. Furthermore, by relieving stress and anxiety, nicotine may even improve performance. And except for the annoyance and slight health risk of second-hand smoke to nonsmokers, the nicotine addict presents no threat to others. I advise heroin addicts to break all social connections, to get out of the heroin-using peer group, to move to a different neighborhood; all those steps are helpful in maintaining abstinence. But none of that will work for nicotine addicts; they have to become abstinent in an environment that offers every opportunity to fail.

A typical addict smokes 10 to 50 cigarettes every day. Each one is linked to a particular time, place, and activity in a way that is reminiscent of the conditioned place preference experiments described in Chapter 4. For example, sitting down to the first morning cup of coffee is a conditioned cue to take out a cigarette and light it. Every meal ends with a cigarette. Sitting down at a desk to work evokes craving for a cigarette. Stepping into the lobby during intermission means light-up time. Just being near other smokers produces an automatic reaching for a cigarette. I call these situations *conditioned association triggers* because—in a pattern that is unique for each person—they trigger the craving that leads immediately to self-administration of nicotine. Thus, the addict smokes on a regular schedule, self-titrating to maintain the blood and brain nicotine level; and the conditioned association triggers make it difficult to break that pattern.

Millions—half of those who ever smoked—have become ex-smokers. Thirty-five years ago, 57% of all U.S. males were smokers; today the figure is down to 28%. The number of female smokers then was 28%, and it has dropped to 23% despite the increasing social acceptance of smoking among females over that same span of years. So quitting is possible. On the other hand, the road to quitting is highly variable. Some can do it neatly and permanently; but the more usual sequence is abstinence followed by relapse, abstinence again, relapse again, until at long last (and unpredictably) long-term abstinence is achieved. What invariably causes relapse is some combination of unusual stress and one of the conditioned association triggers.

Ex-smokers (like other ex-addicts) who relapse are often so ashamed of themselves that they will not admit what happened. For this reason—as with all the addictive drugs—a chemical test is needed to bring the problem quickly into the open for optimal treatment. There are three methods: a test for carbon monoxide in the expired air; a saliva test for thiocyanate (to which cyanide gas in smoke is converted in the body); and a test for cotinine (a metabolic product of nicotine), which can be detected in saliva, blood, or urine.

The "hard-core" addicts—those who have relapsed repeatedly—present a real challenge. People who have never smoked, and especially those who have become ex-smokers, tend to belittle the difficulties. I did it, why can't you? is their unhelpful attitude. Hard-core addicts need sympathetic understanding, not preaching. For such people, who have tried to quit and have relapsed repeatedly, I advocate slow and deliberate reduction of intake as a realistic initial goal, putting off the ultimate quitting decision for later. This can be described as a *harm reduction* strategy, which is applicable to all the drug addictions, as will be explained further in Chapter 15. The rationale is simple. If a person who is smoking 30 cigarettes daily reduces that to 29, and maintains the new level, that smoker has actually accomplished a 3% reduction in the health hazards of the addiction. Then if even a single additional cigarette is removed permanently from the repertoire each week, in four months the health hazards will be reduced by half. Such a program requires discipline and motivation. It requires self-conscious analysis and modification of one's own behavior. One conditioned association trigger at a time has to be eliminated, by repeatedly skipping the cigarette associated with that trigger; that is the classic method of extinguishing a conditioned behavior.*

Some people reject the *controlled-use* approach in principle, on the grounds that addiction is wrong, addictive drugs are bad, and one should not compromise with what is wrong and bad. Others reject it on the grounds that addicts, by their very nature, are unable to sustain moderate intake of an addictive drug and quickly lose control if they

---

* My little "how to do it" book entitled *Learn More, Smoke Less*, listed in Suggestions for Further Reading, describes a harm-reduction program for the intelligent and well-motivated hard-core nicotine addict who despite all efforts relapses repeatedly.

try. This is the position held strongly with respect to alcohol addiction by powerful groups like Alcoholics Anonymous (AA), who are committed to total abstinence. In the face of this strong conviction, medical scientists are afraid even to examine the question objectively—a few brave ones did and were pilloried for it. So although experience and common sense warn us that ex-addicts are at exceptionally high risk for relapse, we don't really have scientific evidence as to whether controlled drug use could be a realistic option for some people in some circumstances, either as an end in itself or as a temporary expedient on the way to total abstinence.

Several kinds of pharmacologic treatments are proving effective in aiding hard-core nicotine addicts to become abstinent, but these drugs are useful only as adjuncts to behavioral therapy:

- *Non-tobacco nicotine agonists.* Nicotine chewing gum was introduced some years ago as an aid to giving up cigarettes. Furnishing nicotine in pure form was seen as a way to assist the addict in breaking the smoking habit completely, while avoiding withdrawal discomfort and sustaining the nicotine dependence. Then eventually, in this approach, the nicotine gum would be stopped. It turned out that the absorption of nicotine from the mouth was irregular and unpredictable; a variable amount of nicotine was swallowed, and some failed to be absorbed at all.

  Now nicotine skin patches are replacing nicotine gum. Patches are highly reliable, and they smoothly establish nicotine blood levels comparable to what the smoker is used to; but they have not been in use long enough to enable us to establish how successful they really are in helping the addict become—and remain— abstinent. Some experts are already advocating a different philosophy. By analogy to the use of surrogate opiates like methadone in the long-term maintenance of heroin addicts, nicotine maintenance is being proposed for the hard-core group of smokers who seem unable to break their addiction. Unlike long-term methadone treatment, however, which has no known adverse effects, nicotine administration may cause cardiovascular problems, as noted earlier. On the other hand, harm-reduction strategy dictates that if it really works, and if it is the only way to get someone to quit cigarettes, those addicts will at least be spared the bronchitis, emphysema, and lung cancer that are caused by smoking.

- *Antagonists.* Nicotinic receptor antagonists like mecamylamine can, in theory, prevent relapse from the abstinent state by blocking the rewarding effects of nicotine. The chief problem with antagonist therapy is securing patient compliance in taking the medication regularly. This reluctance might reflect a dysphoric effect caused by a blocking of the normal actions of acetylcholine on the brain's nicotinic receptors.

■ *Drugs that relieve withdrawal symptoms.* Clonidine is the drug tested most extensively thus far. Its action has nothing to do with nicotinic receptors. Instead, it blocks the receptors that mediate the unpleasant excitatory symptoms of withdrawal, whether from nicotine or from depressant addictive drugs. In some early controlled trials, it has proved highly effective as an adjunct to smoking withdrawal treatment.

■ *Antidepressant medications.* The trials with this class of drugs rest on an interesting finding by A. H. Glassman and others that a great many more heavily addicted smokers than nonsmokers have suffered from episodes of serious depression in their lives. It may be, therefore, that hard-core nicotine addicts are attempting to self-medicate their depression, so antidepressant drugs might in part substitute for nicotine during and after withdrawal.

In summary, the treatment of nicotine addiction is a classic example of the complexities facing the therapist in the field of addiction. Finding conclusively what combination of pharmacologic and behavioral therapy works best, and for whom, is the challenge for future treatment research.

CHAPTER 9

Drink, and Be Merry?

Alcohol and Related Drugs

It is a typical foggy day in Manchester, England. Imagine that you are standing in an open field in the park, watching a pair of orange plastic road markers a few hundred yards away. A red double-decker bus comes bouncing across the field, heading for the gap between the markers. You think: He'll never get through; it's too narrow for the bus. You are right. The bus knocks over one of the markers.

In this famous experiment, each driver was first asked if he thought he could safely drive the bus through. If he said yes, he was asked to try it. If he said no, the markers were moved apart to a separation he himself thought adequate, and then he was asked to try it. On different days and with different drivers the experiment was done "cold sober" and—as in the run we were watching—after drinking a measured dose of whiskey. Under the influence of alcohol the drivers actually needed a wider gap to maneuver the bus through than when they were sober, but at the same time they judged that a narrower gap was sufficient. This result demonstrates the characteristic and dangerous double effect of alcohol—it spoils judgment at the same time that it ruins performance.

How does this simple molecule cause such profound disturbances in behavior? Why are alcohol and its pharmacologic relatives (benzodiazepines, barbiturates, and volatile solvents) so widely used? What is the impact on the drinker and on society? What are the health hazards of long-term heavy use? How and where do these drugs act in the brain? What are the main features of alcohol addiction, and what is known about treating it?

FERMENTATION, DISTILLATION, INTOXICATION

Alcohol is an ancient drug; fermentation has been recognized since the earliest agricultural civilizations. Throughout history, societies have accorded alcohol a position of special respect, hedging its use with restrictions as to time, place, and circumstance. In Judaism and Christianity, the sacramental use of wine illustrates this method of controlling a dangerous drug. Drunkenness is decried universally, whether in the Biblical passage describing Noah's intoxication, or in Islamic law forbidding alcohol entirely. Even in a nonreligious context, the custom of drinking a toast only on special occasions ("to health," curiously, in all languages) is a relic of the special status enjoyed by this drug in former times.

Fermentation is the process whereby yeast cells convert sugar to ethyl alcohol. It is self-limiting because the yeast cells and yeast enzymes are destroyed when the alcohol concentration reaches about 12%. Therefore, wine cannot be stronger than that unless it is "fortified" by adding alcohol, as with port and sherry (about 20% alcohol). To achieve yet higher alcohol concentrations requires distillation—boiling the alcohol out of the fermentation mixture (it boils at a lower temperature than water) and then condensing the alcohol vapor back to liquid in a still. An efficient still, which may yield nearly pure ethyl alcohol, can be put together from the simplest materials by any backwoodsman who wishes to produce bootleg liquor. Whether obtained through legal or illegal channels, distilled liquors (e.g., vodka, gin, whiskey) are usually 80 to 100 proof (40–50% alcohol) and are much more dangerous than wines (12–20% alcohol) and beer (usually 3–6% alcohol).

The history of drinking habits in England provides an interesting example of these relative dangers. As a beer manufacturing and beer drinking country, it did not experience alcoholism as a major public health problem until the introduction of cheap gin from Holland early in the eighteenth century. Then urban drunkenness, especially among the poor, became England's blight, as depicted so well in Hogarth's famous engraving, "Gin Lane." There is a general principle here: the weaker (less concentrated) forms of all addictive drugs, in their natural state, are safer than the purified biologically active drugs themselves.

The easy availability of distilled liquors and the erosion of the cultural protections surrounding alcohol use have had devastating effects. Alcohol is the only addictive drug that dangerously alters behavior yet at the same time is freely and legally available without a prescription. As it is so widely used, it presents the most serious addiction problem for our society.

BEING DRUNK

Intoxication by alcohol is a distinctive behavioral condition, dose-related and easily measurable. In animals as well as in people, the blood concentration of ethyl alcohol is a good indicator of the concentration bathing the brain. And the alcohol vapor in the breath reflects, quite accurately, the concentration in the blood flowing through the lungs. This is the basis of the *breathalyzer* technique for measuring blood concentration, and the close blood-brain relationship is the basis for setting a presumptive blood-level standard for "driving while intoxicated." In most states this is 0.10%, but a few states (California among them) have led the way to the safer level of 0.08% justified by results obtained in driving simulators. Testing by breath or blood sample provides useful and accurate information about whether psychomotor behavior is likely to be disrupted by the drug at the time the sample is taken. In contrast, urine tests for any drug provide only a historical record that a drug entered the body at some prior time.

In alcohol research the single drink is used as a unit of measure because typical drinks of all kinds are roughly equivalent in alcohol content. For example, a typical small jigger (an ounce and a half) of 80-proof (40%) distilled spirits contains 18 milliliters of alcohol.

Equivalent amounts of alcohol would be contained in a 12-ounce can of strong (5%) beer—most beer is 3–4%—or a 5-ounce glass of wine (12%). For most people, this typical single drink represents the smallest amount of alcohol that does anything at all; it is the dosage that people usually take at the outset in social drinking.

With alcohol it is not a question of harmless relaxation at low doses and behavioral toxicity only at higher doses. That very first drink disrupts complex mental abilities and psychomotor coordination; tests requiring calculations, quick memory recall, vigilance, and the like, all show decrements in performance. Harder to measure are the subjective effects, the very ones that people seek from social drinking: loss of inhibitions, a relaxed mood, loquaciousness, and easy sociability. Unfortunately, these sought-after effects are accompanied by poor judgment and greater risk-taking behavior, as the Manchester bus drivers demonstrated.

After a few drinks, the fine control mechanisms that maintain our sense of balance are disturbed. This is the basis for tests like "walking the line" and eyes-closed sway. The disturbance of equilibrium is thought to be due to an action of alcohol in the cerebellum: in this part of the brain, incoming signals from the muscles bringing position information, and those from the inner ear bringing balance information, are coordinated with outgoing messages to the numerous muscles involved in control of posture. Animal tests for this action of alcohol are popular because they are so easy to carry out in the laboratory. One uses a horizontal rod driven by a motor that makes it rotate slowly. A normal mouse or rat placed on the rod has no difficulty maintaining its balance; it walks continuously as the rod turns under its feet. A slightly intoxicated animal falls off the rod. This behavioral deficit can be scored quantitatively—number of falls, time to falling, critical speed of rotation—and the scores relate directly to the blood (and brain) concentration of alcohol.

In humans, as the alcohol dose is increased, speech becomes slurred and incoherent, balance is severely impaired, and inappropriate, foolish behavior develops. Loss of inhibition leads to boastfulness ("Sure, I can drive!") and enhanced aggression ("I can beat him with one hand tied behind my back!")—a particularly dangerous combination. It is estimated that alcohol plays a role in more than half of all homicides in the United States, and it is the cause of half the motor vehicle deaths. At still higher doses, alcohol causes profound sedation, then respiratory depression, eventually coma and death. Alcohol-induced "sleep" (not normal sleep, but rather an immobility like that seen with anesthetics) is an easy effect to measure in animals; the duration of immobility and loss of the righting reflex are related to the alcohol dose.

As to how and where in the brain alcohol causes the psychotropic effects that make it so attractive to so many people, there is no single answer. GABA is the most abundant neurotransmitter, and its receptors are thought to mediate the effects of alcohol. GABA receptors in the brain are ion channels (see Chapter 3) and are composed of several protein subunits arranged to permit the passage of negatively charged chloride ions. When GABA is released from a nearby nerve ending, it binds to this receptor, opening the channel. The sudden inrush of chloride ions increases the negative electrical charge inside the neuron, making it more refractory to the neurotransmitters that ordinarily stimulate it. Alcohol enhances the action of GABA on its receptors.

Since the GABA receptors are found in many parts of the brain, we should not be surprised that alcohol acts in many different brain regions. Alcohol acting on GABA receptors that affect the function of the cerebellum, for example, could disturb equilibrium and posture. Alcohol in the hippocampus could disturb memory formation and retrieval. The serious depression of breathing and of blood pressure by high doses is due to the action of alcohol on the lower parts of the brain that regulate these vital activities. Finally, and not surprisingly, alcohol has been found to stimulate the dopaminergic reward pathways that mediate positive reinforcement by other addictive drugs.

More recently discovered and less well understood is an effect of alcohol on the so-called NMDA receptors, which are also ion channels and normally respond to an abundant excitatory neurotransmitter, glutamate (Chapter 3).

OTHER DRUGS IN THE ALCOHOL FAMILY

Barbiturates and benzodiazepines (like Valium)—although their effects are not identical—both cause a behavioral intoxication very much like that due to alcohol, so it is significant that these drugs have similar effects on GABA receptors. Barbiturates were widely prescribed as sleeping pills before the 1960s. Their easy availability made them favorite drugs for suicide, and accidental deaths from overdose were also not uncommon. Addiction liability was a problem, too. Most important, however, they were not really effective in the treatment of insomnia. Regular use causes dependence, and then attempts to sleep without the medication are frustrated by withdrawal disturbances which include, ironically enough, insomnia. As a colleague who is an expert on sleep disturbances puts it: "Sleeping pills *cause* insomnia."

Benzodiazepines, like alcohol and barbiturates, do not compete with GABA, but they have their own specific binding site on the GABA receptor, different from the barbiturate binding site. The result, however, is like that caused by alcohol—to enhance the effect of GABA in opening the ion channel in the receptor, thus allowing chloride ions to rush in. In 1965, with the abandonment of barbiturates for treating insomnia and anxiety, the first benzodiazepines came onto the market and quickly replaced them, becoming the most widely prescribed drugs in the United States. Advantages of the benzodiazepines over the barbiturates are their safety (overdose deaths being virtually unknown), lesser tendency to dosage escalation and dependence, and less dangerous withdrawal syndrome. In the view of some experts they were greatly overprescribed, both for insomnia and for anxiety; and many patients, especially elderly people, used them daily and became dependent on them. A population survey in 1981 showed that 11% of U.S. adults were using a benzodiazepine (usually Valium); and of these, one in seven had used one daily for the entire year. The reaction to these findings was a drastic reduction in prescribing, so that now—according to a recent report of an American Psychiatric Association Task Force—they are not prescribed sufficiently even for legitimate needs.

The third member of the alcohol family comprises the volatile solvents, which are self-administered by inhalation. They have a long history as mood-altering agents, and their psychotropic actions are quite similar to those of alcohol, barbiturates, and the benzodiazepines. They probably act on GABA receptors in much the same way as alcohol does. The nineteenth century saw ether, chloroform, and nitrous oxide ("laughing gas") become fads for obtaining a quick "high." Nowadays, volatile solvents are used chiefly by children, who have access to glue, correction fluid, paints, fuels, and the like. The "high" is much like alcoholic intoxication, but unfortunately, the solvents are very toxic. Sudden death may occur from heart stoppage. Repeated use over a long period of time is toxic to the liver, kidneys, and other organs. Permanent brain damage, causing loss of balance, tremors, and visual disturbances, is a serious toxic effect of repeated exposure.

ARE THERE ALCOHOL RECEPTORS?

At the neurochemical level, the challenge is to understand how the many and diverse effects of alcohol, especially the psychotropic actions, come about. Ethyl alcohol is a very small molecule, containing only two linked carbon atoms, one oxygen atom, and six hydrogen atoms. No alcohol receptor has been identified, and some scientists doubt that a receptor could bind such a simple and nondescript ligand in a specific manner. Two concrete pieces of evidence speak against a specific alcohol receptor. First, the alcohol concentration required to produce even the mildest of its effects is millions of times higher than the effective concentrations of typical receptor ligands. So, if there is an alcohol receptor, it has remarkably low affinity for its ligand as compared with all known receptors. Second, there is a family of alcohols, progressively larger molecules than ethyl alcohol (ordinary rubbing alcohol, isopropyl alcohol, is an example), which share most or all of the psychotropic effects of ethyl alcohol. Volatile solvents and anesthetic gases (some of which consist of even fewer atoms than ethyl alcohol) also share these effects. The extreme case is the rare gas xenon, which is but a single atom, and moreover is chemically inert, but produces many biologic effects that are indistinguishable from those of ethyl alcohol. This striking lack of specificity is quite at variance with what we expect from ligands that bind to receptors.

However, there is an enzyme in liver, alcohol dehydrogenase, which converts alcohol to acetaldehyde in the first step of alcohol metabolism. Given the existence of such a protein, which accommodates alcohol in a binding site, we can not summarily dismiss the idea that an ethyl alcohol receptor—albeit of low affinity—could be present in brain. The search for such a receptor continues.

If alcohol does not bind to a receptor, how else might it disturb the functions of neurons? Cell membranes, in which receptors, ion channels, enzymes, transporters, and other functional molecules are embedded, are composed of two layers of *lipid* (oily fat), as shown in Figure 9.1. At the inner and outer membrane surface is an array of the so-called head groups of the lipids, which attract and are surrounded by water molecules from the environment. The long "tails" of the lipids—chains of carbon atoms called *fatty acids*—are arrayed in a densely packed parallel manner which gives the membrane a highly ordered structure. The various functional proteins that operate in the

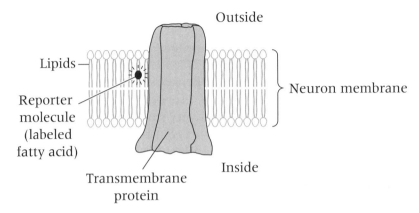

FIGURE 9.1 Measuring fluidity of neuron membranes. A reporter molecule labeling a fatty acid chain gives information about the extent of vibratory motion at a specific depth in the membrane. The transmembrane protein here represents ion-channel receptors, 7-helix receptors, and transporters, described in Chapter 3.

cell membrane ("transmembrane protein" in the figure) are very much affected by the state of this lipid matrix in which they float. Cell membranes can be studied by inserting a labeled fatty acid, as in the figure. The label (called a *reporter molecule*) can be any molecule whose motion is detectable in an appropriate instrument. Suppose the reporter groups are placed at a distance of 10 carbon atoms down the fatty-acid chains; then the vibratory motion of the labeled chains will reflect the motion of all surrounding chains at that depth in the membrane.

A Stanford colleague of mine, Dora B. Goldstein, labeled membranes from neurons in this way and then exposed them to alcohol at intoxicating concentrations. The motion within the membrane was found to increase. In other words, alcohol had a disordering (fluidizing) effect. There is controversy about whether the measured disorder, which is quite small, could be sufficient to account for the psychotropic effects of alcohol. In support of the idea are three key findings:

1. When the experiment is done with a variety of related alcohols, there is an excellent correlation between their disordering effect on the membrane and their biologic potency in causing intoxication.

2. Strains of mice with high natural resistance to alcohol ("short-sleep" mice, described in Chapter 7) have membranes that are resistant to the disordering effect.

3. Membranes from mice that have been made tolerant to alcohol by long-term exposure are less readily disordered by alcohol.

Hard to explain, however, is the fact that small increases in body temperature cause membrane disorder of comparable degree yet do not cause intoxication. It may be that the observed small fluidizing effect, because it represents an average disorder across the whole membrane, obscures a much greater disordering action in the immediate vicinity of some very important receptors. Those could be the GABA and NMDA receptors, whose functions are known to be affected by alcohol.

In attributing a drug effect to a particular molecular interaction, pharmacologists look closely at drug concentrations. We know what concentration of alcohol in the fluid bathing the brain (about 0.1%) is required to cause the characteristic intoxication. Alcohol disturbs numerous biochemical processes at very much higher concentrations, even above the lethal range, but such actions can not be relevant to the intoxicating action. We accept as possibly important the actions of alcohol on membrane fluidity and on the GABA and NMDA receptors because the alcohol concentrations for those actions are in the pharmacologically relevant range.

ALCOHOL DEPENDENCE AND WITHDRAWAL

Chapter 7 outlined some of the evidence for a role of heredity in the predisposition to alcohol addiction. To become addicted requires a pattern of repeated heavy drinking, and this typically develops over a number of years. Most people who enjoy social drinking in moderation, to obtain a mild degree of behavioral disinhibition, do not enjoy—indeed, may even be disgusted by—being drunk, and they dislike losing control. Alcoholics, in contrast, evidently like being drunk, and they drink to get drunk.

Chronic exposure to alcohol produces physical dependence in animals and in people. When someone has been drinking heavily for a long time and then abruptly discontinues, the withdrawal syndrome can be severe to the point of death. Bursts of electrical activity in the brain occur, accompanied by convulsions and sometimes by psychotic phenomena like hallucinations (delirium tremens). With respect to the withdrawal syndrome, alcohol and related substances are the most hazardous of the addictive drugs. It will be recalled that the withdrawal disturbances are instantly relieved by alcohol, by benzodiazepines, or by barbiturates. In like manner, the withdrawal syndrome caused by chronic exposure to either benzodiazepines or barbiturates is relieved by alcohol. This cross-dependence is entirely consistent with a common action of all these drugs—for example, on the GABA receptor complex.

Probably because of its unpleasant taste and the way it irritates the mouth, esophagus, and stomach, mice and rats will not readily drink enough alcohol, in a free-choice arrangement, to become dependent. In order to produce alcohol dependence in experiments like those described for opiates in Chapter 6, mice have to be exposed continuously for at least several days. Dora B. Goldstein accomplished this by housing them in an inhalation chamber, an airtight plastic box through which alcohol was furnished in a continuous flow as a vapor in the airstream. The concentration in the vapor could be held steady, and it could be varied as desired. The blood level of alcohol was measured from time to time in a drop of blood taken from the tail. At various times after removing mice from the chamber, the withdrawal syndrome could be elicited by lifting a mouse by the tail; this provokes a convulsion—a response never seen in normal animals. These studies showed a direct relationship between the alcohol concentration in blood during development of dependence and the intensity of the withdrawal disturbance, analogous to the findings on opiate dependence in animals and humans. Tolerance developed simultaneously with dependence, and both phenomena were reversible over a period of about 24 hours after stopping alcohol administration. Thus, the time course of alcohol tolerance and dependence in mice was much like that seen with opiates.

HEALTH HAZARDS OF ALCOHOL USE

A consequence of long-term chronic and heavy use of alcohol is liver cirrhosis, a condition in which damage to the cells leads to their replacement by scar tissue, until eventually the liver fails entirely, and the addict dies. A complication on the way to that final outcome is severe—even life-threatening—bleeding. Blood circulating from the gut normally flows into the liver on its way back to the heart; but as the liver becomes more scarred and hardened, resistance to the blood flow increases, veins in the stomach and esophagus become distended, and hemorrhage results.

In addition to its psychotropic actions, alcohol—even at ordinary doses, but more significantly as dosage is increased—disturbs the regulation of several hormone systems in the body. Prominent among these effects is a suppression of sex hormone production. In females, menstrual irregularities are common. In males sexual potency is reduced during intoxication; and long-term drinking causes degeneration of the testicles and diminished production of testosterone, enlarged breasts, and decreased sex drive.

A special toxic effect of alcohol addiction is the *fetal alcohol syndrome*, recognized only since 1973. If a woman drinks heavily during very early pregnancy, she is likely to miscarry. But if the fetus escapes that fate, the newborn infant will have low birth weight, with the various medical problems that accompany it. The characteristic marker of fetal alcohol syndrome is a peculiar malformation—a flat face, a thin upper lip, and a peculiar appearance of the eyes and nose. Growth of the infant is abnormally slow, and in later years there are various degrees of mental retardation, hyperactivity, attention deficits, and learning disorders.

A recent major study conducted by Ann P. Streissguth followed affected infants into adolescence and adulthood, with periodic multiple tests of intelligence and mental functioning. The facial abnormalities were accompanied by permanent brain damage, as evidenced by poor test performance. In another study—a prospective one—pregnant women were queried, before they gave birth, about their alcohol use early in pregnancy and also in the month before they knew they were pregnant. Their infants were examined on the first day of life and again periodically until seven years of age. This study showed that even moderate drinking in the earliest weeks of pregnancy had small but measurable and lasting effects on behavior of the newborn, even when the facial abnormalities of the severe fetal alcohol syndrome were not present. Behavioral deficits, learning difficulties, short attention span, impulsivity, and numerous other inappropriate behavior patterns symptomatic of neurologic damage were correlated with the extent of maternal drinking; and these problems persisted throughout childhood. Observations by others, however, have failed to demonstrate any adverse effects on the newborn when maternal alcohol consumption during pregnancy was less than three drinks daily on average. An unavoidable weakness of all such studies is that they depend on self-reporting of drinking during pregnancy, and self-reports are likely be on the low side of the truth. In summary, it is even more obvious with alcohol than with other addictive drugs that the safe course is for the pregnant woman to remain abstinent throughout pregnancy.

There is a general problem here, however, which applies to all drugs that affect fetal development. Figure 9.2 illustrates a normal 28-day menstrual cycle. Ovulation occurs about 14 days from the start of the previous menses, and the ovum can only be fertilized within a short span of time—a couple of days. The time of greatest sensitivity of the developing fetus to serious damage by any drug is during the formation of the body organs, which begins very early—only 20 days after fertilization. Since ovulation and fertilization occur in the middle of the menstrual cycle, this critical time would begin barely a week after the expected start of the first missed period. That is also the earliest time a pregnancy test is likely to turn positive. What this

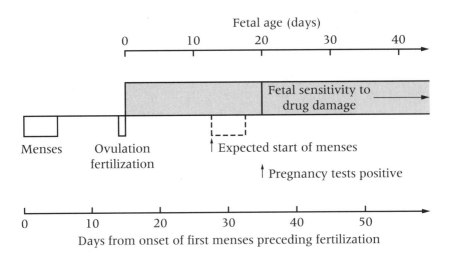

FIGURE 9.2 Critical period for drug damage to the fetus. Diagram is for a woman with normal 28-day menstrual cycles. [From A. Goldstein, L. Aronow, and S. M. Kalman, *Principles of Drug Action*, Harper & Row, New York, 1968, Fig. 12-3.]

means is that even with perfectly regular periods—and the situation is much worse if periods are irregular—a woman can not be sure she is pregnant early enough to prevent serious damage to the fetus. Clearly, then, it is not safe for her to continue addictive drug use, planning to stop if she discovers she is pregnant. Furthermore, if the pregnancy is unplanned, and the woman drinks heavily, she will not even be alert to the urgency of trying to stop in time. This state of affairs really indicates that all female addicts of child-bearing potential are at risk of producing abnormal offspring if they use drugs.

TREATING ALCOHOL ADDICTION

Studying how best to treat any addiction is beset with problems. In addition to the usual technical challenges in carrying out clinical trials in humans, addicts often are poorly motivated and uncooperative, are not amenable to long-term follow-up, and may not be truthful in reporting on abstinence. Thus, clinical trials on the treatment of alcohol addiction are both difficult and controversial. One can not simply assign patients randomly to different treatment modalities, as one would like to do in order to obtain valid comparisons. The reason is that people can not be deprived of free choice of treatment, and most have strong preconceptions about what treatment is best. Moreover, even if it were possible, it would be ethically questionable to deprive anyone of treatments thought to be beneficial merely in order to establish untreated controls against which to measure the effects of treatment. Adding to the difficulty of conducting experimental comparisons of different treatment methods, addicts tend to switch impulsively from one treatment to another, and from treatment to no treatment. Finally, complicating matters further, powerful political constituencies are committed single-mindedly to one approach—total abstinence through a *12-step program* like that originated by Alcoholics Anonymous (AA). It is not surprising, given this situation, that there are no convincing experimental data to tell us which treatments are most effective.

There is a shared impression among most professionals that 12-step programs are the best for most alcohol addicts. The method depends on peer support, honest self-examination, self-accusation, confession, and acceptance of guidance by a "higher power." The only requirement for AA membership is a desire to stop drinking. These are the 12 steps, from the official AA manual:

1. We admitted we were powerless over alcohol—that our lives had become unmanageable.

2. Came to believe that a Power greater than ourselves could restore us to sanity.

3. Made a decision to turn our will and our lives over to the care of God as we understood Him.

4. Made a searching and fearless moral inventory of ourselves.

5. Admitted to God, to ourselves, and to another human being the exact nature of our wrongs.

6. Were entirely ready to have God remove all these defects of character.

7. Humbly asked Him to remove our shortcomings.

8. Made a list of all persons we had harmed, and became willing to make amends to them all.

9. Made direct amends to such people wherever possible, except when to do so would injure them or others.

10. Continued to take personal inventory and when we were wrong promptly admitted it.

11. Sought through prayer and meditation to improve our conscious contact with God as we understood Him, praying only for knowledge of His will for us and the power to carry that out.

12. Having had a spiritual awakening as the result of these steps, we tried to carry this message to alcoholics, and to practice these principles in all our affairs.

Step 12 may well be the most important one, for it makes every alcohol addict a member of a peer support group, reaching out to help other victims of the addiction. Furthermore, central to the AA philosophy is the concept "once an addict always an addict," meaning that one can become a "recovering alcoholic" but never an "ex-alcoholic." Key slogans guide the progress of treatment. "One day at a time" addresses the addict's ambivalence about never being able to use alcohol again. "Easy does it" stresses that recovery from a drug addiction is a long process, requiring patience. "Keep it simple" puts the focus on not drinking, attending meetings, and reaching out to help other alcoholics. "First things first" is a reminder that staying sober has top priority. Usually rejected in the AA approach is any chemical treatment for the addiction, as well as the idea that controlled and moderate drinking may ever become possible. The tenets of 12-step programs are all realistic and practical, and they agree with much of what we know about addiction. Moreover, motivation is strengthened by the evangelistic enthusiasm with which AA groups operate. Yet, as AA's approach to the treatment of alcohol addiction does not rest solidly on a scientific foundation and does not subject itself to objective outcome testing, we can not really assess its validity.

Certain it is that many alcohol addicts have given up drinking through adherence to these programs. Certain it is, also, that many drop out, and that long-term abstinence rates are low; but relapses are accepted as part of the disease, and those who fall by the wayside are encouraged to become abstinent again. Despite the AA explanation that "God" is only a symbolic name for the "higher power," to which alcoholics may attach any meaning they wish, some can not accept this aspect of the basic philosophy, or find the regimentation and rituals unacceptable. The great enemy of treatment success, as in all drug addiction treatment, is ambivalence in the motivation to remain abstinent.

A pharmacologic agent that has been used widely and with partial success in treating alcohol addiction is disulfiram (Antabuse). Alcohol, it will be recalled, is metabolized by two enzymes in the liver. The first is alcohol dehydrogenase, which converts alcohol to acetaldehyde, a very toxic product. The second enzyme is acetaldehyde dehydrogenase, which converts acetaldehyde to acetic acid, a harmless product. Ordinarily, the acetaldehyde is changed to acetic acid almost as fast as it is formed, so very little accumulates even after heavy drinking. Disulfiram inactivates the acetaldehyde dehydrogenase, so acetaldehyde does accumulate—if and only if alcohol has been consumed. In this way, alcohol in the presence of disulfiram produces symptoms that mimic the "Oriental flush" described in Chapter 7—a reaction that is due to an inherited deficiency of the same enzyme.

Disulfiram treatment makes use of the fact that this drug by itself produces no unusual subjective effects, and it can usually be taken safely by mouth once daily. But then even a single drink will cause a dreadful illness. The face and other parts of the body become hot and flushed, and an intense throbbing headache develops, with nausea, vomiting, sweating, dizziness, and trouble breathing. In extreme cases, the blood pressure collapses and the patient goes into shock and may even die. The rationale of treatment, then, is that an addict who in the sober state is motivated to take disulfiram regularly will be unlikely to succumb to the craving for a drink, knowing (perhaps from one bad experience) what is bound to happen. The limited data show that alcohol addicts who take disulfiram regularly maintain abstinence well. Those with poorer motivation present a problem; they either discontinue entirely and relapse, or they skip disulfiram periodically, for several days at a time, in order to be able to drink with only minimal discomfort. A significant limitation is that the drug is toxic in the presence of liver disease—which many alcohol addicts have. Studies of large numbers of alcoholics fail to show effectiveness in preventing relapses, primarily because of failure to take the medication regularly. And thus the real challenge for the therapist is how to encourage compliance. In Chapter 10, a very similar compliance problem is presented—how to get heroin addicts to take naltrexone as part of their treatment.

Recently, an interesting relationship was discovered in animals between alcohol intake in free-choice experiments and the endogenous opioid systems. Low doses of opiates increased alcohol preference, strains of mice with high endogenous opioid activity also displayed high alcohol preference, and opiate antagonists tended to reduce alcohol consumption. The mechanism of these effects is not yet understood, but the findings suggested the possibility that the opiate antagonist naltrexone might be a useful adjunct in the treatment of alcohol addiction.

Double-blind placebo-controlled clinical trials have now been undertaken. Alcohol addicts, after detoxification, were assigned randomly to receive daily naltrexone or placebo by mouth. In addition, both groups received supportive counseling therapy that included behavioral training in methods of preventing a single lapse from leading to full-blown relapse. The trials were continued for three months with regular measures of alcohol consumption by breathalyzer, by self-report, and by reports of family members. Craving was also measured (by self-report). As the subjects were given naltrexone (or placebo) pills to take at home, it was necessary to confirm that they actually took the pills. This was accomplished cleverly, in one study, by incorporating a fluorescent vitamin in the pill, so that a simple measurement of urine fluorescence would confirm that a subject had taken the medication.

The results were very encouraging. Naltrexone had no striking effect in preventing subjects from taking single drinks, but it was dramatically better than placebo in preventing single drinks from triggering binges. It also reduced craving, it was safe, and it was acceptable to the subjects. However, naltrexone was not completely effective; about one-quarter of the naltrexone group relapsed during a three-month period, compared with about half of the placebo group. Thus, much remains to be done before we can safely assert that naltrexone should become a routine adjunct in the treatment of alcohol addiction; and there remains a pressing need to search for still better pharmaco-therapy and for more effective combinations of pharmacotherapy with relapse prevention strategies.

CHAPTER 10

Addictive Tranquility
The Opiates

A passage in the *Odyssey* faithfully captures the peculiar quality of the psychotropic effect of opiates. The scene is the palace of Menelaus, king of Sparta. Telemachus, depressed and miserable after his long and vain search for his father Odysseus, is being entertained at dinner. Then Helen, we are told,

> had a happy thought. Into the bowl in which their wine was mixed, she slipped a drug that had the power of robbing grief and anger of their sting and banishing all painful memories. No one who swallowed this dissolved in wine could shed a single tear that day, even for the death of his mother and father, or if they put his brother or his own son to the sword and he were there to see it done.

The opiate family includes morphine (the chief active component of crude opium from the opium poppy), heroin (a laboratory-produced derivative of morphine), and numerous potent synthetic morphinelike compounds used in medicine. These are powerful pain-killers in the hands of physicians, and as the quotation above suggests, they dramatically relieve emotional as well as physical pain. This property contributes to making them extremely seductive for self-administration.

Heroin is a late nineteenth-century invention. Before the middle of the century, the addict ate or smoked raw opium. The introduction of the hypodermic needle and syringe into medical practice at the time of the Civil War allowed morphine to be injected under the skin or into a vein, flooding the bloodstream with the potent pure drug quickly and efficiently. During the last half of the nineteenth century, many people—mostly middle-class housewives—were maintained on morphine by their physicians and became dependent. This practice probably represented an attempt to treat chronic anxiety, much in the way benzodiazepines (like Valium) are often used today.

By contrast with heroin, morphine passes relatively slowly from the blood into the brain; heroin floods the brain instantly after its injection into a vein. This property made heroin attractive to a new class of addicts who sought its euphoriant actions and self-administered it without medical supervision. Thus heroin became the opiate of first choice for addicts everywhere. Today it is estimated that nearly a million people in the United States are addicted to heroin.

How does a person typically progress from first use of an opiate to full-blown addiction? How can heroin addicts be treated most effectively? Is methadone a solution or is it part of the problem? This chapter addresses these questions, both by reviewing the research findings of others and by citing my own experiences treating heroin addicts with methadone.

PAIN RELIEF BY OPIATES

Even after thousands of years, morphine and its synthetic "look-alikes" are unexcelled for relief of severe physical pain. This characteristic makes them some of the most important drugs at the physician's disposal. Because of their remarkable calming effect on extreme stress and anxiety, they are also used routinely to prepare patients for the operating room. Millions of hospitalized patients have received opiates and have even become physically dependent on them while in the hospital, but after their discharge they almost never seek out opiates again. Thus, medically caused addiction is today truly a rarity, practically a myth. The reluctance of many physicians to use opiates in sufficient dosage and often enough to control pain is therefore unjustified. It is especially absurd for physicians to refuse opiates in sufficient dosage to patients suffering the pain of terminal cancer for fear of addicting them.

When self-administered intravenously, morphine (and even more effectively heroin) acts so rapidly upon the brain that an intense feeling of sublime pleasure is produced—a "rush," which is sometimes compared with orgasm. Then, as the initial drug concentration in the brain declines, a second phase sets in—a peculiar dream state, an emotional disconnection from reality. The addict who injects morphine or heroin under the skin rather than intravenously does not achieve the initial very high brain concentration with its associated "rush"; instead, the predominant effect is the tranquil mood of the second phase.

To understand the feeling of satisfaction produced by opiates, we can go to literature, where the following passage, from Nelson Algren's *The Man with the Golden Arm*, offers a telling description:

> It hit all right. It hit the heart like a runaway locomotive, it hit like a falling wall. Frankie's whole body lifted with that smashing surge, the very heart seemed to lift up-up-up—then rolled over and he slipped into a long warm bath with one orgasmic sigh of relief. ... All he had to do the rest of his life was to lie right here feeling better and better with every beat of his heart till he'd never felt so good in all his life.

Thomas De Quincey summarizes it more succinctly, in his classic *Confessions of an English Opium-Eater*:

> Thou has the keys of Paradise, oh just, subtle, and mighty opium!

Roger E. Meyer and his colleagues conducted carefully designed and meticulously executed experiments on self-administration of heroin by volunteers in a closed research ward. Standardized checklists were employed to follow mood changes. The result, in scientific prose, lacks the romantic hyperbole of the literary descriptions, but makes the same point:

> Subjects reported themselves significantly more carefree, relaxed, calm, elated, clear, and "stoned."

I have asked many addicts to recollect and describe for me their first experience with heroin, which usually occurred during adolescence. Every one of them tried to explain what the feeling was like—an overwhelming sensation of otherworldly bliss—but words seemed inadequate. All of them, at the time, had known perfectly well the dangers of addiction but succumbed to curiosity (often after urging by friends), rationalizing that although others might become addicted, they would not. You can not just try heroin, the way you might try a new breakfast cereal from the supermarket. Someone who is experienced has to teach you the ropes: how and where to buy it, how to dissolve it in a bent spoon, how to cook it over a flame, how to filter it through cotton, how to acquire the syringe and needle. You have to be taught how much to use, an uncertain business because of the unknown strength of the powder you have bought. You have to be shown how to use a tourniquet to make a vein stand out, how to slip the needle into the vein and draw back blood to make sure it is in the vein, how to release the tourniquet, how to inject, and how fast. In other words, heroin use starts out as a very social affair with its own special rituals and techniques.

The first injection of heroin usually provokes nausea and vomiting, but your friend will assure you that this side effect disappears with subsequent injections. One might imagine that if something makes you sick, you would avoid it in the future. Not so with heroin. The drug's effect suppresses the emotional distaste of the nausea and vomiting. Many addicts have told me: "You don't mind puking behind heroin!"

The idea of "just trying it once" is set aside when the second opportunity arises, perhaps the next weekend. After using heroin weekly for a while, you somehow find it in the middle of the week. Gradually the intervals become shorter, leading to tolerance and dependence, as described in Chapter 6, and soon you are "using" daily. One morning you awaken with what seems to be a cold—running nose, a slight feeling of chilliness. You mention it to a friend, who says: "That's no cold. Try some heroin and see how fast it goes away. You're hooked!"

Once you have learned what a mild case of opiate withdrawal is like, and how dramatically it is abolished by heroin, you begin to crave heroin intensely at the very earliest feeling of "being sick." Gradually, as the weeks go by, you find yourself needing more and more heroin to relieve the sickness and to achieve that marvellous feeling of satisfaction. Eventually you become fully addicted. Now you are using heroin three or four times a day, and the cost of each dose, which was originally a reasonable few dollars, has escalated to many times that amount. You have to spend more and more of your time between injections just finding a supply. As a result, you may have trouble holding down your job; but even if you manage that, heroin may be eating up more and more of your income. Unless you are extremely wealthy, you may very well be tempted by the kinds of illegal activity that will raise money quickly—prostitution, theft, robbery, embezzlement, and so on.

The process has to end. Either you are caught and begin a long relationship with the criminal-justice system, or you decide to quit your habit before you are caught. In either case, you have to be detoxified; your system has to rid itself of the opiate. This can be done "cold turkey"; but that requires a kind of discipline and perseverance not often found among addicts. Withdrawal never kills, but it is extremely uncomfortable, something like a very severe case of the flu. And all the while you know that there is an instantaneous cure for the discomfort (heroin, of course!), so you are very likely to give up the attempt to detoxify. It is universally recognized that detoxification on an ambulatory, outpatient, basis—even though the worst of the withdrawal discomfort can be relieved by effective pharmacotherapy—nearly always ends in relapse to heroin use even before the planned 10-day or 21-day detoxification program is completed.

There is an alternative and more effective way to become drug-free—the "half-way house," a disciplined and closed residential therapeutic community in which drugs are not available. The addict who spends enough time (typically at least six months) in such a facility, can become drug-free while there, at the same time receiving the many rehabilitative services that are needed to reconstruct a normal life. Unfortunately, this method is not acceptable to most addicts (so the dropout rate is generally at least 75% of all admissions), it is quite expensive, and it remains unclear what proportion of those who are "cured" in a therapeutic community remain abstinent (and for how long) after they return to the larger community.

A MEDICATION THAT IS TOO GOOD

In previous chapters I described the remarkable opiate antagonists naloxone (Narcan) and naltrexone (Trexan). Both are extraordinarily effective and potent in blocking the opioid receptors, both are remarkably nontoxic, and both are useful in treatment, albeit for different purposes. Naloxone can not be given by mouth because it would be carried in the bloodstream directly to the liver, where it is rapidly destroyed. Its main therapeutic value is for resuscitating victims of heroin overdose. In that application it is the most dramatic antidote known to medicine, instantaneously bringing back to life people who were already at death's door.

In contrast to naloxone, naltrexone is effective by mouth. Pretreatment with it, as we saw in Chapter 4, can completely abolish the effect of a subsequent intravenous injection of heroin. Taken by mouth, naltrexone lasts a few days. This means that if a person drinks a dose of naltrexone a few times a week, that person is very unlikely to use heroin; heroin would be pointless, a waste of money. Like many technologic advances, this one breaks down in the face of human behavior. Since an adequate dose of naltrexone is 100% effective in blocking the rewarding action of heroin, it is completely effective in preventing heroin use. Too effective, perhaps! Faced with the stark choice between naltrexone and heroin, most addicts give up the naltrexone and revert to heroin use. However, in addition to the desire for the heroin "high" there may be another reason: studies have shown a subtle but measurable dysphoric effect of naltrexone, even in normal volunteers. This is presumably due to blockade of endogenous opioids that mediate normal feelings of well-being. In people who are very strongly motivated to remain abstinent, naltrexone has nevertheless proved extremely effective; the typical example of such a favorable result is in an addicted physician, nurse, or pharmacist, whose continued licensure is contingent on complete abstinence from opiates.

METHADONE MAINTENANCE

By the middle of the 1960s, Marie E. Nyswander had devoted most of her career as a psychiatrist to treating heroin addicts in New York City, and she had come to the discouraging realization that no psychiatric treatment seemed to be of any use in getting them to stop using heroin. Vincent P. Dole, a biochemist at Rockefeller University, became interested simultaneously in Dr. Nyswander and in heroin addiction. The result was a marriage of persons and of scientific interests, with profound consequences for the treatment of heroin addicts and for societal attitudes toward them. In brief, the groundbreaking work of Dole and Nyswander established the medical model of heroin addiction.

For 40 years prior to the 1960s, addiction had been wholly the concern of law-enforcement officials. Physicians had been frightened away from treating addicts by sanctions dating back to the early twentieth century, when opiates were first brought under legal control by the Harrison Act of 1914. Of course, physicians were permitted to use morphine for pain control, but they were expressly forbidden from giving an opiate to an addict for the purpose of maintaining the addiction. Physicians who violated the regulation risked losing their medical license as well as facing criminal charges. Heroin addicts were regarded as nothing more than manipulative schemers, criminal sociopaths who had to be locked up to protect society from their predations. Just after World War I, clinics had been opened in some parts of the country to give addicts morphine, on the pragmatic grounds that if they would not give up their habits, they could at least avoid whatever criminal activities they were carrying out solely to obtain the drug. These clinics were all shut down by governmental authorities.

What Nyswander had found so hard to understand was the compulsive, seemingly irrational, irrepressible, drive to obtain and use heroin, even in the face of grave risks to health and of repeated incarceration. Dole brought the rigor of laboratory experimentation to the partnership. Addicts behaved as though they had a real and compelling need for heroin. Was it possible, he speculated, that somehow their bodies actually needed an opiate to function properly? Heroin had two obvious drawbacks and one favorable property. The drawbacks were that it had to be injected intravenously, being poorly and unpredictably absorbed by the oral route, and that it lasted only a few hours because of its rapid metabolism in the body. The favorable property was that, like morphine and other opiates used in medical practice, it was not toxic to any body organs, even on prolonged use, provided reasonable dosages were not exceeded.

In 1967 Dole and Nyswander advanced the heretical hypothesis that heroin addicts might actually improve if they were maintained on a long-acting opiate by the oral route. Such a *surrogate agonist* (a drug similar in action to one for which it substitutes)—methadone—had been studied at the U.S. Public Health Service narcotics hospital in Lexington, Kentucky. Methadone had been developed during World War II in Germany to replace morphine, the supply of opium from abroad having been cut off. It was active by mouth, its pain-relieving action was like that of morphine, and a single oral dose lasted nearly 24 hours. It took courage for Dole and Nyswander to try out methadone, for they faced criminal sanctions if they broke the official taboo on physicians giving opiates to addicts. Their own scientific credentials and the backing of Rockefeller University (and later the New York Medical Society) won the day, and the clinical trials proceeded.

What Dole and Nyswander and their colleague Mary Jeanne Kreek discovered in their first trials in New York has been substantially borne out with hundreds of thousands of heroin addicts all over the world. They reported that after stabilization on a daily dose of methadone, the addicts stopped their frantic search for heroin, seemed to be normalized physically and psychologically, and began to accept rehabilitative services leading to honest employment. Over many years the safety of long-term methadone maintenance was established, largely through clinical studies by Kreek. When heroin addicts are maintained on methadone, all indicators of general health improve, and abnormalities of body systems (for instance of the hormones) tend to normalize. Most important is the finding—by many investigators—that methadone maintenance has no adverse effects on cognitive or psychomotor function, performance of skilled tasks, or memory. Indeed, if ex-addicts maintained on methadone are in the same room as nonaddicts, no observer or psychologic test can pick them out. Court judgments have established in law that methadone patients may not be barred, solely because of taking methadone, from any kind of employment, including—in one famous case—driving a New York subway train.

TREATING HEROIN ADDICTS IN SAN JOSE

In 1969 I established the first major methadone maintenance program in California. This was based in San Jose, a city of half a million at the time, about 50 miles from San Francisco. My purpose was twofold. First, I wanted to confirm what was being claimed about methadone in New York, and to study certain aspects of the use of this drug under rigorously controlled conditions. Second, I saw an opportunity to offer needed help to addicts; who were being hounded and harassed in California as they had been in New York. My colleagues and I had no idea, at the outset, how many heroin addicts there actually were in San Jose and its vicinity. We soon discovered how to find out. By opening a methadone clinic under conditions the addicts would regard as safe, by offering them respect and anonymity, and by making it clear that our aim was to treat rather than harass, we quickly found that many would make themselves known by registering for the program.

Planning and carrying out research in the community and on the streets is far more difficult than doing research in the laboratory. Before we could open the first clinic, my colleagues and I had to enlist the cooperation of the police—the very police whose previous experience with addicts was in a never-ending cops-and-robbers contest. Unless the police stayed away from the clinic, we realized, the addicts would not risk attending. Before we could attempt to deal with the police, we had to establish a solid citizen-support group, an effort that required extensive educational efforts, inasmuch as methadone maintenance was still a novel idea. We also had to get the support of the county mental health center as the official agency that would operate the clinic. And that, in turn, meant convincing the county commissioners and the city council of the expected benefits, especially the likelihood that property crime could be reduced, as the New York experience suggested.

Rigorous clinical research has to be conducted within an ethical framework. Informed consent of the subjects is always required. If a treatment is known to be efficacious, it may not be denied; it would have been impermissible, for example, to have an untreated control group while another group was being given methadone. On the other hand, as optimal dosage was at that time unknown, blind comparisons of different dosages were appropriate.

A special difficulty associated with rigorous research on addicts in a therapeutic setting has to do with training the treatment staff to comply with research protocols. In the laboratory this problem does not arise because the students, research fellows, and technicians who carry out the work have an educational background in the natural sciences and expect to apply their skills to the research at hand. In contrast, the staff in treatment programs are nurses and counselors, who usually have little or no training in scientific methodology and no prior research experience. Moreover, their primary commitment, quite appropriately, is to the welfare of their patients. Therefore, unless they understand the ethical justification for the research and its ultimate benefit to addicts, they are unlikely to insist on the prescribed research procedures, especially if patients object. Moreover, addicts tend to identify those in charge of the research with officialdom, whose edicts and demands they are expert at evading. The only solution to this problem—and I have never seen it work perfectly—is to create an atmosphere in the clinic that commands the respect and confidence of the patients. Insisting on following protocol, and enforcing that even to the point of discharging a recalcitrant patient or staff member, is effective in commanding the respect of the patient group as a whole. In short, clinic personnel must avoid being manipulated—and this rule applies to all addiction treatment, whether or not it includes a research component.

We implemented strict protocols for both comprehensive and random urine testing. The primary purpose of methadone maintenance is to reduce, and if possible eliminate, the use of heroin. Therefore, the only objective measure of success is the presence or absence of morphine (to which the body converts heroin) in the urine. Some methadone programs expel or otherwise penalize patients with "dirty" (morphine-positive) urine—a curious way to react to a treatment failure. However, even in programs that operate on a more helpful philosophy, patients devise the most amazing ways to cheat on a urine test. The incentive to cheat is always present if a condition of parole or probation is never to use heroin. And even in a research program without penalties, cheating may occur simply because it has become a way of life. A simple way to cheat is to drink so much water or beer, for hours before coming to the clinic, that the morphine in urine is too dilute to detect. A complicated way to cheat is to carry someone else's urine, strapped to one's thigh, with a tubing to permit simulating urination, provided one is not watched too closely. The only solution, in the early days, was for a counselor to observe, carefully and directly, the act of urination. This is an invasion of privacy of a most demeaning kind; and even so, the patient who wishes to cheat can easily embarrass the staff monitor into turning away.

This whole situation troubled me, so I determined to invent a better system of urine collection. We established a pass-through window with a sliding shutter between the lavatory and the dispensing station, where a nurse was always on duty. Freshly voided urine is at body temperature. Body temperatures vary somewhat among people, so we first measured hundreds of samples to establish the range of temperatures of freshly voided urine. We also noted the rate of cooling in standard containers. We were then in a good position to assess whether a urine specimen had come directly from a subject's bladder. Someone else's urine strapped to the thigh (for example) was never warm enough. Trying to heat a cold sample with a cigarette lighter usually made it too hot. The system was not unbeatable, but it gave us reasonable assurance of the validity of the urine tests while preserving the dignity of our patients.

Knowing that a urine specimen was genuine, we next needed an immediate method of determining whether morphine was present. The existing method, called thin-layer chromatography, had to be carried out in a chemical laboratory, and it usually took about a week to get a result back. Thus, although urine tests were still useful in documenting the efficacy of the program, the loss of immediacy compromised their therapeutic value. A way was needed to get a test result instantaneously, right at the clinic, in order to confront patients then and there about their use of heroin. I devised a way to do this, based on the principle of immunoassay described in Chapter 3. As immunoassay was practiced, it required measuring radioactive ligand bound to an antibody. That, in turn, required separating the ligand bound to antibody from the free (unbound) radiolabeled ligand, usually by means of a centrifuge. For obtaining an instantaneous result, such manipulations would be unacceptably slow.

I knew, in 1970, that a chemist colleague at Stanford, Harden McConnell, had made several stable free radicals. A free radical is a molecule that has an extra electron, and can be detected in a device known as an *electron spin resonance* (ESR) spectrometer. I knew that the device could distinguish between an immobilized free radical bound to a bulky antibody molecule and one that was not bound but was spinning rapidly in the solution. The same principle is used to study the fluidity of neuronal membranes, as described in Chapter 9. It occurred to me that if we began with morphine labeled with a free radical and bound to an antibody, the ESR spectrometer would detect nothing. If unlabeled morphine were now added, as in a "dirty" urine specimen, the labeled morphine would be displaced from the antibody on the principle of competition. The free-radical morphine, now able to spin freely, would give an immediate signal in the instrument. The new method was all one could hope for. A drop of urine added to a prepared tube containing the antibody and free-radical morphine gave the answer, reliably, in a few seconds. This was one of the first homogeneous immunoassays—assays that did not require separation of bound ligand from free.

Unfortunately, an ESR spectrometer is a very large and very costly machine—out of the question for low-budget methadone clinics. Luckily, it was later made unnecessary by a cheap and efficient homogeneous immunoassay based on color development by an enzyme, and that improved method (called *EMIT*) came into widespread use in clinics everywhere. But there is an interesting twist to the story of the free-radical method. Returning on an airplane from a scientific meeting in Toronto, I found myself sitting next to an old friend and colleague, Jerry Jaffe, who had become President Nixon's "drug czar." I told Jaffe enthusiastically about my new free-radical urine assay, which had been developed by a little company called SYVA, next door to Stanford. I learned from him that heroin use had become a major problem for our ground troops in Vietnam. To avoid returning actively addicted soldiers to the United States, the Army wanted to detoxify them first; but that required a quick and reliable method of identifying heroin users. Jaffe was thrilled to hear my story, and within a few days the ESR spectrometers were on their way to Vietnam. For the Department of Defense, needless to add, the cost was a matter of no concern at all!

To find out what dosage of methadone was appropriate for treating heroin addicts we undertook double-blind experimental comparisons of different dosages. Patients could report whether the methadone "held them" for the full 24-hour period, or whether they felt the early symptoms of withdrawal when they came for their morning dose. These studies and several like them elsewhere established that the proper dosage of methadone for most patients is in the range 60 to 80 milligrams daily. Occasionally, more or less is needed. But addicts tend to view themselves as great experts on drugs; so to avoid being misled by their often inaccurate beliefs, double-blind design is critically important in studies of this kind. There is no great danger in exceeding a dosage of 80 milligrams, as tolerance will develop anyway; and it has been shown that some people metabolize methadone excessively fast, so they actually do need more. On the other hand, too low a dosage is always disastrous. Too often state or federal regulatory authorities have interfered inappropriately with the practice of medicine, and have decreed a maximum dosage—sometimes as low as 40 milligrams. Then the patient is frequently at the very edge of withdrawal, methadone fails to suppress the craving for heroin, and the program is doomed to failure. It is noteworthy that outcome studies conducted under government auspices have consistently shown that the programs with the poorest results are those that give the lowest doses.

Later in the 1970s we tested an improved long-acting methadone, called LAAM. Taken by mouth, like methadone, this opiate lasts for up to 72 hours. We found that patients who had previous experience with methadone uniformly preferred LAAM because—they said—it made them feel better-stabilized. As LAAM was not approved for general use, but only as an experimental drug, we conducted extensive toxicity studies on over 100 subjects and found no untoward effects. Our conclusion, at the end of these studies in 1979, was that LAAM was safe and efficacious and ought to replace methadone for routine use, while methadone should be kept available as an alternative for any patients who might react adversely to LAAM. We tested LAAM in a couple of hundred patients; altogether, throughout the country, LAAM was given to over 4,000 patients in carefully monitored trials, and the same conclusion was reached. However, LAAM had no patent protection, and no pharmaceutical company saw sufficient profit motive to bring it through the elaborate minefield of FDA requirements to final approval. Quite appropriately the National Institute on Drug Abuse took up the project but, as government agencies sometimes do, bungled it again and again. At the present writing, LAAM is still not available on a routine basis for the treatment of heroin addicts, but renewed efforts by the National Institute on Drug Abuse to gain FDA approval have finally succeeded.

An important advantage of LAAM over methadone is that because it need be taken only three times weekly, pressure for "take-home" doses can be resisted fairly easily. With methadone, the need to drink the drug every day in a clinic made it impractical for many addicts to lead normal lives and hold down regular jobs. Consequently, the practice of "take-home" medication began. Most patients handled this responsibly, but some did not. An ordinary dose, to which the patient had developed tolerance during the induction phase of treatment, was lethal for a nontolerant person. Instances of children being killed by a "take-home" dose did nothing to enhance the reputation of methadone in the community. Because of the chronic shortage of treatment "slots,"* methadone had a street value, as a means of preventing withdrawal during an addict's frenetic hunt for heroin. Thus, "take-home" methadone was sometimes divided, and part of it sold, effectively reducing the patient's prescribed dose. The harm to the community from this cause could have been eliminated long ago by authorizing the use of LAAM.

---

* A "slot" is a funded place in a treatment program. Funding may be from federal, state, or local sources. There has always been, and continues to be, insufficient funding to offer treatment to all addicts who want it. Remarkably, despite the increasing need, total funding of heroin addiction treatment has actually decreased. In New York City, with the greatest problem, no new methadone clinics have been opened since 1981.

LONG-TERM RESULTS OF
METHADONE MAINTENANCE

People often ask if methadone "works." To answer that question we need a more precise definition of effectiveness; what should we measure to find out if it works? The simple definition given earlier was that during methadone maintenance, the use of heroin is discontinued or at least greatly reduced. That favorable outcome can be expected only if the dosage is adequate and the clinic environment offers additional support. That means practical counseling about job training and employment, about relating appropriately to the criminal-justice system, about family problems, and about other aspects of daily living.

A different criterion of success has also been proposed—that addicts be able to get off methadone and lead drug-free lives without it. "You're just substituting one addiction for another," critics say, "unless they can live without any opiate at all." It is noteworthy that the need for lifelong treatment with a drug is not questioned for diseases like diabetes or schizophrenia. So in principle, from the medical standpoint, nothing is wrong with lifelong methadone maintenance if it is necessary for a patient's well-being. Dole and Nyswander called heroin addiction a "metabolic disease," implying that addicts might actually have some kind of physiologic need for an opiate in order to function normally. And in earlier chapters I have discussed recent advances in neurochemistry that suggest a possible basis for such a view. If it were proved that opiate addicts really do have a physiologic need for opiates, the arguments against lifelong methadone maintenance ought to subside. In the meantime, I have to adopt an agnostic position on this issue. The truth is that patients themselves, partly because they have accepted the prevalent societal attitude that all opiates are bad, typically try to discontinue methadone or to reduce their dosage.

One common pattern is for a patient to manage for a while without methadone but then to relapse to heroin use and return to methadone treatment. I recall one such case that was truly dramatic. A San Jose man—let's call him Joe Campbell—had a history of years of heroin addiction and difficulties with the law. On methadone maintenance he was able to discontinue heroin completely. To remove himself from the influence of old associates who were still active addicts, he moved to Detroit, where he knew no one. Finding a good job in the automobile industry, he led a stereotypic middle-class life. He fell in love, married, bought a little house and a new car, started a family. Life seemed perfect—for all of four years. Then one day, on his way home from work, he met an old friend from San Jose. "I've got some good stuff in my room," the man volunteered, "come and have a taste." Campbell refused, but the "friend" pressed him, arguing that one "fix" for old times' sake could do no harm. Of course, that one injection soon led to another, and within a few months Campbell had lost job, home, car, and wife. He returned, a broken man, to San Jose and to methadone maintenance.

The story of Joe Campbell is typical of what can and often does happen. His behavior seems so irrational, it defies our understanding. It shows the extreme vulnerability of former addicts to relapse; and this is true regardless of which drug is the culprit. It also tells us that ex-addicts can indeed function well for varying periods after quitting methadone maintenance, but that we must always be ready to re-instate them in a methadone program—quickly, without question, and without red tape—if they relapse to using heroin.

The above account is true but anecdotal. What about systematic studies to find out what eventually happens to heroin addicts who enter a methadone program? How many continue to do poorly and end up dead or in prison? How many change their lifestyles and give up heroin, whether or not they remain in methadone treatment? How long do favorable results last? How frequent is relapse? Follow-up studies on heroin addicts are extraordinarily difficult and expensive to carry out, but several have been done. In general, it is found, some kind of treatment is better than no treatment; but a skeptical interpretation would be that this is because people who are better motivated, who are more likely to succeed anyway, are just the ones who choose to enter treatment. Results are about the same regardless of the treatment modality—methadone or a drug-free residential program; but this may only mean that different people require different approaches, and they all choose what suits them best. A global summary of all methadone outcome studies, including our own five-year follow-up in San Jose might go something like this: About one-third do very poorly, continue illegal activities, often drink heavily, and end up either dead or in prison. Another one-third do well periodically, then relapse, and spend many years—perhaps their whole lifetimes—on and off methadone maintenance. The final one-third are the success stories. They become truly rehabilitated, leave the drug scene entirely (although many may continue taking methadone indefinitely), and become upright citizens in their community. There is no known way to predict, at the outset, which group a person will fall into.

TWENTY YEARS AT
THE FOOT OF SANDIA

Sandia at sunset is one of the most beautiful sights in the world. The red glow turns the mountain into a huge open watermelon—its name means "watermelon" in Spanish. Here in the New Mexico desert, everything is so incredibly vast, it is hard to get one's bearings. The blue sky seems endless, with scattered puffy white clouds, and you can see for hundreds of miles. Then, as you adjust your vision to put things into a human scale of dimensions, your gaze shifts down from Sandia's crest to the sprawling city at its foot. Albuquerque, once a mere stop on the railroad, is now a city spreading over the desert floor, across the Rio Grande, and onto the western side of the river.

Shortly after starting the methadone maintenance program in San Jose, I was asked by colleagues in Albuquerque to come and advise them on starting a methadone program there. Just as the availability of methadone treatment brought a thousand heroin addicts out of the woodwork (so to speak) in San Jose, the same thing happened in New Mexico. Within three years, more than a thousand addicts had registered for methadone in this city of 300,000. What eventually became of them? A 20-year follow-up would be impractical nowadays in most places; the extreme mobility of American urban society would make it very difficult to find people 20 years later. But Albuquerque is different. It is isolated in the vastness of the New Mexico desert. It has a large Mexican-American population with a strong network of extended families. Its people tend to stay; and if they do leave, they tend to return. It seemed possible to go back and track those first thousand methadone patients to find out how many were still (or again) on methadone, how many were dead (and why), how many were in prison (and why), how many were still (or again) actively using heroin, and how many had been integrated into normal society and were no longer drug addicts at all.

The study is still in progress at this writing. Some of the methodologic pitfalls are worth describing. My aim was to track down the first thousand addicts who entered treatment in 1969, 1970, and 1971. The first task, of course, was to find out who they were. The original treatment records had long since been lost or placed in archival storage; just finding them took a year and a half. I felt like a sleuth rather than a medical researcher as we rummaged through the University of New Mexico archives. Let me give a few small examples of the kinds of special difficulty one runs into in tracking heroin addicts. The straightforward method of tracking by names is unreliable because aliases are so common among a group in constant trouble with the law. Date of birth, a customary means of identification, also proved unreliable rather often: a person would give dates that differed by a day or a month or a year on different occasions. Fortunately, those who registered for treatment 20 years ago were assigned sequential numbers from 1 to 1,000, so we at least knew when a number was missing from our list. Eventually, we attached a name to all but six of the sequential numbers, and the real tracking could begin.

Of the original thousand we have by now successfully located more than half—as alive and interviewed, or confirmed dead or in prison. This is what we have found so far; pending completion of the study, these results can only be regarded as an interim progress report. The terms "more than" and "at least" indicate the number already documented as belonging in a certain category—a number that is bound to increase as we locate additional subjects.

- More than one-third of the original thousand are dead, and the most frequent causes of death were violence, drug overdose, and alcoholic liver disease. Considering that the average age of the group 20 years earlier was only 26, this is an amazingly high death rate. It illustrates strikingly the life-threatening quality of heroin addiction and of the associated circumstances of life for so many heroin addicts.

- Nearly one-half of the original thousand appear on the records of the probation and parole office—and half of those committed significant crimes (violent crimes or property crimes) more than five years after their initial entry into treatment. Many are regular clients of the criminal-justice system, on and off supervision, in and out of prison.

- A substantial fraction—at least one-quarter—have been on methadone maintenance at one time or another during the past five years: in other words, 15–20 years after their initial entry into treatment. There is no doubt, therefore, that opiate dependence, whether on heroin or on methadone, is a lifelong condition for a considerable fraction of the addict population.

What about nearly half of the original group, whom we have not yet located? Have they done well or poorly? Here we encounter a major methodologic problem. The people with the poorest outcomes are naturally easiest to find, as indicated in the three categories just listed. Ex-addicts who have been off methadone and drug-free for years, who are well integrated into the community, who have become respected citizens, usually do not wish to be tracked and found. They wisely want nothing to do with the drug scene. Their present acquaintances—even close members of their families—may not have any inkling of their heroin-addict history.

Thus, the outcome of a follow-up such as we are doing will necessarily be biased in an unfavorable direction. The biggest problem is sorting out those who took maximum advantage of methadone treatment from those who merely used methadone on and off to tide them over periods of heroin scarcity. A favorable assessement of the therapeutic value of methadone would exclude the latter group from consideration. But it appears unlikely that we will be able to find an adequate 20-year trail of clinical records to permit that kind of analysis.

Thus, even after the study is finished, we will probably not be able to put a reliable number on the probability that a heroin addict in Albuquerque in 1970 would be an abstinent ex-addict 20 years later. However, we do know, for certain, that there are former addicts who, whether or not still on methadone, have put illicit use of addictive drugs behind them. The experience of one of them—let's call him Michael Romero—makes a suitable ending to this chapter.

At the age of 32, a typical unemployed street addict, Romero registered for methadone maintenance in 1970. At first his sights were set on becoming drug-free without methadone, but it never worked. Whenever he was getting methadone, he stopped using heroin completely. Whenever he quit methadone, he found himself using heroin again. After two years of this, he took stock and made a decision that determined his future. As he explained: "My life didn't seem to be going anywhere without methadone. Why couldn't I just look at methadone as my own insulin, and stop trying to live without it?" His life changed dramatically. Twenty-two years later, Romero owns his own business, a machine shop, in a small town about 75 miles from Albuquerque. His annual personal income is about $50,000. He is a prominent citizen in his community. He has a wife and three children, the eldest of whom is attending a university. Once every two weeks he drives to Albuquerque to pick up 13 daily doses of methadone and leave a urine sample. He has not touched heroin for nearly 20 years. Few of his friends or associates know that he was ever a heroin addict or that he now drinks a dose of methadone every day.

CHAPTER 11

The Wild Addictions

Cocaine and Amphetamines

"They give all that they possess, in order to indulge their mad craving," wrote the German physician and medical researcher Louis Lewin in 1887 about cocaine addicts. That description is just as apt for cocaine users today as it was a century ago, and is true of amphetamine addicts as well. Chapter 4 described how monkeys, given free access to cocaine, self-administer it to the exclusion of all other activities until they reach a state of sleepless exhaustion and die in a couple of weeks. One sees the same frantic, compulsive behavior in cocaine addicts on a binge, the chief difference being that their supply of cocaine is usually (but not always) exhausted before the addicts can kill themselves.

This chapter reviews briefly the history of cocaine and amphetamine use and the advent of "crack." It describes the typical behavior of a cocaine or amphetamine addict, and the paranoid psychosis produced by continued use. The characteristic dependence and withdrawal syndrome are described. What we know and do not know about "crack babies" is summarized. Finally, the difficult challenge of treating cocaine and amphetamine addictions is discussed.

THE MOST POWERFUL STIMULANTS

Amphetamines were the stimulants of choice from the 1930s, when they were first synthesized and introduced into medical use, through the 1970s. Epidemics of intravenous amphetamine use raged in Japan after World War II, and in Sweden and America during the sixties and seventies. This is a class of drugs containing many synthetic compounds that are chemically similar and share the same mechanism of action. Included are amphetamine itself (formerly allowed in inhalers and other over-the-counter cold medications), methamphetamine ("speed," "crank," "crystal"), methylphenidate (Ritalin), and—most recently introduced—a pure form of methamphetamine ("ice") that can be smoked. The pharmacologic actions of amphetamines are very similar to those of cocaine, though not identical in all respects. Amphetamines act on the reward pathways to cause excessive dopamine release and thus to increase the dopamine concentration in the synapses, as described in Chapter 4. Drug discrimination experiments established that experienced human subjects could not distinguish cocaine from amphetamines, confirming the conclusions from animal studies of their pharmacology.

Cocaine is a natural substance found in coca leaves. Chewed by natives in the Andes highlands, the leaf was said to prevent fatigue and to increase energy for laborious physical labor. No doubt its stimulant effects produced a subjective impression of enhanced work capacity, but careful experiments have failed to confirm such an effect objectively in the absence of fatigue. Like caffeine, however, cocaine does reverse impairments of performance caused by fatigue. In the nineteenth century, the active principle, cocaine, was purified and its chemical structure identified. It was found to be a powerful local anesthetic, especially for numbing the mucous membranes of the nose, throat, and eyes. Thus it found a legitimate use in medicine, but its mood-altering effects did not escape attention. A leading exponent of the medical and recreational use of cocaine was Sigmund Freud, who denied it was addictive. Lewin's years of research documenting the powerful grip of cocaine on users helped to counter Freud's misconceptions. Nevertheless, in Europe, and later in North America, use of cocaine as a "tonic" spread widely. As late as 1900 it was still a component of Coca-Cola and similar products. The stimulant actions were well recognized by the public, and Coca-Cola was even referred to in the vernacular as "dope."

Amphetamine was a product of the pharmaceutical industry, a compound invented by laboratory chemists. However, a fascinating discovery of the 1970s revealed that nature makes its own amphetamine. An East African shrub called *khat* (also *kat*) contains a substance (*cathinone*) in its leaves which is almost identical to amphetamine, differing only by a single atom. The native populations of Ethiopia and Somalia have chewed khat leaves since ancient times, much as the Peruvian highlanders chew coca leaves. Cathinone is quite unstable, so the leaves have to be fresh and young; and cathinone is destroyed rapidly in the body. Although all the psychotropic, cardiovascular, and toxic effects of cathinone are identical to those of amphetamine, it is so rapidly metabolized that it is difficult for the khat user to establish high and sustained levels in the brain. Chewing khat is certainly addictive and potentially harmful. However, it is much safer than the intravenous use of amphetamines, much as chewing coca leaves is safer and more socially acceptable than using pure cocaine.

Cocaine—together with other popular psychotropic drugs, especially opiates—was placed under legal restrictions in the Harrison Act of 1914. Its legitimate use in medicine was retained; but synthetic analogues like procaine (Novocaine), which deaden the nerves locally if injected under the skin, have largely displaced it. Their primary advantage is that they do not readily enter the brain, so they have no psychotropic effects. In medical practice cocaine itself is still used as a surface anesthetic for numbing mucous membranes, as in the eyes, nose, and throat, where its effectiveness is unsurpassed. Cocaine continued in use as an illicit stimulant; but until the 1980s it was considered a luxury drug because of its expense, and amphetamines were the illicit stimulants of choice for all but the wealthiest. Then the price of cocaine fell, and a cocaine epidemic in the United States began to spread, peaking in 1979, when 9% of people in the 18–25-year-old age group were using the drug at least once a month. By 1990 this figure had fallen to 2%, for reasons that no one really understands.

There are two chemical forms of cocaine, the hydrochloride salt and the free base. Cocaine itself is the biologically active material in both, but the two forms have different physical properties and are absorbed differently into the body. Cocaine hydrochloride dissolves easily in water. It is used by the nasal route ("snorted") or intravenously. Crack (a form of free base cocaine) can not be dissolved, but it can be smoked, and this fact, which made it easy and efficient to use, greatly expanded the illicit market. Typically, a simple glass pipe is used; a water pipe, which filters the smoke, is also effective because the cocaine does not dissolve when the smoke passes through water. Like cigarette smoking for nicotine, cocaine smoked as crack reaches the brain within a few seconds (even faster than intravenous cocaine hydrochloride), and dosage is controllable. An important advantage— especially in view of the AIDS epidemic—is that smoking eliminates the danger of transmitting blood-borne diseases by needles and syringes.

Crack became enormously popular, from 1985 on, for two main reasons. First, it was manufactured as convenient little "rocks" that could easily be smoked. Second, vast numbers of inexperienced people, who would not even consider putting a needle into their veins, were willing to try a new drug by a long-established and socially accepted route of administration.

By whatever method the cocaine is administered, it is rapidly destroyed in the bloodstream—so rapidly that the effects of a single moderate dose last only ten minutes or so. Amphetamines, by contrast, are destroyed slowly, with the effect of a single dose lasting more than an hour. With both cocaine and amphetamines a special kind of rapid tolerance develops, within minutes: the pleasurable effects die away even before the drug concentration in the blood falls significantly. This phenomenon encourages dosage escalation and binges in some users, who attempt desperately to keep the "high" going. The very large dosage levels attained during binges can cause irregular heart beats and even heart stoppage, and can sometimes cause a stroke because of spasm of the blood vessels in the brain. The widely publicized sudden deaths of a few famous young athletes in the prime of physical condition are attributable to one of these causes. The toxic effects on the heart and circulation are notably more frequent and more severe if cocaine is combined with alcohol. Binge use can also lead to frankly psychotic behavior, such as extreme paranoia, visual and auditory hallucinations, a belief that bugs are crawling under the skin, and other sensory distortions. This kind of bizarre reaction, in an individual whom the drug has made to feel extraordinarily powerful but whose judgment is seriously affected, can produce dangerously aggressive, even homicidal, behavior.

A cocaine binge may last 24 sleepless hours or more (even longer with amphetamine), with several "hits" per hour, followed by a "crash" when the drug supply is exhausted. Intense craving follows, and finding a fresh supply of drug becomes an obsession. Then another binge is initiated. Only a fraction of users go on to this extraordinary, self-destructive, compulsive pattern of use; but as with other addictive drugs, we cannot predict who will go out of control in this way. Frank H. Gawin, an experienced clinician in this field, writes: "Human cocaine addicts report that virtually all thoughts are focused on cocaine during binges; nourishment, sleep, money, loved ones, responsibility, and survival lose all significance."

The immediate effect of a small dose of cocaine or amphetamine is an extremely intense pleasurable sensation (the "high"), a magnification of normal pleasures (especially of sexual feelings), a release of social inhibitions, talkativeness, and an unrealistic feeling of cleverness, great competence, and power. Enhancement of sexual activity and of the intensity of orgasm evidently plays a major role in the attractiveness of these stimulants. Extravagant sexual fantasies are common, and are often acted upon, so that all sorts of uninhibited and aberrant sexual behaviors may be indulged in, which the user would not ordinarily condone.

A DRUG TO DRIVE YOU CRAZY

A remarkable experiment at Vanderbilt University in 1971 taught us something important about amphetamine. In animal testing, amphetamine had seemed to be a reasonably safe drug; and regular administration for a long time had not produced any remarkable toxicity—no liver damage, no kidney failure, no heart stoppage; no cancer. As the drug was popular as an illicit stimulant, and at that time was still available in over-the-counter dieting aids and cold remedies, it was important to find out if there were any significant adverse mental effects of regular use. Heavy users of "speed" were known, sometimes, to become psychotic; but arguments raged over whether that was really a direct effect of the drug, whether it was due to other drugs used at the same time, or whether amphetamines only triggered psychotic behavior in those already prone to serious mental illness.

In order to meet the ethical requirement of not introducing anyone to an addictive drug for the first time, only subjects who had used amphetamine before were recruited. However, only the most stable were selected, with no history of mental illness, and healthy in all other respects. In order to ensure complete control of drug intake, and for safety, the subjects lived in a closed hospital ward. Nine young men, volunteers, were first maintained under close observation for six weeks to make sure that all drugs were eliminated from their bodies, and that no drugs of any kind were taken. Careful baseline records of physical and psychologic measurements were made. Then regular dosage of amphetamine was started and continued for up to five days. Dosage was high, but not out of the range used by many street addicts.

All subjects showed increases of blood pressure and heart rate and a low-grade fever. No big surprises there! But amazingly, a full-blown psychosis developed before the fifth day in eight of the nine subjects. They became hostile and paranoid. They believed that the investigators were engaged in a conspiracy against them. They thought they were being poisoned. One subject complained of a giant oscillator in the ceiling, placed there to control his thoughts and behavior. Another insisted on guarding the window and door against a hired assassin. Two subjects believed they were being discussed on television, and one that he was being photographed through a mirror. In similar experiments carried out elsewhere, the same kinds of reaction occurred, which are much like those seen in classic paranoid schizophrenia. Sometimes the more suspicious of the subjects had powerful delusions of persecution, were terrified of what might be done to them, and even expressed homicidal or suicidal thoughts. Meticulous inspection of the surroundings—as though looking for dangerous concealed items—was a common expression of the paranoia. The subjects also felt they were gaining sudden insight into "deep meanings" of common objects that were not apparent before. For example, one subject used a magnifying glass to examine every period and comma in a newspaper article to discover the hidden codes inscribed on them.

Of course, in these experiments the amphetamine was stopped immediately when a psychotic reaction occurred. Then, as the drug was eliminated from the body, over a period of 24 hours, the mental processes of all the subjects returned to normal. At the end of the experiment the investigators carried out exhaustive psychologic testing but found no evidence of persistent abnormality. And the subjects, looking back on their experience, recognized it for the abnormal reaction it was. However, when amphetamines or cocaine are used for a long time and then stopped, it is not unusual to find persistent depression, lack of energy, anhedonia, and episodes of intense craving. As with the long-term aftermath of addiction to other drugs, we can not yet say whether this clinical depression reflects long-term neuro-chemical brain damage caused by the drug, or whether a preexisting deficit in the dopamine reward pathways contributed to the excessive use of stimulant drugs in the first place.

The important lesson of the experiment described here is that con-tinuous intake of high-dosage amphetamine eventually produces psy-chotic behavior in everyone; no special predisposition is required, nor prior mental instability. Similar experiments have not been conducted with cocaine, so we can not draw on direct experimental evidence to decide if it is also true that everyone who uses cocaine at high dosage is at risk for psychosis. However, in view of the close pharmacologic similarity of cocaine to amphetamine, that is likely to be a real danger.

NOT ADDICTIVE?

The myth that cocaine was not addictive enjoyed wide currency throughout the medical profession and in society at large for a long time. Some accepted this notion as late as the seventies and eighties despite the knowledge that regular users experience intense and irre-sistible craving. The confusion arose because in contrast to withdrawal from opiates and alcohol, the cocaine withdrawal syndrome is not dramatic, obvious, and physical, but primarily behavioral. The imme-diate "crash" upon exhausting the drug supply is followed by de-pression, anxiety, agitation, and suspiciousness (sometimes actual paranoia). As abstinence continues, there is extreme boredom, lack of motivation, and depression. Recalling what the "high" was like pro-vokes intense craving, as do numerous conditioned cues (people, ob-jects, and situations associated with cocaine or amphetamine use). Often these conditioned association triggers provoke a new binge, and vulnerability to relapse probably persists for a lifetime.

CRACK BABIES

It is early dawn in New York City. A faint light gives the bridges across the East River a mystical hushed beauty. Not far from the river, at Bellevue Hospital, a woman in the seventh month of pregnancy ap-pears, alone, in the emergency room. She is writhing in pain, obviously about to go into premature labor. Her last crack binge ended barely an hour ago and she is still "high" on the drug. She reaches the delivery room only just in time to give birth. Her baby is not only premature, its weight is low even by standards of prematurity. Its head is small, it has trouble breathing, it seems to have some kind of congenital heart malformation, and its chance of survival is uncertain even with all of modern technology thrown into the battle to rescue it. The physician in charge, when satisfied that the baby's condition has been stabilized, goes to the ward to report to the mother. The sun has just risen. The woman is gone.

Scenes like this are enacted every day in every large city. The intensity of the "mad craving" can be judged by the astounding and totally unbiologic behavior of a mother abandoning her newborn infant to go out in search of cocaine.

Cocaine—whether injected as the hydrochloride or smoked as crack—provokes premature delivery, and many cocaine babies are abnormally small and have unusually small heads. What becomes of these babies if they survive infancy? The media have reported extensively on "crack babies" and their future, but surprisingly, we still have little scientific information about them. There is some evidence—though not overwhelming—that babies born with this syndrome have long-term behavioral problems as they grow up and suffer from learning deficits when they get to school. From the point of view of the impact on society, it makes little difference whether such problems are actually due to cocaine, to the premature birth of an underweight and underdeveloped infant, or even to associated factors in the mother's life only indirectly related to cocaine. For the scientist, however, it is important to know how much of the problem is due to cocaine itself. Many animal studies have shown that cocaine is capable of causing fetal damage—even death of fetal brain tissue due to impaired circulation. And there is no doubt that cocaine use by a pregnant woman causes complications due to spasm of her own blood vessels, including those of the placenta, where such a spasm can result in miscarriage. The disturbances of placental circulation could well account for some of the observed damage to the fetus, for its health and normal development is dependent on a normally functioning placenta.

Furthermore, as can well be imagined, many women addicted to cocaine do not maintain adequate nutrition, do not get prenatal care, use other drugs that harm the fetus, and neither breast-feed nor establish normal maternal bonding with their newborn. Then, when developmental deficits occur in the growing child, it is nearly impossible to say what role was played by these associated factors rather than by cocaine itself. Problems of methodology extend even to evaluating the published information, for researchers tend not to report and publish negative results (i.e., results that show no adverse effects); therefore, the medical literature is bound to give an exaggerated picture of toxicity in the fetus. On the other hand, drug-induced abnormalities may be missed for a long time; for instance, the very existence of the fetal alcohol syndrome—now an undisputed reality—went unrecognized until 20 years ago. It is important to devise better ways to learn the truth. But until proved otherwise, it is prudent to take a common-sense position and accept as probable that cocaine is dangerous to the fetus during pregnancy and may impair a child's normal physical and intellectual development.

TREATING COCAINE AND AMPHETAMINE ADDICTION

In the United States, immediate toxic reactions to cocaine and amphetamine account for 40% of all drug-related episodes seen in hospital emergency rooms and for half of all medical examiner cases (unexplained sudden deaths) in which a drug is involved. Immediate treatment for cocaine users consists of life-saving measures at the hospital. Most treatment, however, is directed toward alleviating withdrawal symptoms in addicts who are trying to discontinue the drug. As withdrawal is characterized by profound depression, standard antidepressant medications may be used. However, as these do not take effect for two or three weeks, the initial period after stopping cocaine or amphetamine self-administration may be the most difficult to manage. Later in the post-withdrawal phase, according to a few studies, antidepressants reduce craving and increase the abstinence rate; but other studies have failed to replicate these encouraging results.

As with most addictive drugs, detoxification can be carried out fairly easily; but preventing relapse is the heart of the problem. Recent research has focused attention on conditioned association triggers, which were described in connection with nicotine addiction in Chapter 8—the principles of deconditioning are the same for cocaine as for any conditioned behavior. In one experiment, carried out by Charles P. O'Brien, cocaine addicts were hospitalized for two weeks in a closed ward while the cocaine cues were systematically presented in daily "extinction sessions." This was accomplished by exposing the subjects to audio tapes, video tapes, and play-acting depicting situations that had been associated with securing and using cocaine. For example, a video presentation might show an addict preparing cocaine hydrochloride powder for injection. Actors might pretend to be purchasing crack or smoking it. Subjects were then exposed to sessions on an outpatient basis once weekly for eight weeks. Classic psychologic theory based on animal studies predicts that by doing this repeatedly in a "safe environment"—that is, in a situation where no cocaine is available—the cues should lose their power to evoke craving.

The experimenters could actually measure a drop in skin temperature (reflecting emotional arousal) that is evoked by cues associated with cocaine administration, as shown in Figure 11.1A. Video presentations without any cocaine-related content ("Neutral video" and "Neutral activity") had little effect. In contrast, scenes of cocaine purchases and use ("Cocaine video") and scenes related to subjects' own cocaine experiences ("Cocaine activity") caused significant skin temperature change.

Craving, as measured by subjects' reports on a numerical scale, was virtually abolished by the extinction sessions, as shown in Figure 11.1B. The ability of cocaine cues to cause a drop in skin temperature was also reduced during the treatment period (not shown in the figure). Then, for seven months after completion of the 28-day treatment, the researchers conducted follow-up assessments of abstinence, as confirmed by urine tests. Most promising, subjects who had participated in the extinction sessions had a higher proportion of cocaine-free urine samples at follow-up than did control subjects who had also been in treatment for 28 days but without the specific deconditioning program.

A question often asked is whether full hospitalization is required during the initial stage of treatment, or whether a less expensive alternative is equally effective. Arguing from common sense, many professionals have advocated round-the-clock hospitalization as the best way to provide a drug-free environment in which to establish abstinence. But common sense must always give way to actual experimental proof. Experiments showed that coming to the hospital for several hours a day but being free to return home in the evenings was at least as effective as full hospitalization. Half of the subjects reported no cocaine use at the 7-month follow-up, and that degree of abstinence was confirmed by urine test—an unusually good outcome.

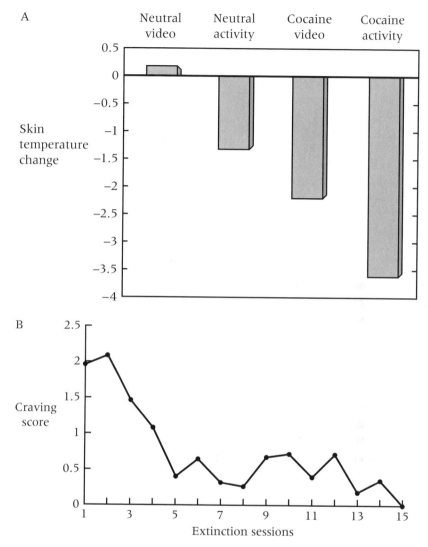

FIGURE 11.1 Extinction of responses to cocaine cues. (A) Cocaine cues cause drop in skin temperature; (B) deconditioning reduces craving. See text for explanations. [From C. P. O'Brien et al., *Journal of Clinical Psychiatry* 49: Suppl. 2, 17–22, 1988]

Another question that often arises is whether treatment must be conducted by fully trained professional psychologists and psychiatrists or whether standard drug counseling by paraprofessional staff suffices. Here again we are dealing with an issue of great practical importance because of the relative costs. Preliminary studies have suggested that standard drug counseling works as well as more sophisticated techniques.

Animal experiments have revealed that long-term cocaine administration causes an irreversible destruction of dopamine neurons. This has suggested that persistent depression and craving even after years of abstinence might be due to a persistent dopamine deficiency. Accordingly, numerous attempts have been made to prevent relapse by long-term treatment with standard antidepressant medications, which modify the dopamine or serotonin systems, and some groups have reported favorable outcomes. There is also an ongoing search for some kind of long-acting cocaine-like surrogate agonist that would be analogous to methadone in heroin addiction; or alternatively, an antagonist that would block cocaine reward, much as naltrexone blocks opiate reward.

Recent animal studies have suggested that naltrexone or other opiate antagonists (especially one called *buprenorphine*) may have therapeutic value in cocaine addiction. Although the mechanism is not understood, these drugs cause animals to reduce their cocaine intake in self-administration experiments. They also make cocaine less effective in producing conditioned place preference—the tendency an animal acquires to prefer being in the place where it receives injections of a reinforcing (rewarding) drug. A few clinical trials with cocaine addicts have yielded promising results in reducing relapse rates.

A novel and interesting approach to treatment would use the recently developed technology of *catalytic antibodies*. These are antibodies deliberately fashioned to combine specifically with a certain molecule (in this case cocaine) and at the same time destroy it. In theory, if such an antibody were injected into the bloodstream it could protect a person (at least partially) from the effects of cocaine by destroying the drug more rapidly than do the enzymes already present in the blood. This is really a variation on the naltrexone theme (Chapter 10)—the idea that depriving a drug of its rewarding effect will cause the addict to give up the drug rather than quit the treatment. This approach might have a limited application for highly motivated patients, but the inability to administer an antibody by mouth will impose a further limitation on its use.

There seems to be general agreement that, pending some breakthrough in pharmacotherapy, rehabilitation counseling and 12-step programs such as those used for alcohol addiction (see Chapter 9) will remain the mainstays of treatment. In 1991 a leading expert, Herbert D. Kleber, offered the following assessment:

One can sum up the status of the pharmacotherapy of cocaine abuse by noting that a number of positive clinical reports exist, but most reports are anecdotal and uncontrolled ... the nature of addiction requires that pharmacotherapy be combined with appropriate psychological and behavioural therapy. It is unlikely that any "magic bullet" will stop drug addiction in and of itself.

CHAPTER 12

Highs and Lows of Getting Stoned
Cannabis

A professional airplane pilot sits in a simulator, the kind used to check the abilities of the men and women who fly for the military and the airlines. The task is to bring an aircraft safely down onto a runway through clouds or fog without being able to see anything outside. As the aircraft descends, the pilot has to watch for the smallest deviations of instruments on the panel, and correct for them quickly with more or less power or with slight movements of the control yoke. A continuous scan of instruments is required to make sure that all aircraft systems are operating correctly. An approach chart has to be consulted continuously without interrupting the other tasks being attended to. And while all this is going on, the pilot has to communicate by radio with a controller on the ground and must be prepared to carry out unexpected instructions. Furthermore, if in the pilot's judgment anything at all seems wrong, an immediate climb must be initiated, rather than gamble on reaching the runway safely.

Before the test begins, the pilot reports that he feels up to par, that he would feel comfortable flying a real airplane right now, and that he has no doubt about his ability to carry out the standard instrument landing procedure. But he is wrong. His performance is so poor that if he were flying an actual airplane there might be real danger. Yet the only thing different today is that—as part of an experiment—he had smoked a single marijuana cigarette, and that single exposure to cannabis had occurred 24 hours before. While cannabis—marijuana and hashish—is not as dangerous as some other addictive drugs, it clearly impairs judgment, and long-term heavy use may have adverse consequences.

BEHAVIORAL EFFECTS

That a single exposure to cannabis the day before can disrupt performance on the complex flight-simulator task may sound like the kind of scare story used to frighten children about the dangers of marijuana. But it is not. The same result was confirmed with many other pilots. Marijuana users know that performance on complex tasks suffers after smoking a "joint." When simulator tests were carried out immediately after smoking, the pilots themselves realized they were impaired. However, the marijuana "high" is largely gone a few hours after a single joint, as the blood levels of THC (tetrahydrocannabinol, the biologically active material in cannabis) fall to a point supposedly below what is needed to cause psychotropic effects. Experiments like this one with pilots showed not only that subtle effects of marijuana on a complex coordination task persist for a very long time, but of even greater concern, that such persistent effects may not be recognized by the individual. This finding contradicts a common belief among cannabis smokers. "When you're drunk," they say, "you think you can do anything perfectly, including driving a car or flying an airplane. But when you're high on grass, you know better than to try." No doubt that statement is true during the period of obvious intoxication, but the simulator experiments point to a dangerous false optimism that persists after the gross behavioral changes have disappeared, but while subtle disturbances of performance remain.

The leaves of the hemp (*cannabis*) plant contain many chemicals, of which THC is the principal psychotropic one. Typically, THC is self-administered by smoking cigarettes packed with finely ground cannabis leaf. The concentrated hemp resin called *hashish* can also be smoked, usually in a pipe; and because THC does not dissolve in water, a water pipe is often used to filter the smoke. The THC content of the leaves varies greatly; most wild cannabis is derived from plants originally grown for hemp fiber, which contain less than one percent THC. But cultivated strains may contain five percent or even more, while hashish and "hash oil" are even richer in THC. For users, apart from the question of getting their money's worth, the THC content really does not matter much because—as discussed in connection with nicotine in Chapter 8—smokers can adjust their intake to the desired effect, and they can inhale more deeply or take more puffs if the drug content of the material smoked is low. A few milligrams of THC taken into the lungs with smoke, and entering the brain readily, are sufficient to activate the cannabinoid receptors. Pure THC is used in research because one wants a standard dosage, and because it is almost impossible to make laboratory animals inhale smoke. All the evidence indicates that THC produces the same biologic effects as smoking the whole leaf.

THC acts on a seven-helix receptor (Chapter 3), which has been identified in those parts of the brain that could reasonably mediate the changes of mood and perception caused by marijuana. The amino-acid sequence of this cannabinoid receptor was determined so recently that very little information has been obtained yet about the functional role of the receptor. A proposed endogenous ligand has been identified, a compact molecule related structurally to the family of hormones called prostaglandins. Thus, in some way not yet understood, THC mimics or blocks the normal effects of an endogenous brain hormone or neurotransmitter.

Why do people use cannabis? They seek a sense of well-being (euphoria)—a relaxed, calm, drowsy, dreamlike state, with a feeling of disconnection from the ordinary world. Thoughts ramble out of control. Things seem funny to the smoker that are not especially humorous to an observer. The most obvious behavioral abnormality displayed by a subject under the influence of cannabis is difficulty in carrying on an intelligible conversation, perhaps because of an inability to remember what was just said, even a few words before. The problem has been described by one investigator as "impaired ability to think in a connected fashion to a goal."

A characteristic feature of being "stoned" is a distortion in the sense of time, associated with profound deficits in short-term memory and learning. In experiments to define more precisely the mental disturbances caused by cannabis, it was found that new information is learned very poorly or not at all while under the influence of the drug.

This is obviously relevant to the education of students who smoke marijuana.

A consequence of the memory and time-sense disruptions is loss of the alertness, coordination, and judgment that are required for complicated tasks. Thus, driving a car or train, and operating other kinds of complex equipment, are seriously affected; and numerous studies have found, among those involved in highway accidents, a disproportionate number of drivers with detectable THC in the blood.

The smoker typically has a sense of enhanced physical and emotional sensitivity, including a feeling of greater interpersonal closeness. Increased sensitivity to all kinds of sensory stimuli can be demonstrated, and this may be related to reports of enhanced sexual pleasure. Increased sex drive is also claimed, but this is controversial; it is unclear if the effects of cannabis as perceived by the user are objectively real or merely part of the altered mental state.

Especially confusing in assessing the immediate effects of smoking marijuana is a very strong influence of expectation. A study compared a group of subjects who had never had marijuana with a group of experienced, chronic smokers. At the very same dosage, the experienced smokers showed greater effects than the first-time smokers. This curious phenomenon had been observed frequently and had been attributed to some sort of "reverse tolerance." In the present experiment, however, placebo "joints" were included; and that shed a very different light on matters. The first-time smokers showed very little effect from the placebo cigarettes. The experienced smokers, in contrast, reported many typical cannabis effects from the placebo. Thus, social setting, previous experience, and expectation contribute heavily to how chronic users react, and "reverse tolerance" is no longer given credence.

Ordinary dosages cause increased heart rate and dilation of blood vessels in the eyes, but redness of the eyes may be caused in so many different ways that this effect is not useful in the diagnosis of marijuana use. High levels of cannabis intake can cause psychotic reactions, with hallucinations, paranoia, depersonalization (the feeling of being outside one's own body), and panic attacks.

THC remains in the body for a very long time, and some of the behavioral disturbances linger surprisingly long, as in the experiment with pilots. The long persistence is due, in part, to storage of THC in fatty tissues, with traces leaking out into the blood and excreted in the urine for many days, even for weeks, after stopping intake. For this reason, although urine tests tell positively that a person did smoke cannabis, they tell little about when that was. Also, differences among people in their sensitivity to THC make it difficult to set sharp legal standards for likely impairment. This is quite different from alcohol testing, where breath or blood analysis tells not only the concentration of alcohol to which the brain is exposed at the moment the test is conducted, but also the relationship of the measured levels to known deficits in psychomotor performance.

LONG-TERM USE

Does regular use of cannabis for a long time have serious long-term adverse consequences? Why is there so much controversy surrounding this question? In trying to decide if an addictive drug has long-lasting behavioral toxicity, the fundamental difficulty is that we never have comparable groups to begin with. How could we? For studies on current users we can never distinguish cause from effect; whatever behavioral abnormalities we see might not be due to the drug at all, but might have been present before drug use—indeed, might have been factors predisposing to the addiction in the first place. And to conduct a proper prospective study, we would have to start with a large number of children, before they begin using drugs, deliberately expose a randomly chosen group of them to a drug for many years, and then test the outcome. Moreover, the young subjects in such an experiment would have to be isolated in a closed environment—just as experiments with volunteer adult subjects have to be done in a closed ward—to guarantee that the drug and control (no-drug) conditions were maintained. I mention such a fantasy experiment with children only to highlight the problem; any such experiment would, of course, be unethical as well as impractical.

Let's look at one famous example of a controversial study. In 1971 M. I. Souief, Egypt's leading cannabis researcher, studied a population of nearly 2,000 prisoners. He sorted them into two groups—those who had been long-term cannabis users and those who had not. Then he carried out various standard psychological tests. He found that the former users did more poorly than the others on tests of psychomotor performance and on visual coordination tasks. He drew the conclusion that chronic use of cannabis by these Egyptian prisoners had affected brain function adversely. Studies like this, with any addictive drug, have political impact—and that makes it doubly important that the science be good, that the results be valid. People who believe passionately that cannabis is dangerous and should be tightly controlled cite studies like this one in support of their position. People who believe cannabis is harmless and should be legalized find plenty to criticize. In this study, for example, as the two populations were not necessarily comparable to start with, how can cannabis be blamed for the difference? Could one not argue just as well that the less capable people were just the ones who had turned to cannabis in the first place?

Cannabis smoke contains more carcinogens than tobacco smoke, so lung damage and cancer are real risks for heavy users. Disturbances of hormone balance have been well documented, especially of the sex hormones; these effects result from actions of THC in the hypothalamus, the part of the brain that controls the secretion of pituitary hormones. Repeated administration of THC under controlled conditions to normal volunteers caused a reduction of sperm count, a depressed testosterone level, decreased libido in males; menstrual cycles in females were disturbed. All these effects were reversed when the drug was discontinued.

In one study, when monkeys were forced to inhale the smoke of a single marijuana cigarette every day, five days a week for six months, structural damage was evident in their brain cells. In a similar experiment, the monkeys were found to have a significant reduction in the number and size of brain cells, with the result that the ventricles (the central cavities) of the brain became dilated—an indication of tissue loss. Comparable findings were reported in rats after administration of THC by mouth for 90 days at a dose that established blood levels comparable to those found in smokers of several marijuana cigarettes daily. The microscopic changes observed in the brain were evident principally in the hippocampus, where the nerve cells were shrunken and the number of synapses reduced. This finding was consistent with long-term effects on rat behavior, which were similar to the known effects of destroying parts of the hippocampus. Furthermore, it is of interest that cannabinoid receptors are especially dense in the hippocampus and cerebral cortex, areas of the brain specialized for memory and cognitive skills. The other brain area rich in cannabinoid receptors is the cerebellum, a region concerned with balance and fine control of muscle movement. On the other hand, cannabinoid receptors are virtually absent from parts of the brain that control the heart rate, the constriction or dilation of blood vessels, and the rate and depth of breathing; this may well account for the lack of immediate serious toxic effects on these vital systems—no overdose deaths due to marijuana have been reported.

Even though brain damage has not yet been convincingly shown in humans, the findings in rats and monkeys are disturbing. They indicate that although occasional use of this drug has relatively mild effects, frequent high-dose use for a long time could have serious permanent consequences. A possible long-term effect about which there has been much controversy is the "amotivational syndrome." The existence of such a syndrome is not supported by scientific evidence; and, unfortunately, relevant scientific evidence is impossible, in principle, to obtain. There is no doubt that chronic heavy marijuana users often reject the goal-directed lifestyle and ethos of our modern urban civilization. But who is to say if that is consequent to cannabis use or if it was part of the reason for cannabis use in the first place? The evidence of brain damage in animals, however—especially if it stands up to replication under varied conditions and with multiple species—is very concrete and points to a real possibility of serious irreversible alterations in brain function and personality in humans.

The special problem of possible fetal damage requires consideration with any drug, as discussed with respect to cocaine in Chapter 11; and marijuana is no exception. The difficulty in establishing clearly whether the drug is harmful to the unborn child arises chiefly from the fact that pregnant women who use marijuana generally use other drugs (especially alcohol, caffeine, and nicotine) as well. THC crosses the placenta readily, and prematurity and low birth weight are associated with maternal marijuana use. Animal experiments also suggest that the course of pregnancy may be affected adversely, but truly convincing studies on fetal brain damage by THC have not yet been reported.

On discontinuance of cannabis after chronic heavy use there is a mild withdrawal syndrome, with irritability, restlessness, loss of appetite, sleeplessness, tremor, perspiration, and sometimes nausea, vomiting, and diarrhea. Most of the withdrawal symptoms are behavioral rather than physical, much as with nicotine or cocaine; and therefore the very existence of a withdrawal syndrome has been questioned by some.

Finally, cannabis is like the opiates in being an addictive substance with potential (though limited) therapeutic uses. Controlled clinical trials have shown a beneficial effect in patients suffering from severe nausea and vomiting during cancer chemotherapy. It is not entirely clear, however, if marijuana or THC has a substantial advantage over other well-established anti-nausea medications. The other therapeutic use is for glaucoma, where THC reduces the damaging excessive pressure in the eyeball. Again, it is unclear if this treatment is superior to existing medications.

How Dangerous is Cannabis to Society?

There is a curious discrepancy with regard to some of the addictive drugs between actual danger to the individual or to society and the perceived danger, as reflected in their legal status and in the severity of penalties for violating the laws. The discrepancy with respect to nicotine and alcohol has already been suggested in previous chapters: considering the seriousness of their damaging effects, the law treats them very leniently. Cannabis presents a discrepancy in the other direction: considering what we know about the harm it causes, the law is in some respects excessively harsh. In the past, cannabis education in the schools was characterized by extreme exaggerations. Even today, people are serving prison terms for possession of small amounts for personal use.

Governmental commissions are established from time to time to study the cannabis question, and they always arrive at the same conclusions and recommendations. As long ago as 1894 the Indian Hemp Commission, appointed by the British parliament, published an exhaustive report of 3,281 pages, which concluded that moderate use of cannabis was not injurious to the majority of users. The La Guardia commission in New York City in 1944 found no evidence that cannabis was the terrible menace it was claimed to be at the time. In 1962 a *White House Panel on Narcotic and Drug Abuse* reported:

> It is the opinion of the Panel that the hazards of marihuana per se have been exaggerated and that long criminal sentences imposed on an occasional user or possessor of the drug are in poor social perspective.

Similar findings emerged from official committees of inquiry in the subsequent two decades in Britain and in Canada. The periodic reports of such expert groups do not oppose legal restrictions on cannabis; they certainly do not suggest that it is a safe drug for general use. But they do address—and forcefully—the discrepancy between true danger and perceived danger, as reflected in the law. In this connection Chapter 17 describes the Dutch approach to cannabis regulation—an interesting alternative to the U.S. system.

CHAPTER 13

The Gentle Stimulant

Caffeine

It is 7 P.M. Twenty Stanford medical students are sitting around a conference table, pencil and paper at the ready, intent on a large movie screen on the wall. The film rolls. The screen is blank. Suddenly, in the upper left corner, the number 15662 flashes for a fraction of a second, and the screen goes blank again. The students try to write down all five digits of the number. Suddenly, a few seconds later, the number 70597 flashes—this time at the center bottom of the screen. After 50 numbers have been flashed in this way, the room lights go up. Everyone gets a coded sample of instant coffee to drink. An hour and a half later, the group gathers around the table again for another test with 50 new numbers. This is a scene from just one of many experiments that examined whether caffeine enhances performance, whether—and how consistently—caffeine disturbs sleep, whether caffeine is rewarding (as are other addictive drugs), and how caffeine dependence and withdrawal are manifested.

EFFECTS ON PERFORMANCE

Caffeine is the most popular and least harmful of all the addictive drugs. Others are either illicit (cocaine, heroin, marijuana, hallucinogens) or have a social stigma attached to heavy use (alcohol, nicotine), and this complicates research. Because caffeine is legal and so widely used (by 90% of the population), it is relatively easy to find subjects for experiments. Also, the oral route of administration makes it possible to give subjects coded samples to take at home, as for experiments on sleep. Most important, study of the biologic aspects of caffeine addiction is but little confounded by the sorts of social factors that complicate research on illicit drugs. Consider the key question of why some people become addicted heavy users of a drug, whereas others do not. With illicit drugs, not everyone has equal access to them in the first place; and even among those who do, the willingness to break a legal taboo may vary in ways unrelated to any biologic predisposition to use and become addicted to the drug. With caffeine, on the other hand, virtually everyone (except for adherents of certain religions) has socially acceptable access during childhood or adolescence, following which, by self-selection, only a few become chronic heavy users, become addicts.

My first studies on addiction, over 25 years ago, were experiments on caffeine in volunteers. To prepare for double-blind experiments, it was first necessary to develop coded caffeine and placebo samples that were truly indistinguishable by appearance, taste, or any other property. Starting with a decaffeinated instant coffee base, we added caffeine in the usual amount to one set of samples, a bitter white powder (to match the added caffeine) to the other set. We set up a coffee bar in our medical student lounge and offered everyone free coffee on condition that they examine and taste two coded samples and tell us immediately which they thought was real coffee and which decaffeinated, and which of the two samples they preferred. Day after day, we made adjustments to the mixture until the students were guessing right only half the time, and expressing no consistent preference. Then we were ready to start the real experiments.

People presumably take caffeine to obtain a rewarding effect, usually described as feeling more alert and competent. But are they really more alert and competent, or do they only feel that way? The flashing-numbers procedure described above is a form of vigilance test. Each group of five digits is taken from a table of random numbers. The location where each number is flashed on the screen is also chosen randomly. Finally, the intervals between presentations are randomized. Thus, to see and read a number flashed so briefly (1/32 second) requires extraordinary vigilance because a subject does not know when or where it will appear, and a momentary lapse of attention may result in missing the number entirely. To inspire maximum effort I offered a monetary prize for the best performance at each of the nine sessions.

Another test, administered at each session, required good eye-hand coordination and fine control. Subjects had to draw a continuous line through a zigzag maze on paper as fast as possible. Scoring was based on speed of completion, with penalties for touching the edges of the maze. Finally, a questionnaire surveyed mood. Both of the performance tests and the mood survey were administered once before and then again an hour and a half after drinking the coded coffee sample.

Caffeine (as compared with placebo) did not enhance performance on either of the tests. Nonetheless, subjects who had taken caffeine reported that they felt more alert, more active, and better coordinated than those who had taken placebo. In short, caffeine did not improve the subjects' mental or physical abilities beyond their wide-awake norm, and our tests were conducted under wide-awake conditions. The chief effect we observed was a favorable mood state, unaccompanied by any real improvement in performance.

As the primary effect of the drug is to enhance the state of wakefulness, improvements in performance are seen best in subjects who are fatigued and sleepy, whose performance is already degraded. In addition, caffeine seems to improve certain kinds of performance more than others; thus, different results are obtained depending on the test used. A recent study demonstrates this nicely. Taking advantage of technologic developments in sleep research, the investigators measured sleep latency—the time required to fall asleep, where sleep was defined by standard changes in the brain-wave pattern. Time to bed and time to wake in the morning were strictly standardized, and a device that could record movements was attached to the wrist in order to measure periods of activity and inactivity during the night. At 9 A.M. each day, subjects were given caffeine or placebo. Then at several times during the day they were placed on beds in a quiet darkened room and instructed to relax and fall asleep. If they did, the time it took was recorded, and they were awakened immediately; otherwise, after 20 minutes the attempt was terminated. Interspersed with these opportunities to fall asleep were two vigilance tests. One was a 15-minute visual presentation on a computer monitor, much like our flashing-number procedure. The other was a 40-minute auditory vigilance test, in which the subject had to detect long tones that were presented randomly during a continuous series of short tones.

Caffeine consistently increased the sleep latency as compared with placebo; in other words, caffeine made it harder to fall asleep. The drug also improved performance on the auditory vigilance test, but not, interestingly, on the visual test. (The different results in these two tests could be due to the much longer duration of the auditory one, with more time for boredom and more opportunity for sleepiness to interfere with vigilance.)

Numerous experiments carried out since my initial studies have confirmed the description of caffeine as a mild stimulant that, by overcoming fatigue, can improve vigilance and the performance of some mental and physical tasks. Likewise, athletic performance is generally unaffected when maximum exertion is required for a very short time, as in a 100-yard dash, but is measurably improved if continuous prolonged effort is called for, as in a marathon.

SLEEP DISTURBANCE

Ask any group of people if caffeine affects their night-time sleep. You will hear a confusing multiplicity of answers, ranging from "If I drink any coffee after noon, I toss and turn all that night," to "I can drink coffee all evening and sleep like a baby." According to their own accounts, people differ greatly in their sensitivity to the drug. My aim was to find out whether sleep disturbance by caffeine was real, and if so, whether people actually differed as much in their sensitivity as their accounts suggested. I gave out coded coffee samples to medical students, asking them to drink one before bedtime, and then the next morning to fill out a questionnaire about how well they had slept.

Caffeinated coffee (containing the usual amount of caffeine) did cause wakefulness, as compared with placebo, in most of the subjects. But there were large and consistent differences in sensitivity; "consistent" means here that if a subject was kept awake (or not kept awake) by caffeine, the same result was obtained on several nights. Were the intrinsic differences among people due to differences in brain sensitivity to caffeine, or did they reflect differences in absorbing and metabolizing the drug? To answer that question I measured caffeine in the subjects' blood after the standard dose, and found only minor differences. Since the blood bathing the brain contained about the same amount of drug in all subjects, I could conclude that the brain itself is responsible for a person's sensitivity to caffeine.

As the previous subjects were male, another double-blind study was carried out with 239 young women, mostly wives of students. Coded coffee samples were drunk shortly before bedtime, and questionnaires were filled out each morning. The habitual coffee drinkers described coffee as an enjoyable, pleasant-tasting beverage that helps one to wake up and get going, that gives one a feeling of well-being and a certain lift, that also induces relaxation and a reduction of irritability. Those who habitually drank the most coffee were the least disturbed in their sleep. One's first reaction to this finding might be that it demonstrates tolerance. Not necessarily. A quite different interpretation would be that these people are intrinsically less sensitive to caffeine, and were that way even before they began using the drug. That would explain why they have to drink so much coffee to get the desired stimulant effect in the daytime, and why coffee is less disturbing to their sleep at night.

Here we confront a familiar "chicken-and-egg" problem in the study of addictive drugs. Which came first, relative insensitivity to a drug, or heavy drug use leading to tolerance? One way to distinguish the two possibilities would be to test children before their first contact with a drug, make a record of their sensitivity, then follow them to adulthood and see how their drug-using habit develops. This would be nice, but as previously noted, such experiments would be difficult to conduct, very expensive, ethically dubious, perhaps entirely impractical. Another way would be to recruit addicts who are willing to abstain from caffeine for long enough to allow the withdrawal syndrome as well as any drug-induced tolerance to dissipate, and then to carry out the controlled trials. But getting addicts to give up their addiction for the sake of science is a dubious proposition, and it would also require regular testing of urine to confirm abstinence. Furthermore, even with so mild an addictive drug as caffeine, some would think it unethical to readminister it for experimental purposes to ex-addicts who might wish to remain abstinent.

Important advances in sleep research have been made in recent years, and careful quantitative measures, chiefly introduced by my Stanford colleague William C. Dement, have added greatly to the precision of sleep experiments. However, the sleep studies described above, despite their crudity, were conclusive and demonstrate an interesting point about scientific method. Good science does not require expensive sophisticated equipment and highly precise measurements.

What are needed are a testable hypothesis, a sound experimental design, a clear decision in advance about what are to be the outcome measures, and valid statistical analysis of the results. A useful result can not come from a poorly designed experiment, no matter how precise the measurements. A well-designed experiment, which (as with the double-blind technique) has eliminated all sources of subjective bias, can yield decisive results even when the measurement technique is necessarily as crude as asking subjects how well they slept the night before.

REWARDING EFFECTS

Although extracts of coffee beans had probably been consumed for at least a thousand years in East Africa and Yemen, the custom of drinking coffee first flourished in the urban centers of the Middle East in the late fifteenth century. One of the earliest descriptions notes that "it drove away fatigue and lethargy, and brought to the body a certain sprightliness and vigor." Coffee reached England in the middle of the seventeenth century, and coffee houses were established on the Middle Eastern model. The founder of London's first coffee house advertised that it "quickens the spirits, and makes the heart lightsome."

When a novel psychotropic drug enters a society, it often arouses opposition. Despite the mildness of caffeine's stimulant actions, coffee houses were the objects of suspicion from the beginning. In 1511 they were actually prohibited for a short time by the religious authorities in Mecca. And in England in 1675 they were shut down by Charles II in response to a strong temperance movement, coffee being regarded as a kind of intoxicant, one that made people too lively and loquacious, and which promoted dangerous literary and political discussions.

For a drug that is as widely used as caffeine, it may seem foolish for scientists to devise complicated experiments to show that it is a reinforcer. After all, it is freely chosen by millions of humans, and free choice is the criterion used to demonstrate that a drug is a primary reinforcer in animal experiments. Caffeine, however, has peculiar properties. Although animals can be made to self-administer it, the drug is certainly not a powerful reinforcer. That it acts on the mesolimbic reward pathway is indicated by the fact that it causes dopamine release there. In humans it is a weak stimulant, with nothing like the effects of cocaine or amphetamines. People respond to it in different ways. Some like it, some don't. Some are sensitive to low doses, some respond only at high doses, and many find high doses distinctly unpleasant. Careful experiments with human subjects were needed to understand these curious differences.

One such study was conducted recently by Roland R. Griffiths. In order to avoid any complicating pharmacologic actions of compounds other than caffeine in coffee, the experiment employed pure caffeine at various doses (or a placebo) in distinctively colored capsules. The basic unit of the experimental design was a three-day sequence. A subject might be given a blue capsule on day 1 containing (for example) a low dose of caffeine. On day 2 the subject might be given a red placebo capsule. Of course, neither the subjects nor the experimenters knew the color code, and it was different for each subject. Then on day 3 both colors were presented. The question was whether, on the basis of subjective effects experienced on the first two days, a subject would choose caffeine or placebo.

There were 12 subjects, 10 independent trials at each dose level, and four doses were tested. As a trial took three days, this meant 30 days for each caffeine dose for each subject—120 experimental days in all. This was truly a major undertaking. Questionnaires about subjective effects were filled out a few hours after taking a capsule, and again later the same day. Saliva tests were done to determine circulating caffeine levels. If caffeine had neither rewarding nor aversive effects, a subject would be expected to choose caffeine or placebo about half of the time.

At the low dose (100 mg), which corresponds to the average amount in a cup of coffee, caffeine was clearly reinforcing for four of the 12 subjects and was aversive to none. Reported subjective effects were "stimulated, energetic, talkative, vigorous." As the dose was increased, the preference for caffeine over placebo decreased in most (but not all) subjects, as aversive effects became predominant ("jittery, nervous, shaky"). These interesting results are summarized in Figure 13.1. Panel A shows the overall decrease in caffeine selection as the dose was increased from 100 mg to 600 mg (corresponding to from one to six cups of coffee). Panel B shows the increase in stated dislike for caffeine as the dose was increased. Panel C shows how the higher doses made subjects feel jittery, nervous, and shaky. In addition (not shown), at a moderate dose (corresponding to about two cups of coffee) caffeine was selected most often by subjects who initially had scored lowest on a test of anxiety, but it tended to be rejected by the most anxious subjects.

This elegant experiment thus demonstrates the following: First, mild stimulant effects of caffeine are reinforcing for some people,

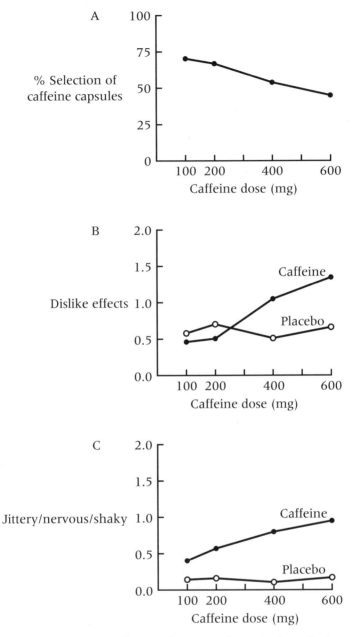

FIGURE 13.1 Dose effects in human subjects in free-choice caffeine selection. (A) Overall selection results on free-choice days; (B) expressed dislike of caffeine or placebo effects on forced-choice days; (C) specific unpleasant effects—jittery/nervous/shaky—on forced-choice days. [Adapted from R. R. Griffiths and P. P. Woodson, *Journal of Pharmacology and Experimental Therapeutics* 246: 21, 1988, Fig. 2.]

chiefly those who are of a calm and relaxed temperament. Second, caffeine becomes aversive to most people as the dose is increased to the amount contained in six cups of coffee, and perhaps it would be aversive to all at some higher dose. Third, sensitivity to caffeine dosage varies greatly among people. By direct experimentation, and in a much more thorough manner, therefore, this study confirms many of the conclusions of my early experiments.

TOXICITY AND DEPENDENCE

In my studies, those who habitually drank the most coffee complained of headache, drowsiness, fatigue, and a generally negative mood state on awakening the morning after placebo had been drunk, but not the morning after caffeine. These withdrawal symptoms were quickly relieved by morning caffeine, but they became worse after morning placebo. This confirmed earlier work by others showing that dependence develops with habitual caffeine consumption. More recent research has confirmed the same finding, especially the triad of withdrawal symptoms—headache, drowsiness, and fatigue. Most interesting, mild withdrawal symptoms of the same kind have been documented when caffeine is abruptly discontinued even in some subjects who take the caffeine equivalent (in coffee, tea, or carbonated beverages) of less than a single cup of coffee a day. Since 90% of the population, including young children, take caffeine daily, one has to conclude that a large fraction of the entire population is dependent on this addictive drug.

How concerned should one be about the nearly universal dependence on caffeine? Much effort has been expended in large-scale epidemiologic studies throughout the world to see if caffeine is a "risk factor" for coronary heart disease, high blood pressure, or cancer. To say that coffee drinking is a risk factor for coronary heart disease, for example, would mean that a greater proportion of coffee drinkers than of abstainers develop this serious medical problem. It would not mean that coffee drinking causes the disease: the term "risk factor" merely denotes an association, nothing more. Sophisticated statistical analysis tries to tease out what other factors may also be associated, and to remove them from the analysis. For example, coffee drinkers often smoke, and smoking is certainly associated with heart disease. Then the question is: After accounting for the effect of smoking, do coffee drinkers still have a higher likelihood of developing heart disease? No matter how many other factors can be recognized and accounted for, one may still be left with unknown associated factors. After all, coffee drinkers are different from people who do not drink coffee in many aspects of lifestyle and personality. For example, coffee drinking is found to be associated with a diet high in animal fat—itself a risk factor for heart disease.

The results of these large-scale studies show that no toxic effects of any kind have been associated unequivocally with modest use of caffeine. Only at extremely high dosages may the drug cause irregularities of the heart beat, anxiety states, and occasionally mental confusion. Moreover, caffeine—like nicotine, but unlike alcohol, cocaine, marijuana, or hallucinogens—causes no socially dangerous changes in behavior. And finally, when caffeine is used on a long-term basis—unlike alcohol or tobacco—it causes no evident organ damage.

The possible risk of caffeine use during pregnancy, however, requires special consideration. Many drugs that are harmless to adults at moderate dosages can be dangerous to the fetus, especially during the very early period of organ development, which takes place even before a woman may know she is pregnant. Caffeine consumption at a very high level—for example, more than 10 cups of coffee daily—can cause miscarriage and premature labor, as well as chromosome abnormalities, congenital malformations, respiratory difficulties, and problems with the heart and circulation of the newborn. At moderate dosages, however, the finding of fetal damage is subject to all the uncertainties arising from factors associated with the use of a drug (as discussed already in Chapters 8 and 11), such as differences in lifestyle, prenatal care, nutrition, and use of other drugs.

Animal studies help to resolve some of the ambiguities, but extrapolation to humans is problematic because of the many differences between species in responses to any drug. With that caveat in mind, we can summarize the animal experiments as follows: When monkeys were given caffeine in their drinking water at a dosage corresponding to about five cups of coffee daily in humans, early fetal death and stillbirths occurred more often than with controls. Numerous experiments in rats have shown deleterious effects of maternal caffeine intake, but only at dosages corresponding to about 10 cups of coffee daily in humans. These effects included reduced body weight and delayed development of the newborn pups, as well as depressed motor activity and sleep disturbance, but no significant changes in learning or memory. An interesting finding was an increased number of adenosine receptors in the brain, a condition associated with increased sensitivity to adenosine; this would be expected as a response to an adenosine receptor antagonist. In discrete brain areas a decrease in dopamine content was also observed. Taken together, the human and animal data are suggestive enough of fetal damage to indicate that—as with other addictive drugs—the prudent course is to avoid caffeine entirely during pregnancy, beginning (if possible) even before conception.

A key challenge for future research is to demonstrate conclusively where in the brain each typical effect of caffeine is mediated, and to confirm that blockade of an adenosine receptor (of whatever subtype) is responsible. A recent study with human subjects measured blood flow in the forearm. Adenosine given intravenously caused a fivefold increase through its well-known ability to dilate blood vessels. Caffeine dramatically reduced this effect of adenosine, confirming that caffeine is an antagonist at adenosine receptors. But the experiment does not tell us if adenosine receptor blockade accounts for its effects in the brain, nor do we yet understand the role of adenosine in normal brain function.

Another key problem for study is the extent to which genetic predisposition accounts for the striking differences in habitual caffeine self-administration and in sensitivity to the alerting and wakefulness caused by caffeine. This question is relevant to all the addictive drugs, as discussed in Chapter 7, but it might be studied most easily with caffeine, for the reasons outlined at the beginning of this chapter.

CHAPTER 14

Chemical Fantasies
The Hallucinogens

An anthropologist studying a native tribe in the jungles of South America observed the ceremonial use of an intoxicating drink called *ayahuasca*, made from a certain vine. "The natives," he wrote, "see big snakes curling upward on their house posts, and on the walls appear colored butterflies and creatures that are aggregates of snakes, jaguars, and birds. ... A man saw a cat climbing a wall, then turning into a leopard, when in fact, not even the cat existed." To understand the custom better, he drank some himself. The world around him took on an extraordinarily vivid appearance. Colored geometric designs seemed to soar before his open eyes. With his eyes closed he saw quickly moving small figures, as in a cartoon—abundant imagery, with bright-colored red-green or blue-orange contrasts. There were long dream-like sequences. Buzzing sounds occurred. Most remarkable was the superimposition of images on walls, or imaginary scenes and objective scenes appearing simultaneously.

The ritual use of hallucinogens is embedded in many cultures. Remarkably, indigenous peoples in all parts of the world have discovered natural products that thrived locally and that possessed the ability to alter the sense of time and place and to produce visual, auditory and other sensory distortions. Some hallucinogens may not be addictive in the sense of producing an irresistible craving or leading to a frank withdrawal syndrome. Yet one, at least, is powerfully addictive; and some addictive drugs of the other families may cause hallucinations at high doses. At the end of this chapter I shall consider the arguments about their classification. But let us first examine the hallucinogens for the light they shed on how psychotropic drugs can disorder normal brain function.

There are two groups of hallucinogens with effects like those just described, and the compounds in both groups are related to neurotransmitters. The first contains chemical structures related to serotonin (5-HT), the other to dopamine and the closely related amphetamine structure. Both groups seem to mimic the effects of serotonin on one subtype of serotonin receptor. A few hallucinogens do not fit into these two categories. This chapter describes the main groups, the ways they are used, their typical effects, and what little we know about their mechanisms of action.

SUBSTANCES RELATED TO THE STRUCTURE OF SEROTONIN

In 1956, a German anthropologist made his way to the upper reaches of the Amazon to study the Yanomami Indians, an isolated tribe living deep in the rain forest. There he discovered, and filmed, the ceremonial use of a snuff called by the Indians *epena*. To prepare this material a certain rare tree has first to be located. Its bark is stripped and the fibrous substance on the inner side of the bark is scraped. The scrapings are dried slowly over a fire, then crumbled to a fine dust by rubbing between the hands. Next, the bark of another tree (only a certain kind of tree) is burned to ashes, and these ashes are mixed in equal parts with the crumbled scrapings. The resulting snuff powder is then stored in a bamboo tube.

The hallucinogenic epena snuff is used in the following curious way. With a special blowpipe about five feet long, one man blows a portion of the powder forcibly into another man's nostrils. The snuff produces severe headache, salivation, vomiting, and profuse sweating.

The subject stares fixedly and he begins a vigorous stamping dance accompanied by a chant. This is interrupted every few minutes by a fierce yell, while he spreads his arms toward the sky. The anthropologist learned that during the intoxication the Indians are convinced they have grown to an enormous size, big enough to converse face to face with the spirits in the sky—spirits that they report being able to see.

In contrast to the natural epena snuff, *LSD* is a highly potent synthetic hallucinogen. On Friday, April 16, 1943, the chemist Albert Hofmann, working for the Swiss pharmaceutical firm Sandoz, in Basel, was engaged in a project to synthesize a large variety of compounds related chemically to lysergic acid. Lysergic acid is derived from chemicals in a fungus called *ergot,* which grows on spoiled rye grain. For many years extracts of ergot, and more recently pure compounds isolated from ergot, had been used in obstetrics to stop uterine bleeding after childbirth. By altering chemical groups on lysergic acid systematically, the Sandoz chemists hoped to learn more about the relationship of chemical structure to biologic activity. They were trying to find safer and more effective ergot drugs, because the existing ones had undesirable side effects, including the serious one of shutting off circulation to various parts of the body.

Ergot toxicity was well known in Europe since the Middle Ages, under the name "St. Anthony's Fire." When bread was made from rye flour that was contaminated with ergot, an entire village—all the villagers would have patronized a single bakery—would become seriously ill. Disturbances of the circulation were prominent, with terrible burning sensations (thus the name of the affliction) in the intestines and elsewhere in the body, and gangrene of the fingers and toes. The most severely affected victims also developed hallucinations and bizarre psychotic behaviors. An epidemic of ergotism was recorded as recently as 1951, in the little French village of Pont-Saint-Esprit, where several hundred people were affected. Some became delirious and confused, seeing imaginary animals and flames and other macabre visions, and a few of them died.

Hofmann had to leave his laboratory early that Friday afternoon because he felt oddly agitated and slightly dizzy. At home he lay down and tried to sleep, but weird things began to happen. Fantastic pictures appeared before his eyes, with a play of extraordinary, kaleidoscopic colors. Hofmann was clever enough to recognize that the toxic psychosis was probably due to some chemical he had come in contact with in his laboratory. He was surely aware of the profound hallucinogenic effects of ergot, and one of the compounds he had made and crystallized that day was an ergot derivative, lysergic acid diethylamide (LSD). However, as the total amount he had worked with was only a few milligrams, it seemed to him most unlikely that enough could have gotten into his system to poison him.

Hofmann felt better the next morning, so to check out his suspicions about LSD he returned to the laboratory. He dissolved what he considered a tiny amount—250 micrograms—in water, and drank it. (We know now that this was ten times the effective hallucinogenic dose.) Forty minutes later, his notebook entry was:

> Slight giddiness, anxiety, hard to focus my thoughts, disturbance of vision, impulse to laugh.

Here the notebook record stopped abruptly. A few days later he described why:

> Words could only be written down with great effort. I asked my laboratory assistant to accompany me home, for I expected the thing would run the same course as the disturbances of the previous Friday. But it was clear, even as I rode home by bicycle, that all the symptoms were worse than the first time. I had great difficulty speaking clearly, and my field of vision wavered like an image in a crooked mirror.

After he reached home, the visual disturbances became more vivid. Fantastic images appeared, colored bright blue and green. Most remarkable of all, sounds, as of passing cars, were somehow transmuted into optical sensations, "so that for each tone and each noise a corresponding kaleidoscopic form and color was produced." After a night's sleep, Hofmann felt completely normal again.

It turned out that LSD was by far the most potent hallucinogen ever discovered. Even the 250 micrograms taken deliberately by Hofmann would be no bigger than a grain of salt, and the more typical dose of 25 micrograms would be practically invisible. Thus it was clear how, on that first Friday, he might accidentally have contaminated himself, perhaps by merely touching a dirty finger to his lips.

It was the same Hofmann, of LSD fame, who first identified *psilocybin*, the psychotropic principle of a *"magic mushroom."* This chemical is related to serotonin. Psychotropic mushrooms have been used since prehistoric times, especially in Aztec and other South American religious rituals; in modern times they have entered the drug culture in the United States and Europe.

When someone not too familiar with mushrooms mistakenly eats one of these, the effects can be quite alarming. Unexpectedly, a tingling numbness develops throughout the body, vision becomes blurred, and brilliantly colored images appear. Victims may panic, fearing they are going insane, especially when they experience feelings of disembodiment. In one reported case, a young woman "thought that she was a banana and that somebody was attempting to skin her." A three-year-old child was frightened by "seeing colored lights on the ceiling, seeing cats that were not there, and feeling that she was bigger than she really was."

Deliberate use of the mushrooms—as by cooking them into soups or omelettes—more often than not produces effects that are regarded as pleasant and interesting, since they are anticipated and desired. Colorful hallucinations are common, often accompanied by a sense of elation and uncontrollable laughing. However, the potency of psychotropic mushrooms varies unpredictably, as does the way different people react, so that "bad trips" are an ever-present threat. Panic attacks and "flashbacks" occur; these are psychotic reactions that occur days or even weeks after the drug has worn off.

Animals trained to discriminate LSD respond to psilocybin as if it were the same, and the effects in humans are much like those of LSD and other LSD-like drugs. For this reason, "psilocybin" sold on the street is almost always actually LSD, and ordinary mushrooms laced with LSD may be sold as "magic mushrooms."

SUBSTANCES RELATED TO THE STRUCTURES OF DOPAMINE AND AMPHETAMINE

The *peyote* cactus, native to the southwestern states and Mexico, has an ancient history of use for religious purposes among the North American Indians. Spanish explorers along the Rio Grande valley described the peyote rite in 1560, and archeological data obtained with carbon-14 dating now suggest a history that goes back 7,000 years. Among the Navaho, the peyote ceremony is today the central ritual of the Native American Church, founded about 1880. A meeting typically lasts all night, with chanting, drumming, prayers, and the eating of peyote "buttons" in strictly limited amount according to a prescribed ritual. The peyote experience was described by one participant as follows:

The appearance of vision with closed eyes was very gradual. At first there was merely a vague play of light and shade which suggested pictures, but never made them. Then the pictures became more definite, but too confused and crowded to be described, beyond saying that they were of the same character as the images of the kaleidoscope, symmetrical groupings of spiked objects. Then, in the course of the evening, they became distinct, but still indescribable—mostly a vast field of golden jewels, studded with red and green stones, ever changing ... all sorts of odd and grotesque images passed in succession through my mind ... five or six fish, the color of canaries, floating about in air in a gold wire cage.

According to anthropologists who have studied peyotism, frank hallucinations, like those described above, are the exception rather than the rule. The essential psychotropic effect that is sought is rather the seeming endowment of ordinary objects and events with profound significance. This subtle change in the way participants view their surroundings is considered to be an aid to introspection and to making prayers more efficacious. Probably—except for people who are unusually sensitive to the drug action—hallucinations occur only at higher dosages than are normally used in the ceremony.

Mescaline is the active compound in peyote. Its molecular structure is nearly identical to that of amphetamine, which, in turn, is closely related to that of the neurotransmitter dopamine. The first experimental administration of pure mescaline to a human was conducted—on himself—by the German pharmacologist Arthur Heffter in 1897. The effects of hallucinogens are so modified by personal experience, and in today's drug-taking youth culture so exaggerated by subjective anticipation and shared mythologies, that it is interesting to read Heffter's unbiased account. He was reputed to be rather staid, stern, and objective, a no-nonsense scientist with a rigid personality and no preconceptions about what he would experience.

Violet and green spots appear on the paper during reading. When the eyes are kept shut there are visions of carpet patterns, ribbed vaulting, etc. ... Landscapes, halls, architectural scenes (e.g. pillars decorated with flowers) also appear. ... Nausea and dizziness are at times very distressing. The appreciation of time is reduced. ... Both mescaline and the crude drug (peyote) produced the characteristic visions.

Heffter considered whether peyote would "become popular amongst cultured people as an intoxicating drug." He thought it unlikely because the side effects were so pronounced that "they considerably spoil the appreciation of the beautiful visions."

Nutmeg contains a substance that is metabolized to a mescaline-like compound in the body. The seeds of a handsome East Indian tree, nutmeg had medicinal uses in ancient times, especially among Arabic physicians. The neuroanatomist Johannes Purkinje tried some in 1829, and wrote: "My movements ... were lost momentarily in dream pictures, from which I had to extricate myself with considerable force in order to keep on walking ... dreams and physical activity battled one another." Distortions of space are especially common, described thus by one subject: "The kitchen was cathedral-like in its dimensions ... and I was unusually tall, my feet were small and far away, it was like looking through the wrong end of binoculars." Often reported are sensations of floating, being transported aloft, or having one's limbs separated from one's body.

MDMA ("ecstasy"), which enjoyed a wave of popularity recently on college campuses, is also related chemically to dopamine, amphetamines, and mescaline. For most people, the sense of disembodiment and the visual hallucinations are less extreme than with LSD or mescaline, and the feelings of elation are greater; but the effects are qualitatively very similar. In rats, MDMA causes massive destruction of serotonin neurons; and although we do not know if this alarming brain damage occurs in humans, it is worrisome to think it might. The neurotoxic effect may be due, not to MDMA itself, but rather to a product of the metabolism of MDMA in the body.

All the LSD-like hallucinogens act, directly or indirectly, on serotonin receptors (especially on one receptor subtype) in the brain, which belong to the 7-helix family (see Chapter 3). For substances chemically related to serotonin, this mode of action is not surprising; but it is not understood why compounds with structures related to dopamine and amphetamine should behave in the same way. Compounds of both groups cause a massive discharge of serotonin from the endings of the serotonin neurons, followed by prolonged depletion of this neurotransmitter. As it is so difficult to study hallucinations in animals, research on the true mechanisms of action has progressed very slowly. There is not even agreement about whether the psychotropic effects are due to the massive release of serotonin, or to a deficiency resulting from serotonin depletion. And it is even still controversial if the hallucinogens that act directly on brain serotonin receptors do so as agonists (mimicking) or as antagonists (blocking).

PHENCYCLIDINE
(PCP, "ANGEL DUST")

This substance, although capable of producing hallucinations, is rather different from the hallucinogens discussed above. One difference is that PCP acts consistently as a primary reinforcer in animal experiments: it is self-administered, whereas most other hallucinogens are not.* Drug discrimination experiments also set PCP apart. Animals trained to recognize one LSD-like hallucinogen usually can not distinguish between it and others in the group, whereas they clearly perceive PCP as different. Human subjects seek euphoria from PCP and become truly addicted to it. It enjoys periodic popularity on the street, but unpredictable adverse reactions tend to limit its use. Unlike the relaxed euphoria and emotional blunting caused by opiates, and unlike the euphoric stimulation caused by cocaine and amphetamines, the PCP "high" combines an ecstatic euphoria with feelings of unreality, accompanied by distortions of time, space and body image. Judgment and intellectual capacity are strongly impaired. Strange and bizarre behavior may occur, with thought disturbances, paranoia, and even violent (homicidal or suicidal) actions.

At low doses, the balance between pleasant and unpleasant effects is unpredictable. Higher doses consistently produce restlessness, disorientation, panic, fear of impending death, obsession with trivial matters, paranoid thinking, belligerence, and impaired judgment. The full-blown PCP psychosis may include bizarre, violent, assaultive behavior, incoherent speech, blank stare, and compulsive repetitive movements. After recovery from the immediate drug psychosis, there is usually amnesia for the whole episode. An alarming feature is persistence of the delusional state for as long as a week or more, with recurrent panic attacks, hallucinations, and even the possibility of suicide during this period.

PCP resembles the opiates in producing a physical withdrawal syndrome in animals, but a less florid one than opiates produce in humans, in whom intense craving, depression, and extreme sleepiness are typical. Newborn infants of PCP-addicted mothers are irritable,

---

* However, this distinction is not absolute, for baboons will, indeed, self-administer a few compounds of the LSD group, even displaying what appears to be hallucinatory behavior, such as trying to catch imaginary objects.

with a characteristic high-pitched cry. They are jittery, they have hyperactive reflexes, they feed poorly, and they suffer from diarrhea. Major developmental deficits soon become evident in these children—trouble with adaptive behaviors (and impaired learning), poor motor control, retarded acquisition of language skills, and problems in interpersonal relationships.

The chemical structure of PCP is unique and unrelated to that of any known neurotransmitter. In the search for specific PCP receptors it became clear, about five years ago, that this compound interacted with two types of receptor in the brain. One type could also bind various opioid ligands; the other was more selective for compounds closely related to the structure of PCP itself. This latter PCP binding site turned out, remarkably, to be part of the NMDA receptor complex (see Chapter 3). The natural ligand of this receptor is glutamate, a major excitatory neurotransmitter in the brain. Like the GABA receptor also described in Chapter 3, the NMDA receptor is an ion channel composed of several subunits. Presumably, PCP blocks this ion channel; but how that leads to hallucinations and psychosis remains obscure.

The identification of a PCP receptor initiated a search for an endogenous ligand, on the conceptual model of opioid receptors and endogenous opioids. Intense interest attaches to this search because the behavioral disturbances caused by PCP resemble those of schizophrenia in so many ways. Thus, it has been proposed, although not yet demonstrated, that schizophrenia itself might be due to excessive production or defective removal of an endogenous PCP-like ligand.

ANOTHER MAGIC MUSHROOM

Fly agaric (Amanita muscaria) is a large, bright-red mushroom with a long history of ceremonial use by shamans in Siberia and Northern Europe. Some anthropologists speculate that its history goes back to ancient times in India. The psychotropic principle of this mushroom, known as *muscimol*, is unrelated to serotonin or dopamine but, interestingly, is an agonist at the GABA receptor. It will be recalled that the GABA receptor is also thought to be the site of action of alcohol; yet muscimol intoxication presents a very different picture. There is a peculiar kind of half-sleep accompanied by colored visions and feelings of elation. Under the influence of this drug one has the impression of being able to perform amazing feats of physical effort, even to fly. One pharmacologist has described his own experience as follows:

There was dizziness, speech was inarticulate, concentration was difficult. There were endlessly repeated echo-pictures of situations observed a few minutes before ... hearing was noisy ... there was confusion, disturbance of visual perception, illusions of color vision, disorientation in time and space, weariness, fatigue.

A curious property of the hallucinogenic substance in fly agaric is that it passes intact into the urine. Body metabolism removes various toxic impurities so that muscimol extracted from urine is actually purer than it was in the mushroom. This unusual property (most drugs are destroyed as they pass through the body) was discovered in ancient times, so that drinking the shaman's urine and thus recycling the psychotropic substance became a part of the religious ritual. (I am reminded of my days as an Army physician in 1944, when penicillin was first being introduced into medicine. This antibiotic is also excreted intact into urine. During those wartime years it was so scarce and precious that we actually recovered it routinely from patients' urine and used it again.)

HALLUCINOGENS AND ADDICTION

It is a remarkable fact that plant products should have the power to alter the way the human mind functions. Like all the addictive drugs, the hallucinogens are closely related chemically to the natural neurotransmitters, and they act by disturbing the finely regulated chemical systems of the brain. Even the synthetic hallucinogens, by and large, are chemically modified natural plant products. How amazing it is that of the million or more species of plants on the planet, humans should have discovered just those few that contain psychotropic substances!

Wherever anthropologists have gone, in whatever remote region of the world, they have found people using mind-altering drugs derived from natural sources. The great physician William Osler once said, jocularly, "The chief thing that distinguishes humans from other species is their desire to take medicines." A whole field of research, called *ethnopharmacology*, is devoted to searching out and studying natural drugs used by native cultures. In the story of *epena* snuff, it is noteworthy—and typical—that unschooled people were able to discover, and pass on from generation to generation, the kind of detailed knowledge that modern ethnopharmacologists now seek. Which rare tree was required? What part of the tree produced the psychotropic substance? How was the product to be prepared for use? Very likely the active material is destroyed when taken by mouth, so it has to be absorbed through the membranes of the nose. But this can only occur after a chemical treatment with alkali. But then, which other tree will produce an ash that is alkaline enough to be effective when mixed with epena ash? One is awestruck by the amount of experimentation that must have been needed, over the centuries, to develop this one hallucinogenic snuff for ritual use.

Does a chapter on hallucinogens belong in a book on drug addiction? Most would argue for including PCP, because it causes dependence and an opiate-like withdrawal syndrome. Many would argue for omitting the LSD-like and dopamine-related hallucinogens. However, clear-cut categories are difficult to establish because of the many overlapping actions of the psychotropic drugs. The brain is so complex, with so many subtypes of neurotransmitter receptors, that no single substance will ever have only a single biologic effect. At the lowest dosages, for example of LSD, only visual hallucinations may occur. But as dosage is increased, quite different mental and physical disturbances come into play. Thus, some drugs are primarily hallucinogenic at the lowest effective dosages, while others are primarily reinforcers at low dosage but may be hallucinogenic at higher dosage. Sometimes high-dosage hallucinations are part of a toxic psychosis, accompanied by serious thought disorders. Marijuana, for example, at low dosage produces only relaxation, altered mood, and some disturbance of time sense; whereas high dosage can produce frank hallucinations. Cocaine and amphetamines are powerful reinforcers, producing an intense "high" at ordinary dosages; but greater dosages or continuous binging use cause outright paranoia, with hallucinations and manic behavior.

Hallucinogens share with all addictive drugs the property that they are self-administered for the purpose of altering mood, perception, and emotions. But there are significant differences in the social context in which they are used. Among native peoples all over the world, hallucinogens are chiefly used ceremonially, on infrequent occasions, and under strict control of a shaman or other religious leader. A similar mode of controlled drug use is seen in the way sacramental wine is used in the Jewish and Christian religions. These traditions seem to reflect an understanding, assimilated into human culture over centuries, that unrestricted use of any psychotropic drug is dangerous.

In our own culture, in contrast, hallucinogenic drugs are often used in an out-of-control fashion. Then craving may become a prominent feature between occasions of use, and panic reactions and toxic psychosis can be significant hazards, at least for some users. Long-term brain damage may be a real possibility with high dosage and repeated use, and "flashbacks" during periods of abstinence may reflect such irreversible disturbance of brain function. Fads in the use of one or another hallucinogen come and go. No one understands why LSD, for example, should have been so popular in the sixties, fallen off in popularity in the seventies, and made a partial comeback in the eighties. Nor is it clear why drugs of this class can become popular in one geographic area but not at all in another.

Hallucinogens have been popularized as somehow being able to reveal mystical or symbolic aspects of the mind that are normally hidden from introspection—thus the term *psychedelic*, meaning "mind-revealing." The person on a "trip," as described by a knowledgeable psychiatrist, "passively watches as a range of novel emotional, perceptual, and cognitive events are intensely exposed." One subject, a scientist, described his hallucinations as follows:

> What I was seeing was more clearly seen than anything I had seen before. At last I was seeing with the eye of the soul, not through the coarse lenses of my natural eyes. Moreover, what I was seeing was impregnated with weighty meaning. I was awe-struck.

Much as dreams are based on personal experience, the content of drug-induced hallucinations varies greatly from person to person. In the sixties, with the rise of the youth drug culture, some psychiatrists used hallucinogens to access what they considered to be aspects of a patient's mind that were otherwise inaccessible. Such therapeutic use has waned, perhaps because psychiatrists—like the rest of us—found it too difficult to draw valid conclusions from the productions of chemically disordered brains.

PART THREE

Drugs and Society

CHAPTER 15

Just Say No?

If you walked into one of a number of Kansas City sixth-grade classrooms a few years ago, you might have observed the following scene. Under a teacher's guidance, and with the whole class watching, a child pretends to offer a cigarette to a friend. The friend hesitates, uncertain what to do. The teacher intervenes. "Sally," she suggests, "you know that smoke makes people cough. Try saying that." The role-playing is repeated. The cigarette is offered. Sally says, boldly, "No thanks, I don't like the way smoke makes me cough." Then Sally turns her back and walks away with a determined air.

The slogan "Just say no!" expresses a valid goal, but by itself it is too simplistic. Although usually considered as a deterrent only for first use of drugs by children, this slogan really applies at all times of life— to occasional users, to those who have become addicted, to addicts in treatment, and to those who are in danger of relapse after treatment. Furthermore, in each of these situations a set of skills has to be taught in order to make "Just say no!" a reality. What has actually been learned about how to prevent children and adolescents from using addictive drugs in the first place? What are the various methods of treatment for people who have become addicted, and how effective are they in the short term and in preventing relapse?

PREVENTION

There are two distinct questions about the use of addictive drugs—why does a person take such a drug the first time, and why does a person continue drug use and become addicted? Obviously without first use there could be no addiction, just as there could be no addiction if the particular drug were totally unavailable.

Usually first use occurs during adolescence or even earlier as an expression of natural curiosity, a desire to imitate grown-up behavior, or a daring venture into a forbidden realm. The degree of social deviance represented by first use is different for each drug and varies from one cultural context to another. In the United States and many other societies, first use of alcohol or tobacco usually signifies only a minor transgression of accepted social standards. An exception is in families where such substances are strictly taboo on religious grounds; in that case first use may signify a more serious break with social convention. Even with these legal drugs, however, the age of first use typically precedes the legally sanctioned age, and therefore use must be associated—to some extent at least—with a willingness to break the law. A recent survey showed that, of children below ninth grade, 30% had used alcohol and more than half of those had actually gotten drunk at least once. About 40% had smoked cigarettes, and one in seven of those were smoking daily. Blatant advertising, as well as more subtle media messages extolling the virtues of drinking and smoking, no doubt contribute to making these dangerous addictive drugs seem acceptable to minors.

Although marijuana is a prohibited drug, its use is so widespread in some circles that first use requires little or no sociopathic behavior; and the route of administration—smoking—is already commonplace for tobacco. At the other extreme, first use of drugs like cocaine or heroin requires a high degree of deviance. Their illicit status forces the would-be first-time user into criminal behavior at the outset. Just to "learn the ropes"—where and how to find the drug, how to prepare it for use, how to use it—requires experienced associates who are often already deeply involved in antisocial and criminal behavior. And if cocaine or heroin is to be used intravenously, the route of administration itself presupposes a high degree of social deviance; inserting a needle into one's own vein is a strange, unnatural act not casually performed.

Recruiting of new users to an addiction is made easier if the route of administration is socially acceptable. When tobacco was first introduced, people did not take to it readily because smoking seemed a strange and unpleasant behavior. Over the years, thanks to the tobacco industry's vigorous promotional efforts, smoking became a normal custom in society. This process will be obvious to older readers, who have seen, in their own lifetimes, how a habit that was socially unacceptable for women before World War II became as commonplace for them as for men. Today most people view intravenous drug self-administration as bizarre behavior and are reluctant to cross that line, but they have no such inhibitions about smoking. This probably accounts, at least in part, for the sharp increase in cocaine use when crack cocaine was introduced for smoking, whereas cocaine for intravenous use or for "snorting" had been limited to a much smaller number of users.

Everyone would like to prevent kids from using drugs, but how to accomplish that goal is not entirely obvious. In the sixties it was common practice for uniformed police officers to come into the classroom with exaggerated and untruthful stories about the "evil" effects of marijuana on the body and mind. Their accounts of the criminal sanctions on marijuana possession and use, although more accurate, were also meant to terrify. At a time when the use of cannabis was growing among adults, and when children learned from other sources that legal alcohol and tobacco were probably more harmful to health than illicit marijuana, any positive effects of the teaching were thus undercut by the appearance of hypocrisy.

In the early 1970s the pendulum swung. An ambivalent stance about drugs was introduced into the classroom. Many argued that the mere use of addictive drugs was not necessarily bad, that children had to be encouraged to learn all they could about the favorable and unfavorable effects of drugs in order to be able to make their own decisions about drug use. This view is no longer prevalent, in part at least because of political pressures from organized anti-drug groups, especially parents' groups. Their position, grounded in a moral perspective on drug use, is stated cogently by Phyllis Schlafly, who has been a leading exponent of opposition in principle to drug use. Her major objection is the failure of today's schools to teach old-fashioned values, as schools used to do. However, there have been no experiments to test whether returning to earlier methods of education would be effective in reducing drug use in children. Two extracts, one from Schlafly's own writings and one from material issued by her *Eagle Forum*, capture the flavor of the principal arguments:

Contrary to what most people believe, drug education is not drug *prevention* education; it is telling children *about* drugs and telling them they can make their *own* decisions.

Society has already decided that illegal drugs such as crack and cocaine are wrong. It is evil to tell a fourth grader that it's *his* decision and not give him any guidance. What this does is to leave the child a sitting duck for the peddler out on the street and for peer pressure.

In the mid-1970s researchers began to consider seriously how to design experiments to find out what were the best ways of preventing drug abuse. Cigarettes and alcohol—because they are so easy to obtain—are always the first drugs to be used, and therefore they are called "gateway drugs." Blocking that first gateway might prevent progression to marijuana (which may be considered a second gateway) and then to the other illicit addictive drugs. The gateway concept owes much to the systematic long-term studies of Denise Kandel, who showed that adolescents who become addicted to heroin or cocaine as they enter adulthood have almost always, when they were younger, used cigarettes and alcohol first, then marijuana. Regardless of gateway theory, however, preventing young people from starting to drink or smoke, and reducing their drinking and smoking if they have already started, are important goals in their own right because of the major health hazards posed by the use of these two drugs.

Social psychology research on ways of changing human behavior has revealed that many different influences have to be brought to bear in the prevention effort. According to modern social learning theory, behavior is shaped in a social context; and therefore changing children's behavior must involve teachers, peers, parents—indeed the whole community. Scare tactics alone are certainly not effective and even in a diversified program are probably not very useful, given the natural striving of adolescents for independence and their natural tendency to rebel against adult authority. Three steps are necessary:

- Basic information has to be imparted—truthful information—to generate motivation for behavior change. Only honest, straightforward, and full information about the health risks of the addictive drugs will meet this requirement.

- The means for behavior change have to be provided. Here many techniques have proven effective, especially teaching children how to resist peer pressure. It is important to promote a redefinition of drug-using peers as not "cool."

■ Methods for reinforcing the new behaviors have to be employed. This means, in short, that children need recognition, praise, and other rewards for not using drugs. Emphasis on how drugs detract from a healthy body and an attractive appearance, for example, appeals to adolescents' interest in athletics as well as to their developing sexuality and their striving for intimate peer relationships.

An important and relevant finding of social learning theory is the importance of *self-efficacy*. This quality, which is related to self-esteem, is the expression of people's belief that they are in charge of their own behavior, that they are capable of actually making a desired change. Those who have that self-confidence are more successful than those who doubt their own ability. If a child believes and asserts that he or she is capable of turning down a proposal to drink beer or smoke marijuana with a friend, that is likely to happen. Most important, self-efficacy can be enhanced through training and practice.

Self-efficacy has interesting biochemical correlates. A rat can be taught that when a warning light comes on, an electric footshock will follow. If the rat is helpless to prevent the shock, the light itself becomes very stressful; and the rat's endogenous opioid pain-suppressing system is turned on, as though in anticipation of the painful shock. However, if the rat is taught that by pressing a lever when the light comes on, it can prevent the shock—in other words, that it has self-efficacy in this situation—stress is reduced and endogenous opioids are not activated.

Similar results have been obtained in humans. People who give themselves a high self-efficacy score have lower levels of stress-combating hormones in their blood (as though they are not needed) than people who rate their self-efficacy as low. In Chapter 5, experiments with the opioid antagonist naloxone in human volunteers were described, showing that stress activates the endogenous opioid pain-suppressing system, as evidenced by the fact that stressful pain is made worse by naloxone. Recently, the following interesting experiment was conducted by Stanford psychologist Albert Bandura. Subjects were given mathematical problems to solve. Group A could regulate the level of difficulty of the problems, thus matching their own self-efficacy to the task at hand. Group B were given difficult problems that frequently exceeded their capacities; this was evidently stressful, and they rated their own self-efficacy as low. Then experimental pain was inflicted on both groups. In group A naloxone had no effect, indicating that no endogenous opioids had been mobilized. In group B naloxone made the pain worse, even intolerable, showing that the stress associated with feelings of low self-efficacy had activated the opioid system.

Among studies of educational techniques aimed at modifying children's first use of drugs, the Kansas City drug prevention program is one of the few carefully designed school-based experiments to be carried out, as such experiments must be, on a very large scale. Directed specifically at eleven- and twelve-year-olds, this program had many components. The skills of resisting peer pressure were taught through role-playing (as illustrated in the introduction to this chapter), and especially through the use of peers as group leaders. Parent organizations were enlisted to reinforce the classroom experiences at home through participation in special homework assignments. Community organizations were involved and the mass media were employed. The program was implemented in the sixth and seventh grades of 24 schools (nearly 2,000 students), chosen randomly, while another 18 schools served as controls.

The measure of success or failure was to be the rate of increase in the use of cigarettes, alcohol, and marijuana in the experimental schools as compared with the control schools. The study began with children who had barely begun drug use of any kind. From sixth grade on, drug use typically increases substantially each year. Successful prevention in the experimental schools would mean reducing this rate of increase, compared with that in the control schools. Self-reports by the children were used as the primary data; but how reliable would self-reports be? There was obviously no possibility here for double-blind design, as children in the experimental schools were well aware that they were participants in a special program. They therefore would know what was expected of them. Might they then fabricate or shade their reports to please the researchers? This was a major concern.

To address this concern, the investigators took a common-sense approach to enhancing the reliability of the students' self-reports: they taught the children about breath testing for carbon monoxide and saliva testing for thiocyanate (described in Chapter 8)—these are reliable indicators of recent smoking. Then saliva samples were actually collected. Other studies have shown, as one might expect, that the very act of collecting saliva (or urine, in other drug studies) improves the veracity of self-reports. Accordingly, the researchers found very good agreement between self-reports and chemical measurements for frequent smokers, whose intake could be monitored reliably by the tests. Parents were also queried about their children's drug use; but this seems of dubious value, since drug users are unlikely to confide illicit behavior to their parents. The important finding concerning parents was, not surprisingly, that a child's drug use (cigarettes, alcohol, marijuana) was likely to be similar to that of the parents.

At the outset, the experimental and control groups were comparable. One year later, as expected, more children in both groups had used drugs. However, the increase was considerably less in the experimental schools than in the control schools. Smoking in the previous month, for example, increased from the initial 13% to 24% in the control schools but only to 17% in the experimental schools. For alcohol, the initial 8% increased to 16% (control), compared with 11% (experimental). For marijuana, the initial 1% had become 10% (control) compared with only 7% (experimental). It can be concluded that for all three drugs, after one year, roughly half the children who would have started using were deterred from doing so. Three years later, although the school component of the program had not been continued, and the community and mass media components affected children from both experimental and control schools, some effects of the experimental intervention persisted: children in the experimental schools smoked less tobacco and marijuana—but there was no difference in alcohol use.

It is not yet known how well the positive prevention effects observed in this and numerous similar studies will carry forward into the high school years and beyond. Unfortunately for demonstrating effects of the intervention (but fortunately for the health of the nation) there had been, at the time, and continues to be, a steady decline in the use of all addictive drugs across all segments of the population. This is recorded in the *High School Seniors Survey*, conducted annually for many years now, with funding from the federal government's National Institute on Drug Abuse. The declines in drug use revealed by this survey are large and continuous, reflecting a general change in societal attitudes toward drugs.

Figure 15.1 shows the trend, over the years 1975–1991, for daily use of tobacco, alcohol, and marijuana among high school seniors. For both males and females, cigarette smoking reached a peak of around 29% in 1976–1977, then fell steadily to about 18% in the years 1988 to 1991. The decline in both daily use and heavy daily use (more than

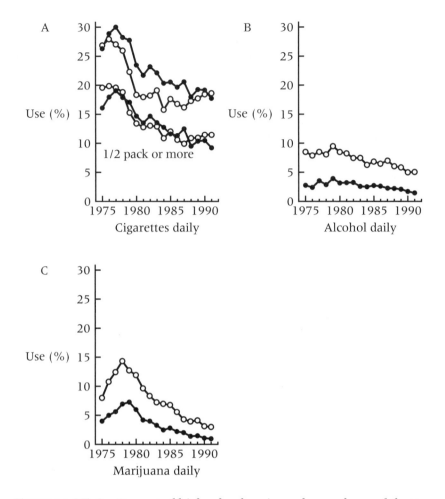

FIGURE 15.1 Percent of high school seniors who used any of three addictive drugs daily, 1975–1991. (A) Cigarettes, total users (upper curves) and those who smoked half a pack or more daily (lower curves); (B) alcohol; (C) marijuana. Open circles, males; solid circles, females. [From L. D. Johnston et al., *Smoking, Drinking, and Illicit Drug Use among American Secondary Students, College Students, and Young Adults, 1975–1991, vol. I, Secondary School Students* (National Institute on Drug Abuse, Publication No. 93-3480, Washington DC, 1992, Fig. 10).]

10 cigarettes) seems to have stopped in recent years. Daily use of marijuana increased to a peak of 14% for males and 7% for females in 1978; then the trend reversed, and the numbers fell to only a few

percent by 1991. Daily drinking peaked in 1979 at 10% for males, 4% for females, then declined slowly and continuously. PCP, LSD, cocaine, and all other drugs (not shown) had similar trends. Heroin has never been used by more than a fraction of a percent of the high school population.

A striking feature of this epidemiologic research has been the finding of a strong inverse relationship between perceived risk and drug use. For all the drugs, over this same period, as increasing numbers of students perceived use as harmful, fewer students used them. At the same time, there was no evident change in drug availability. Typical data are shown for marijuana in Figure 15.2. The overwhelming majority of students reported having seen or heard anti-drug commercials in the previous month, and about three-quarters of them stated that the commercials had to some extent made them less likely to use drugs.

These results show that large-scale efforts on the community or national level can bring about behavior change by tapping into the health concerns of young people. Such change occurs gradually but steadily, and it affects the whole population (though with some ethnic,

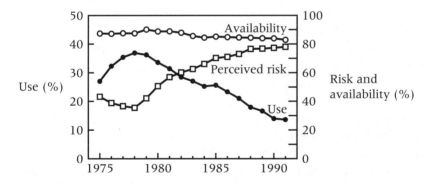

FIGURE 15.2 Percent of high school seniors who used marijuana during the past month, perceived risk, and availability; 1975–1991. Here "Use" means percent using once or more in the previous month; "Perceived Risk" means percent saying there is great risk of harm in regular use; "Availability" means percent saying marijuana is fairly easy or very easy to get. [From L. D. Johnston et al., *Smoking, Drinking, and Illicit Drug Use among American Secondary Students, College Students, and Young Adults, 1975–1991, vol. I, Secondary School Students*. (National Institute on Drug Abuse, Publication No. 93-3480, Washington DC, 1992, Fig. 23.)

class, and geographic differences). Cigarette smoking is the prototypic example. At the peak of its popularity, in 1964, when the first Surgeon General's report focused public attention on the health risks, 53% of adult males in the United States were smoking, and 32% of adult females. Over the subsequent 28 years, these figures fell steadily, to 29% and 26%, respectively, by 1991.

What about the cost-effectiveness of prevention education for the young? Several excellent research studies have taught us that it is possible, through appropriate methods of prevention education in the schools, to reduce drug use. However, whether the extent of reduction obtainable is worth the extra effort and expenditure for special programs is a difficult question to answer. Consider cigarette smoking. As noted above for high school seniors, fewer than one-fifth now become daily smokers. Thus, in terms of health benefit, special smoking prevention programs for the early grades seem to be unnecessary for four-fifths of the children, who will not become smokers anyway. Moreover, much prevention education is already being done, routinely, at low cost, in most schools at all grade levels.

In order to prove anything conclusively, the prevention research projects had to be planned with meticulous care and carried out on a massive scale. While that kind of research design was necessary to learn what actually works, it was also extremely costly. Society would certainly not be willing to pay for special programs on that scale in all the nation's schools. The key question, therefore, is whether the procedures that work in the research projects can be implemented on a national basis by regular teachers within the regular curriculum. To find out will presumably be the next step in prevention research.

Some experts have suggested that actions such as enforcing bans on cigarette sales to minors and raising taxes on cigarettes and alcohol might be more cost-effective than across-the-board prevention education in the schools. The laws prohibiting sales of cigarettes to minors are rarely enforced. In a county-wide study conducted by a Stanford University group and a similar study in the Washington, D.C. area, it was found that when obviously under-age children were sent around to supermarkets and small stores they were able to purchase cigarettes in over 80% of the cases. An informational campaign directed at the store owners and clerks and also the posting of prominent signs at the check-out counters reduced the number of violations; but when children were sent out again, they were still able to buy cigarettes 30% of the time.

In my opinion, the main lesson to be gotten from research on drug abuse prevention during the critical years of childhood and adolescence, when curiosity is a driving force and drugs are first tried and then used increasingly, is this: Classroom education to teach children why to say no and how to say no is essential, but it is not enough. Nor can it have more than marginal effects unless it is supplemented by broad parental and community-wide efforts. We can hardly expect to prevent children from using drugs unless they can actually see that adults are willing to set a consistent example in their own behavior and are prepared to enforce the laws that are supposed to restrict access of minors to addictive drugs. Drug prevention education in the schools has to be viewed as an integral part of bringing about a pervasive change in societal attitudes toward all addictive drugs.

TREATMENT

Treatment presents a different problem from prevention. The challenge is to move addicts from an addicted to a drug-free state, if possible, or at least to free them from the compulsion of drug use, which dominates their lives. Changing established addictive behavior is a complicated business, and removing the addictive drug is only one part of an overall treatment plan. Moreover, speaking of "the addictive drug" is a gross oversimplification because a pattern of using several drugs simultaneously (polydrug abuse) is so common, especially among alienated young people with troubled histories and disorganized lives. Treatment then requires not only addressing each drug appropriately, but also dealing with the many ways that the drugs affect each other. And because people vary so greatly in the total circumstances of their addiction, what works well for one may not work at all for another. Therefore, the skilled therapist is flexible, nondogmatic, understanding, supportive yet demanding, patient, and willing to discover by trial and error what is best for the individual patient. A central theme of treatment is expressed in the slogan "Different strokes for different folks."

Treatment programs may be divided into *residential* and *outpatient*. Programs of both types may be publicly or privately funded. For budgetary reasons, residential programs (the most costly) are usually reserved for the most recalcitrant addicts, who can not deal effectively with their addiction in the same setting that nourished their drug use in the first place. Some programs insist on immediate total abstinence, with alleviation of the withdrawal syndrome followed by efforts to sustain abstinence. Others encourage slow reduction of drug use with ample counseling support. Some programs employ surrogate agonists like methadone for short or extended periods. Some make use of various other pharmacologic agents (for example to allay withdrawal discomfort), while others absolutely reject medication of any kind. A nationwide network of groups dealing with various drug addictions by the 12-step (Alcoholics Anonymous) model accepts no public funds and uses no professional counselors. Model self-directed residential therapeutic communities for rehabilitation of drug addicts are Phoenix House in New York (and elsewhere) and the Delancey Street Foundation in San Francisco. Because of this great variety of approaches to treatment it is hard to estimate the total number of programs in operation in the United States. According to official U.S. government sources, about 2.8 million drug users in 1992 needed and would probably benefit from treatment. At any given time, 600,000 addicts could be served in "slots" funded by public sources, with a total capacity to treat only 1.7 million addicts during the course of the year.

"Cold turkey" withdrawal is unlikely to be accomplished successfully without extraordinarily strong motivation, strong external support, and—again—self-efficacy. Virtually all addicts have tried, at some time, to discontinue use on their own, but the discomfort of the withdrawal syndrome, with its accompanying intense craving, makes success rare. If there is a solid supportive environment, some argue, the best treatment system begins with "cold turkey." Even addiction to heroin and other opiates, which is reputed to have intolerable withdrawal distress, is often treated this way in residential facilities devoted to self-help with intensive peer support.

The most widely used treatment methods employ slow detoxification combined with chemical means of reducing withdrawal distress. For nicotine addiction this may include the temporary use of nicotine skin patches. For heroin addiction it may include substitution of methadone for heroin, followed by slow dosage reduction of the methadone to zero over a period of a few weeks. To make withdrawal syndromes characterized by agitation and anxiety more tolerable, clonidine or mild tranquilizers may be used. Benzodiazepine tranquilizers (e.g., Valium) are traditional mainstays of managing alcohol withdrawal. Antidepressant medication is effective in withdrawal from amphetamines or cocaine, where depression is a major problem. To summarize and generalize: whatever the addictive drug, the first step in treatment is to remove it, with pharmacologic and social support, as gradually as may be necessary.

Powerful forces are struggling within the addict—a real Jekyll-and-Hyde situation. If there is no motivation to give up the drug, there is no way to begin treatment. But even if addicts present themselves for treatment, it is usually with ambivalent feelings. Some kind of pressure brought them to the treatment facility—perhaps insistent urging by family, perhaps the cost of a drug escalating out of control, perhaps loss of job, perhaps trouble with the law, perhaps health concerns, perhaps dissatisfaction with self. But counterpressures are also hard at work—craving the next smoke, injection, snort, or drink; wanting to remain a member of an addict peer group; being depressed just thinking about a future with never another taste of the drug. As long as the addict can just walk away or fail to keep the next clinic appointment, the negative forces may well win out. Treatment personnel have to anticipate this self-defeating behavior and be prepared to start treatment again and again.

Then what about compulsory treatment, which is often proposed as a solution? In fact, we already have such a system for the illicit drugs. When an addict engages in criminal activity, the criminal-justice system requires abstinence as a condition of probation in lieu of incarceration, or of parole after early release from prison; and continuous participation in treatment is obligatory. Alcohol addicts who are habitually arrested for driving while intoxicated are typically required to attend Alcoholics Anonymous or some other treatment program. Legally mandated supervision has been found, in several research studies, to be an extremely effective method of ensuring abstinence. However, it is difficult to see how compulsory treatment could be instituted, in our free society, in the absence of a court conviction and sentence.

The same principles of social learning theory that guide prevention education in the classroom are also relevant to treatment. To be motivated is not enough. The addict has to be taught, explicitly, the many day-to-day techniques of living without drugs. A system of contracts is established, whereby the addict agrees to comply with a step-by-step program of progress, worked out jointly with the therapist counselor. Here, tailoring the approach to the individual becomes important. For many heroin or cocaine addicts, a major part of counseling will be to promote the practical skills that are needed for rehabilitation after a life of crime. These include job training and education, legal assistance, counseling to restore disrupted family life, attention to neglected medical conditions, advice about HIV risks, and prenatal care.

Objective tests of drug use—saliva, urine, or breath tests—are essentials in effective treatment programs. Their purpose is to confront the addicts with reality, for the expert therapist does not necessarily accept their self-reports as the truth. Patients with organic or mental disease are usually eager to communicate accurate information to the physician or other therapist. But with Jekyll-and-Hyde drug addicts, of whatever socioeconomic class, of whatever educational level, and whatever the drug of addiction, this straightforward honesty can not be assumed. I have been asked repeatedly, often angrily, by heroin addicts, "Don't you believe me when I tell you I haven't used heroin in the past week?" My answer is, "No! Why should anyone believe you at this point? The record of your recent life doesn't exactly inspire trust. Let's work together to change that situation, but it takes time and effort to earn trust."

The need for objective evidence is not limited to the illicit drugs. If smoking is likely to be under-reported, as was noted earlier, the reports become more truthful when saliva, urine, or breath samples are taken for testing. The same principle applies to drinking. For the therapist, it is absolutely essential to know accurately about drug use. As urine tests tell about recent previous use of nicotine, marijuana, opiates, cocaine, amphetamines, and PCP, so saliva, blood, and breath tests tell about recent smoking, and the breathalyzer test measures the current blood level of alcohol.

The general approach to addiction treatment can be described as breaking a big task into manageable bits, each tailored to the needs of the individual patient. If a surrogate agonist is available—the same kind of drug as the one to which the subject is addicted—it can make the task easier by stabilizing the chemical dependence while changes are made in the addict's lifestyle. Substituting methadone for heroin permits the addict to discontinue intravenous injections, since methadone is taken by mouth, and breaks the cycle of seeking and using heroin several times daily. Withdrawal is put off to a later time, when the addict will have better support systems and greater self-efficacy. After personal and social rehabilitation is well under way, and when absolutely no heroin has been used for many months, one can think about tapering off the methadone. At that point some people will be able to give up the methadone quickly and easily; but others may take a very long time, and some may actually require it indefinitely (see Chapter 10).

The same principles apply in treating nicotine addiction. Many people can quit, cold turkey, and never smoke again; fine, that's what they should do. Others find it harder. Substituting a nicotine patch for cigarettes maintains a stable blood and brain nicotine level and permits many addicts to discontinue smoking without discomfort. But there are some hard-core, heavily addicted smokers who are not yet ready to face life without smoking; they can at least be helped to reduce their intake. This is a *harm reduction* approach. After all, smokers who cut down from two packs a day to one pack a day reduce all their tobacco-related health risks by half. The principles of behavior modification dictate that the conditioned cues that control the lighting of every cigarette, as described in Chapter 8, must be recognized and then extinguished, one by one.

Antagonist treatment has been thoroughly developed only for opiate addiction but it is now being tested also for nicotine addiction, as noted in Chapter 8. Experience with naltrexone (see Chapter 10) has not been encouraging. Naltrexone can not even be started until no opiate dependence remains, else precipitated withdrawal would result; so slow withdrawal followed by a period of successful abstinence is a precondition for its use. Although highly effective in blocking the re-warding actions of heroin—and perhaps for that very reason—it is dropped quickly by most addicts who try it. Part of the problem may be poor motivation; but in addition, blocking the normal functions of the opioid receptors may cause subtle negative mood changes, as suggested by research on normal volunteers.

Aversive treatment is illustrated by disulfiram (Antabuse) (see Chapter 9). Alcoholics who take Antabuse regularly are deterred from drinking because of the knowledge that they will become very ill if they do drink. Antabuse is an important tool in the therapist's kit; but as with antagonists, compliance is a major problem. For reasons that are not clear, disulfiram is more often prescribed and used in Europe than in the United States.

Drug addiction is much more than just using a certain addictive drug; it involves total behavior, social interactions, lifestyle. Whatever the form of treatment, therefore, treating drug addiction, like preventing it, entails much more than "Just say no!"

RELAPSE

There is some truth in the saying "Once an addict, always an addict." The formerly addicted person has drug-related memories and experiences not shared by those who have never been addicted. And these—

under the right conditions—can trigger a relapse. Recognizing this vulnerability is important for protecting the once-addicted person against relapse—a view emphasized by Alcoholics Anonymous in their insistence on calling their members "recovering alcoholics," never "former alcoholics." If we knew how to prevent relapse reliably, it would be a great deal easier to solve the drug addiction problem once and for all.

Relapse is, of course, always preceded by a decision to use, however vague and inchoate that decision may be. It is an impulsive decision, not a rational one; and it is provoked by craving—the intense and overwhelming desire to use the drug. Although craving is a constant feature of withdrawal, it may also occur from time to time even years after the last drug dose. That kind of craving, which is obviously not part of a withdrawal syndrome, is poorly understood but enormously important, for it can drive the ex-addict into relapse even after long-sustained successful abstinence. Animal and human experiments reveal a "priming effect" of a drug to which the subject was previously addicted. This means that a small dose of the drug, administered to an abstinent ex-addict, can immediately initiate self-administration behavior. This is, of course, the very phenomenon that AA warns of— that abstinent alcoholics can not resume occasional drinking without losing control.

For the abstinent ex-addict any of the circumstances and environments surrounding former drug use can lead to relapse. These may have become conditioned stimuli for the rewarding effects of the drugs themselves. It is thought that such stimuli, by activating the reward systems, can mimic drug action and thus produce what is tantamount to a "priming effect" even though no drug was taken. This phenomenon is very likely related to the conditioned place preference described in chapter 4. The consequence is a return to drug-seeking and drug-taking behavior.

Also of interest in understanding recurring craving in the abstinent ex-addict is the *conditioned withdrawal syndrome*, which is elicited by cues that were associated with drug availability and drug use in the ex-addict's previous experience. Here is a typical case. One of my patients (let's call him Charlie T.) had been stabilized on methadone, had discontinued all heroin use (as proved by regular urine tests), had gotten a job, and had been doing well by all the indicators. One day, to my great surprise, his urine test showed that he had used heroin. He admitted the truth, but he was at a loss to understand why he had suddenly been overwhelmed by an irresistible craving and had rushed out of his house to find some heroin. His description was fascinating; it was as though he were driven by some external force he was powerless to resist, even though he knew while it was happening that it was a disastrous course of action for him. "Well, Charlie," I asked, "can you recall what you were doing just before you rushed out of the house?" He tried to recall, then said, "I guess I was watching TV." "And what, exactly, were you watching?" There was a long silence before he replied. "Oh, yes," he said, "now I remember. It was a program about addiction. They showed an addict fixing, putting the needle into his vein. And suddenly I felt sick, just like needing heroin. I got that craving. I broke out in a sweat. I had that old feeling that only a fix would cure me."

Conditioned withdrawal has been demonstrated in the laboratory. Ex-addict volunteers who had not used opiates for months or years were shown, on the video screen, a scene of someone using heroin. They displayed many of the signs of withdrawal—sweating, chills, a running nose, and goose bumps. They felt that they were undergoing actual opiate withdrawal, and they experienced intense craving for heroin. Such observations help us understand why addicts so often relapse when they are immediately returned after detoxification to the previous environment, with all its drug-related associations.

The medical management of withdrawal can be so smooth and painless that all addicts, whatever their drug, can be brought readily and relatively painlessly to a drug-free state. But then a sudden attack of craving can start the whole cycle over again. Therefore, the therapist has to teach the techniques for eliminating conditioned craving by *desensitizing*—by *extinction* of the conditioned cues. That requires being exposed to the situation that was formerly associated with drug use, but without drug being available.

Watch a smoker as she gets into her car in the morning to drive to work. She reaches into her purse, takes out a cigarette, lights up, and inhales deeply. Before long, getting into the car becomes a conditioned cue for smoking that cigarette. Getting into the car provokes immediate craving for nicotine; and with cigarettes available, the craving leads immediately to nicotine use. To desensitize, to break the conditioned association to that cue, means regularly and consistently not smoking that particular cigarette.

I heard a convincing story from a colleague who had been a nicotine addict but hadn't smoked for years. He had abstained from cigarettes in a variety of situations where he had smoked in the past, and thus he had desensitized himself to a variety of conditioned associations—

cigarettes at parties, cigarettes at morning coffee, cigarettes at the desk, and so on. One day he went to the beach and was suddenly over-whelmed by an intense craving to smoke. He found this beyond un-derstanding until he realized that smoking on the beach had been an important pattern at one time in his life, and that he had not had the opportunity to eliminate that particular conditioned association.

Contrary to what most people might think, craving is not provoked by the absence of the drug to which a person was addicted, but by its presence—that is, by its availability. This is illustrated by the nicotine addict who goes skiing for a whole day, leaving cigarettes behind. No thought is given to cigarettes—they are simply unavailable. Then back at the lodge, where nicotine is available again, intense craving strikes, and the addict lights up. In the story of Charlie T., even the conditioned craving would soon have passed were it not for his knowledge that he could actually go out and find heroin. With nicotine, someone else's smoking is a potent conditioned cue for light-ing up; and that is why regulations that establish smoke-free environ-ments are so helpful to nicotine addicts and ex-addicts in reducing their consumption or maintaining their abstinence.

Relapses will occur; there is no perfect preventive. The important thing is for a relapse to be contained. Airplane flight instructors tell about how students differ in their reactions to making mistakes. Learn-ing to fly is a challenging and difficult undertaking, and mistakes are inevitable along the way. Students who dwell on every mistake, who keep castigating themselves, who think up excuses, who simply won't put the mistake behind them, invariably wind up making more mis-takes. Instead of paying attention to business and going forward, their minds are fixed on the past. The successful student notes the mistake, learns a lesson from it, and gets on with the job. A relapse from ab-stinence is just a mistake. Some people panic, taking it as a sign that they can not remain abstinent after all. They let the relapse destroy their self-efficacy. Then, instead of a single episode of drug use, which would have done no great harm, they end up with a total relapse, severely addicted again. That pattern of successful abstinence, a single relapse, and then reversion to full-blown addiction is all too common. Training in how to handle relapses when they occur is, therefore, an important part of drug addiction treatment.

This chapter has explored the many ways that a determination to "Just say no!" has to be implemented successfully. The same principles apply to prevention education in the schools, to the various stages of treatment of established drug addictions, and to preventing relapses and dealing effectively with them when they occur. In the next chapter we examine some special problems posed by the use of illicit drugs, especially of those used intravenously. Then in the final chapters we consider some possible ways of making drug policy more effective, first as tried in Great Britain and the Netherlands, then as might be implemented in the United States.

CHAPTER 16

Lessons from the Street

The stereotyped drug addict whose image fills the newspapers, magazines, TV screens, and politicians' speeches is only part—and a small part at that—of our addiction problem, as I have pointed out throughout this book. Drug addiction afflicts all economic classes, all educational levels, and all ethnic groups. But although nicotine and alcohol, not cocaine and heroin, affect society on the largest scale, it must be acknowledged that the street addict (the "junkie") is a conspicuous reality, one whose very existence frightens and disgusts many citizens. This chapter focuses on some of the problems street addicts present to the larger society. These include the addicts' criminal activities, difficulties encountered by health professionals in establishing treatment facilities, and intravenous drug use as a major factor in the epidemic spread of AIDS.

CRIME AND PUNISHMENT

There are essentially two kinds of crime committed by addicts. One kind is crime by definition, since buying, selling, or possessing an illicit drug is illegal. According to FBI sources, there were about a million arrests for drug violations in 1990; approximately one-third of these were for trafficking, the remainder for possession. We could think of these as crimes against society but without direct and identifiable victims. Sometimes they are called "victimless crimes"; but there are frequently innocent victims such as members of the addict's family and others who are affected by the addict's behavior or by the health consequences of the addiction. The other kind of crime is not uniquely related to drugs, but it is often committed to obtain money for drugs, as well as for other purposes. The common crimes in this category are theft (especially shoplifting), burglary, robbery (often with personal violence), and homicide (incident either to robbery or to battles over trafficking), as well as prostitution.

Are street addicts criminals first, so that the use of illicit drugs is essentially a part of their antisocial behavior pattern? Or are they addicts first, who innocently became enmeshed deeper and deeper in the drug scene, and then become criminals to raise the ever-increasing sums needed to support an addiction? There is no simple answer, but studies of those addicted to the illicit street drugs do reveal a pattern. Most inner-city street addicts belong to the lower socioeconomic class, so it is not surprising that there is a high proportion of ethnic minorities. Most street addicts were juvenile delinquents first, with records of truancy, gang activities, fighting, stealing cars for joy rides, and petty shoplifting even before their first contact with an addictive drug. Most had a juvenile criminal record before the age of sixteen and were unemployed when not in custody. Often they are victims of child abuse, products of broken families, and dropouts from school at an early age. Leading lives without apparent goals, they frequently became members of street gangs. Nearly all of them used alcohol and smoked cigarettes—the two classic gateway drugs—at a very early age, before it was legal for them to do so. Next came marijuana, and then heroin and either cocaine or amphetamines. The addict-to-be was typically introduced to each new drug by a friend, rarely by a "pusher."

Middle-class and wealthy addicts go through the same progression of drug use, beginning, usually in high school, with the same two gateway drugs, nicotine and alcohol, then graduating to marijuana and finally to cocaine and heroin. Gross antisocial behavior is not so evident in this group before they began using drugs, but a troubled psychiatric history and severe personality problems are common. Then, as the use of illicit drugs becomes more intense, drugs come to occupy more and more of a person's time at the expense of educational or employment activities. With these addicts, serious criminality starts when the cost of supporting an addiction escalates and becomes a real burden. Then one generally sees white-collar crimes, not burglaries and street muggings. Typical are embezzlement, theft from a family member or employer, writing bad checks, and running up enormous credit-card and other debts.

For all the illicit addictive drugs there is a common pattern of progression from experimental use to increasingly frequent use, and finally to full-blown addiction. Fewer and fewer people move to each successive step, so that by and large only the most sociopathic, the most mentally disturbed, the least educated, the habitual losers, go all the way. As a simple illustration, consider the 1991 statistics on the use of marijuana in the 18–25-year-old age group. Fifty percent had tried it at some time in the past, 25% had smoked it during the previous year, 13% during the previous month, and only 7% during the previous week. This same pattern also applies to the progression from licit to illicit, from nicotine and alcohol to marijuana, and then to heroin and cocaine (or amphetamine); and likewise from the socially acceptable smoking or drinking route of administration to the intravenous route.

A major issue, concerning which there is uncertainty in the court system, is to what extent addiction exculpates crimes committed either under the influence of a drug or in the course of obtaining the drug. I sat on a jury once, in an open-and-shut case of drunk driving. After the defendant was found guilty, the public defender argued for leniency on the ground that her client was an alcoholic and therefore could not help drinking. True, no one had been injured by this defendant's irresponsible actions, but many innocent people had been placed in jeopardy. Fortunately, the judge was not persuaded by the defense attorney's peculiar logic. Fortunately, too, it is becoming increasingly common to hold drunk drivers fully responsible for the consequences of their behavior. Thus, the idea that alcoholism exculpates crime is being rejected, and the same principle should apply to all the drug addictions.

A few years ago I was asked to meet with a committee of the Santa Clara County (California) Bar Association to discuss drugs and crime. These lawyers were deeply interested in the problem, and they had plenty of first-hand experience defending drug addicts. I was astonished to hear them express the naive notion that an addict who "needed" a drug had no alternative to criminal activity. "He had no choice," they told me in effect, "He had to mug the old lady for her money, else he would have gone into withdrawal." In other words, these lawyers had actually come to believe the exaggerated and self-serving accounts of their clients. A less kindly way to put it would be that the addicts had "conned" their attorneys.

I pointed out that although cold-turkey withdrawal from heroin is unpleasant, it is by no means intolerable; and it is life-threatening only in the most extraordinary circumstances. Indeed, cold-turkey withdrawal is actually the method preferred by certain ex-addict groups (for example, Synanon and some other therapeutic communities) that try to help addicts become abstinent. And although cocaine withdrawal is unpleasant and is associated with intense craving, its physiologic symptoms are milder than those of heroin withdrawal. Thus, there is no medical reason that could justify doing physical harm to other human beings or depriving them of their property in order to obtain funds to purchase an addictive drug.

I explained to the lawyers that addicts should be expected to bear full responsibility for their crimes, whether they are in treatment or whether they have chosen to reject treatment. What I was saying was pretty simple—that the alternative to committing crimes is not to commit crimes, that addiction does not force a person to be a criminal. Moreover, if treatment were available to all who want it, even the weak defense of "needing" the drug would collapse. Studies in Baltimore and other cities have shown dramatically that criminal activities decline substantially while heroin addicts are enrolled in a methadone maintenance program but increase again if they leave the program. Those studies, incidentally, make a strong case for the cost-effectiveness of addiction treatment: it costs a lot less to keep an addict in treatment than society loses—not only directly but also through the expensive arrest, prosecution, and incarceration process—when that addict, left untreated, continues to engage in criminal activities.

"NOT IN MY BACK YARD"

It is one thing to say, as a statement of principle, that addiction should be treated like any other disease. It is quite another to put the principle into effect. Negative societal attitudes toward certain kinds of addicts create real obstacles. And the antisocial attitudes of some addicts make matters worse. The story of my research clinic is an instructive example of how the "NIMBY" ("not in my back yard") syndrome operates.

Picture the neighborhood. Stanford Medical Center with its medical school and hospital occupies a large area on the edge of the Stanford University campus. A stone's throw from the hospital is Welch Road, attractively manicured, with trees and green lawns, a quiet and refined suburban street. Here you find physicians' and dentists' offices and many kinds of business offices, but no private residences.

In the 1970s my Addiction Research Foundation occupied one of the Welch Road office buildings. The purpose of our clinical research was to test the efficacy of two maintenance drugs for heroin addicts—LAAM, a long-acting relative of methadone, and the opiate antagonist naltrexone. The clinic was supported by federal grants, and treatment was free. Even then, at the height of federal funding, it was the experience everywhere that demand for treatment exceeded the capacity of treatment programs. Thus, within weeks of opening our doors, addicts were coming to us from as far as 10 or 20 miles away, and we soon reached our limit. Every Monday, Wednesday, and Friday 120 patients attended the clinic. As both LAAM and naltrexone needed to be taken (by mouth) only three times a week, all medication was consumed on the premises. This eliminated any possibility of LAAM's being diverted into illicit channels, of drug trafficking in the vicinity, or of accidental poisoning of addicts' children or others—all major problems with "take-home" methadone.

Almost at once, the landlord began complaining. He said that we were bringing unsavory characters into the neighborhood, that his other tenants were frightened, that the comings and goings of our patients three times a week were inappropriate to the Welch Road environment. Of course, many more people came and went every day at the hospital next door, at the bank across the street, at the ice cream parlor, at the doctors' and dentists' offices. So the problem was not the numbers. Obviously, our patients were the wrong kind of people. They were a mix of Latino, Oriental, African-American, and Caucasian ethnicity. This was unusual enough for Welch Road. But far more upsetting, they came from the "lower" classes of society. Most did not follow the Welch Road dress code, and some wore tattered clothing and presented an unkempt appearance. Some also behaved in an offensive manner, without consideration for others. The vernacular of the streets, not typically heard in this neighborhood, was used freely and loudly. Occasionally even a fist fight would break out between patients.

The landlord sought an injunction to close the clinic, alleging it was a nuisance to his tenants. In addition, he sued our Foundation for compensatory damages (because of the supposed effect on the value of his property) in the amount of a million dollars—considerably more than our total endowment. I refused to take all this seriously. It seemed so unjust, so obviously motivated by class and racist biases. Surely we had a right to conduct a humane and socially useful treatment program, especially right next door to a hospital. Surely the law would uphold our good deeds against the crass position of the landlord.

Unfortunately, some of our patients played right into the landlord's hands. A few of them, with criminal records and deft fingers, wandered the halls of the buildings; and wallets and purses began to disappear. Some patients, despite our earnest explanations and warnings, began to loiter in the parking lot. In one memorable confrontation, a patient urinated against a car—the landlord's car, no less! When the landlord objected, the patient swore at him, using obscenities. This particular episode was described in lurid detail in the depositions that initiated the legal proceedings.

Soon I began to get advice from colleagues throughout the country. What was happening, they told me, was not at all unusual. Moreover, in every case that had actually gone to trial, injunctions were indeed issued; and clinics had to shut down or move. I had better take this seriously, they warned. And even I had to admit that the antisocial attitudes of some street addicts—although I could understand that some of their hostility was a reaction to the way they were treated by society—would make it nearly impossible to operate a clinic in harmony with this neighborhood.

Reluctantly, I closed the clinic. In the four years we were able to operate, we had accomplished a great deal, both in treatment research and in humane services to heroin addicts. The main lesson I learned was that even a compassionate recognition that addiction should be treated as a disease leaves unchanged the deep gulfs that separate the middle class from the underclass in our society and that divide ethnic minorities from the white majority. Well-to-do addicts from Silicon Valley, coming for treatment to physicians on Welch Road, attract no attention. If one wishes to treat typical street addicts, one had better do it either in a large public health facility or in a run-down part of town, where the residents and the proprietors of small businesses are too powerless to object. This is a depressing reality, but it is hard to envision a practical alternative, given the present atmosphere.

CLEAN NEEDLES, SAFE SEX

Tacoma, Washington—the first needle exchange program in North America. Started privately by a citizen concerned about the spread of

AIDS, this program was taken over in 1988 by the Tacoma County Department of Health. At five locations throughout the county, hundreds of addicts who use heroin or cocaine intravenously come to exchange their used syringes and needles for a fresh supply and also to get free condoms. Similar programs have now come into being at many locations throughout the United States and Canada. Even before 1988, needle and syringe distribution schemes had been established in the Netherlands, the United Kingdom, and elsewhere in Europe.

Although returning used needles and syringes is encouraged, few needle exchanges actually require that. Of course, all programs try to capture and destroy as many used drug paraphernalia as possible, in order to prevent their being used again or being discarded in public places. Return rates vary between 50% and 90%. Thus, one should really speak of the free distribution of syringes and needles, and of condoms, for that is what it actually is.

The idea of distributing the very equipment that is needed for intravenous drug use aroused bitter opposition at first, opposition that persists in some circles today. In New York City in 1990, for example, although more than two-thirds of intravenous drug users were known to be infected with HIV, the mayor responded to strong public pressures by canceling a newly instituted needle exchange program. Two years later it was reinstated. Opposition arguments centered about the fear that such official programs would legitimize drug addiction, would "give the wrong message," would attract naive young people to become intravenous drug users.

If it could be shown that needle exchanges do not attract new users, one might argue that nothing is lost by establishing them, that a harm-reduction strategy is always worthwhile. However, substantial costs are involved. At a minimum, therefore, we ought to know if—and to what degree—such programs are effective in reducing HIV transmission or in accomplishing other beneficial results.

The rationale for needle exchange (the term always implies syringe exchange as well) is straightforward. Intravenous drug users typically share syringes and needles, and the AIDS virus (HIV) is spread readily by this route. If addicts have sterile needles and syringes—so the argument goes—they will stop sharing, and the transmission of HIV will be interrupted. At the same time, the other mode of transmission, sexual contact, which can spread the virus to sexual partners (homosexual or heterosexual) of intravenous drug users, will be blocked if condoms are made freely available and are used regularly.

The basic question is whether the exchange programs actually do reduce the spread of HIV. That is not easy to answer. As with so much social science research, controlled experiments, the kind one could do in the laboratory, may not be practical. Ideally, here is what one would want to do. Find two comparable groups of addicts, perhaps in different cities but of the same age, gender, ethnic composition, socio-economic status, educational level, and so on. Ascertain that the HIV seropositivity rate (the percent of people testing positive for the virus) is substantially the same, and low, among addicts in the two cities. An initially low seropositivity rate is essential in order to have a large range of possible rates of conversion from seronegative to seropositive. Flip a coin, and establish a needle exchange in one city, keeping the other city as a control for comparison.

Even if the needle exchange were effective, it would take years to accumulate the data to prove it. Meanwhile, the addicts in the control city are by no means isolated from the many sources of public-health information; so their behavior may well change, based on that information. Quite unrelated to the needle exchange, then, we are likely to find that the rate of new HIV infection decreases in both groups. A similar methodologic problem in prevention education research was discussed in Chapter 15.

Another difficulty arises from the fact that the needle exchanges have to be voluntary. This raises a serious question of whether addicts who decide to participate are representative of addicts in general. They are not. In one study that examined this question it was found—not surprisingly—that participants had a lower infection rate initially than those who allowed themselves to be tested but then declined to participate. Participants presumably had a less chaotic lifestyle, engaged in less risk-taking behavior, and had more concern for personal health. Thus, the value of needle exchanges could well be greatest for those who need it least, and least for those who need it most.

Natural epidemiology—as opposed to controlled experiment—offers some fascinating information, but few firm conclusions. Let's look at a specific case, in which the lack of equivalence of two cities frustrates any scientifically valid interpretation. In Glasgow in 1989, the HIV seropositivity rate among addicts who came into contact with a treatment facility or the criminal-justice system was only about 3%, approximately the same as for other British cities at that time. In Edinburgh, however, only 40 miles away, the rate was over 50%, and by 1990 had reached 85%. In Glasgow a municipally sanctioned needle exchange had been operating for several years. In Edinburgh the city fathers and police took a different line. Their policy was not only opposed to needle exchanges, they forbade the sale of injection equipment entirely, in the hope of thus stemming the increase in intravenous drug use. As the HIV infection rate climbed, a few needle exchanges were belatedly established, but even these operated in so half-hearted a manner as not to attract and hold many clients.

Enthusiasts for needle exchange schemes have pointed to these two cities as evidence in favor of their position. One article states categorically: "If needles and syringes had been readily and legitimately available in Edinburgh during the 1980s, the rate of HIV infection would be substantially lower than that found today." However, deeper analysis reveals that addict behavior in the two cities was quite different, and that difference existed before 1983, when HIV first appeared on the scene. Edinburgh (but not Glasgow) had a tradition of "shooting galleries," communal gathering spots for addicts, where needle sharing was routine. A large new group of intravenous drug users, mostly youngsters, came onto the drug scene in Edinburgh, into this fertile field for epidemic spread of blood-borne infection, just at the moment when HIV first arrived. We have no idea how the virus was introduced into this discrete pool of intravenous drug users already sharing needles (and sex) promiscuously—presumably it was one infected person coming to Edinburgh from somewhere else. Therefore, although the contrast between Edinburgh and Glasgow is interesting, the complicated differences in history and addict culture between them frustrate any attempt to draw firm conclusions about the effectiveness of needle exchanges.

During the first few decades of a novel disease that is transmitted by sex and body fluids, pockets of high and low infection rates are to be expected. It may be, for example, that the difference between Edinburgh and Glasgow was simply due to relative lack of mobility—thus relative isolation of each pool of infection—with the high rate in Edinburgh due to the accident of early introduction of the virus. Albuquerque, New Mexico, is a city of half a million in an isolated location on the desert, with a tradition of low population mobility. At the present writing, when well over two-thirds of intravenous drug users in New York City are HIV seropositive, only a few percent in Albuquerque carry the virus; and this number seems to be growing extremely slowly. The reasons are unclear, but it may be that the virus first appeared in this community only after education had brought about relevant behavior changes. It is also interesting, and perhaps significant, that in New Mexico it has always been legal for anyone to purchase needles and syringes over the counter at pharmacies. Indeed, the states with the lowest HIV rates among intravenous drug users are those in which purchase or possession of such drug paraphernalia is legal.

There is not the slightest hint of credible evidence that needle exchanges promote intravenous drug use by those who would not otherwise become addicts. In many programs that have been in operation for years, the average age of new applicants, which would be expected to decrease if young people were being recruited to intravenous drug use, has not done so. For example, data from a needle-exchange program in New Haven, Connecticut, reveal that the average age of new participants remained constant, as did the six-year average duration of their intravenous drug use.

Sophisticated research is not needed to tell us that behavior change is the key to stopping the spread of AIDS—in all segments of society, not only in the addict group. Behavior change requires that new information be disseminated and—most important—accepted. In the gay community, AIDS education brought about major changes in sexual behavior (less promiscuity, more use of condoms), which resulted in a dramatic reduction of new HIV infections. However, it does not follow automatically that addicts could achieve a similar result; we just don't know. In the state of intense craving provoked by having heroin or cocaine in hand, how many addicts will stop to take precautions? For some addicts, needle sharing has a ritual significance as a token of intimacy; how many will give it up willingly? And when about to engage in sex under the stimulatory influence of cocaine, will a man stop to put on a condom, even if he has one? Many health workers wish such prudence were possible but have come to believe, from their own experience, that addicts are too impulsive, too prone to take risks, too undisciplined. After all, hepatitis B, other life-threatening blood-borne infections, fatal overdoses, and lethal adulterants are nothing new to addicts—yet they continue to inject themselves intravenously with unsterile needles and syringes. Ironically, HIV is not even a robust virus; it is easily killed by even the most perfunctory methods. Rinsing a syringe and needle with readily available household bleach would take only a few seconds and would be effective. If addicts will not take the trouble to do that, argue the pessimists, why would they bother to use fresh sterile syringes and needles even if they had them?

The optimists, while agreeing with these characterizations of addict behavior, argue that many addicts are indeed amenable to behavior change, that addicts as a group are not suicidal. The optimists see the needle exchange as a vehicle for reaching out—carrying an educational message about AIDS, raising consciousness about health risks, offering counseling and other services—and so even leading addicts to take the first step towards treatment. And ideally, treatment would put an end to the addict's intravenous drug use. The message of the needle exchange, they argue, is "We care about you here."

Are needle exchanges worth the cost and the effort? In Britain, the rationale in their favor has been formulated by the official Advisory Council on Misuse of Drugs as follows:

> We have no hesitation in concluding that the spread of HIV is a greater danger to individual and public health than drug misuse. Accordingly, services which aim to minimize HIV risk behaviour by all available means should take precedence in development plans. ... The containment of the spread of the virus is a higher priority in management than the prevention of drug misuse.

Common sense tells us that all possible means are in order to try to check the worldwide AIDS epidemic. In this desperate situation, even though (for reasons explained earlier) a scientifically valid cost-benefit analysis will probably never be possible, the chance that needle exchanges will reduce existing harm is probably substantially greater than of their causing harm. Thus, they are a legitimate weapon in the public-health approach to the drug addiction problem. However, it remains an open question whether, with treatment funds limited, funding should be diverted to needle exchanges at the expense of other services to addicts. Whether or not needle exchanges are in operation, these other services play the key role in stemming the spread of AIDS. Well-run methadone maintenance programs are especially important because we know that heroin addicts substantially reduce or discontinue intravenous heroin injections while they are taking methadone.

The three social consequences of addiction "on the streets" examined in this chapter—crime and how we deal with it, negative societal attitudes that impede treatment, and the role of street addicts in the spread of AIDS—have something in common. All three call for policies that focus on *harm reduction*—minimizing the damage addicts do to themselves and others—while at the same time balancing humane treatment of addicts and respect of their human rights against the rights of other members of society. This theme will be developed further in the final chapters, first by considering some innovative drug policies in other countries, then by focusing sharply on issues of drug policy in the United States.

CHAPTER 17

Lessons from Abroad

Drug addiction is unbounded by geography, form of government, politics, ethnicity, economic status, or degree of formal education. In other words, it is a problem of the human condition. Might we learn something from countries that seem less victimized by drugs than we are? Two other advanced industrial nations—Great Britain and the Netherlands—stand out as having a rather different way of dealing with some aspects of drug addiction. In particular, their governmental policies are based solidly on public-health considerations—on a pragmatic attempt to reduce harm wherever possible, without the moralistic crusading that typifies our own "war on drugs." This chapter explores the similarities and differences between their approach and ours, with a view to seeing what we can learn from them. Then I describe a radical experiment in a conservative country—the park in Zurich, Switzerland, where (until it was closed down) addicts were free to buy, sell, and use whatever drugs they wished.

THE BRITISH APPROACH

Proponents of legalizing addictive drugs often point to Britain as an example that we should follow. They usually put forward one or more of the following assertions about the British:

- That they have brought their drug problem under control.

- That they have legalized the drugs that are prohibited in the United States.

- That by legalizing these drugs, they have broken the connection between addiction and crime, virtually eliminating drug-related crimes.

- That by letting addicts have their drug of choice under hygienic conditions they have greatly improved the addicts' health.

- That they have rehabilitated the addicts in a social and economic sense, integrating them into society as productive citizens, by treating them as patients rather than as criminals.

A lovely picture! Unfortunately, although there are elements of truth here, the assertions are—by and large—false. Since the myth of the successful British system is repeated so often, we need to examine it, point by point, get the facts straight, and then see what useful lessons we can learn.

Addictive drugs have not been legalized in Great Britain. It is true that heroin, which is totally prohibited in the United States, is approved for medical use there. Double-blind studies have shown repeatedly that for the control of pain in hospitalized patients, heroin has no advantage over morphine. The American medical profession accepts this conclusion, but the British medical profession disputes it and continues to prescribe heroin for relief of severe pain. However, whether heroin is or is not approved for medical use in relieving severe pain has no bearing on the problem of heroin addiction.

Britain is signatory to the same United Nations Single Convention on Narcotic Drugs as is the United States. This is the uniform international treaty with which drug laws in the signatory nations are required to comply. In Great Britain, law-enforcement action is vigorous, not only on trafficking, but also on possession. There are customs seizures at the ports and airports, and special narcotics squads in every local police force. Penalties have increased significantly over the past

25 years, so that trafficking now carries a sentence of 14 years to life. Marijuana seizures exceed those of all the other illicit drugs, as do convictions for marijuana possession. In all these respects the British and American policies are quite similar.

Despite the formal similarities in the drug laws, history has shaped attitudes differently in the two countries. In the United States, drug addiction was once regarded (in the nineteenth century) as an unfortunate disease requiring medical attention, and addicts were objects of sympathy. Many of the addicts were middle-class women, for whom physicians furnished morphine on prescription. Radical changes in public perception and in U.S. government policy began in the first decades of the twentieth century. This coincided with the height of the temperance movement and the adoption of a nationwide prohibition of alcohol. It also coincided with a spread of marijuana and heroin to inner-city populations, to lower socioeconomic classes, and to ethnic minorities. This demographic change, which is documented in D. F. Musto's classic, *The American Disease: The Origins of Narcotics Control* (see Suggestions for Further Reading), and elsewhere, provoked a panic reaction, which was exacerbated and fed upon by government agencies. Harry Anslinger, head of the Federal Bureau of Narcotics, conducted a propaganda campaign to persuade the public that heroin, cocaine, and especially marijuana (which he dubbed the "killer weed") were undermining youth and threatening the very foundations of society.

In the wake of this onslaught, politicians responded by enacting and enforcing stronger prohibitions. Especially troubling to them were the maintenance clinics, at which opiate addicts were being given morphine; these were summarily shut down. New federal statutes and legal interpretations, and a few well-publicized prosecutions, made physicians fear to treat addicts. Thus, responsibility for dealing with the drug addiction problem was shifted from the medical profession to the law-enforcement agencies, where it remained, exclusively, until the 1960s. Then methadone maintenance had a strong impact in redefining the drug addictions as medical disorders (see Chapter 10).

Although British urban life after World War II was transformed by the immigration of large numbers of ethnic minorities from all over the former British Empire, drug addiction was (and remains) distinctly uncommon in those groups. A situation so different from the American experience obviously creates a quite different public perception of the problem. For this and other reasons, the American denial of the right of physicians to treat addicts never became an issue in Britain.

Instead, although the same tensions between medicine and law enforcement existed, the medical profession resisted every attempt by the Home Office (the law-enforcement branch of the national government) to criminalize addiction. A balanced system evolved, with good cooperation between the public-health and law-enforcement authorities. Physicians retained their right to treat addicts according to their best medical judgment even if treatment included long-term prescribing of the addict's drug of choice. At the same time, physicians were required to notify the Home Office of the identity of addicts under their care. In consequence, an official statistical database was maintained, a resource for following national trends and for tracking drug traffickers. In practice, the local police exercised discretion in not arresting addicts for simple possession, provided they were being treated and were not involved in trafficking. If they confined their drug use to what was prescribed legitimately for them, there would presumably be no reason for them to resort to the black market.

It did not quite work out that way. Until about 1960, the total number of users of heroin, cocaine, amphetamines, and all the other illicit drugs was so small that it was claimed, with some justification, that Britain really had no significant problem. For example, according to official estimates for 1960—amazing as it sounds now—the total number of known heroin addicts in the entire British Isles was 94, and of addicts to all reportable drugs only 437. The few heroin addicts, most of them in London, were managed well enough by physicians in ordinary medical practice, who often prescribed heroin, syringes, and needles as part of an overall plan of treatment and rehabilitation. In the late sixties, however, there was a sharp increase in the number of heroin addicts. Clusters of new addicts were appearing, owing their existence to a few unscrupulous or gullible physicians who were prescribing heroin willy-nilly to all who asked for it. As the availability of black-market heroin grew, addicts under treatment who could not get all the drugs they wanted from physicians began to supplement their prescribed heroin or amphetamines with drugs purchased on the street. With increasing demand on the street, some addicts were selling off a portion of their prescribed drugs. The government responded, in 1968, by restricting the right to prescribe addictive drugs for addicts to a small number of physician experts based at specially authorized clinics.

By the 1980s, the epidemic of heroin addiction had continued to escalate, and it spread beyond London to other parts of the country. As illicit imports rose, a significant black market in heroin developed. The attempt to maintain addicts on heroin was deemed a failure. At the clinics, which were operated in good faith by health workers devoted to the welfare of the addicts—and despite the provision of psychiatric and counseling services—true rehabilitation was a rare event. Criminal activities continued, the spread of diseases by needle sharing continued, the chaotic and antisocial life style of a large fraction of the addict population continued. Some British clinics simply switched from injectable heroin to injectable methadone, failing to grasp the therapeutic importance of the oral route in helping break the needle habit. But most of the clinics—as one option in a menu of diverse treatment procedures—did eventually adopt oral methadone maintenance, thus following the path pioneered in the United States by Dole and Nyswander (see Chapter 10).

Today Britain is no longer very different from the United States in the magnitude of its addiction problem. With a population of 57 million, the United Kingdom is estimated to have 100,000 to 150,000 heroin addicts, around two per thousand population. In the United States, with a population of 250 million, there are estimated to be between a half million and a million heroin addicts, approximately the same ratio. One interesting difference from the United States (as noted earlier) is in the ethnic distribution; despite a large immigrant minority from India, Africa, and the Caribbean, heroin use in Great Britain affects primarily the Anglo-Saxon majority. Another difference is the extraordinarily low numbers for cocaine (including crack) users—less than one-tenth the number of heroin users—with amphetamines remaining the principal addictive stimulant, as it was before the 1980s in the United States. The dismal outlook for heroin addicts is no different from that in the United States. Two out of every hundred die each year—60% by overdoses, the remainder from infections of the blood and heart valves due to unsterile syringes and needles, from suicide and homicide, and from complications of alcoholism.

All estimates of how many addicts there really are in any country have to be taken with many grains of salt. If one recalls the raging arguments about undercounting after the 1990 U.S. census, where it was simply a matter of counting heads, it is easy to see how difficult it must be to count accurately those engaged in an illicit activity like heroin use. In Britain, the statistics depend largely on reporting by physicians; but confidential surveys have shown that only about one-quarter of addicts in treatment are actually reported. Moreover, addicts who have not yet sought treatment are missed—especially young people just embarking on an addiction career. In the United States, the data come from national questionnaire surveys, clinic attendance, emergency room admissions for adverse drug reactions and overdoses, and arrests, most of which are likely to produce underestimates. The British are just now installing a more comprehensive set of regional databases, which—it is hoped—may yield more accurate information on illicit drug use.

Contrary to what is often asserted in the media, what we can learn from Britain's policies has nothing to do with legalizing drugs—that never happened there. It has everything to do with regarding addiction as a disease. This unambiguous position, which is held by all branches of the British government, contrasts with the view still prevalent in many influential circles in the United States that drug addicts deserve punishment more than they do sympathetic treatment. The British medical orientation is reflected in the composition of the several government commissions which, from time to time, have examined the drug addiction problem and offered recommendations; medical and public health experts have always played a prominent role. Moreover, there is an official permanent expert group, the Advisory Council on Misuse of Drugs, upon which the government relies for continuous monitoring, analysis, and recommendations for changes in policy.

Another important difference from the American drug addiction scene is the existence of the National Health Service in Great Britain. Established fifty years ago, this system guarantees free and unlimited medical care to everyone and therefore provides—as a right—universally available treatment for addicts. By informal agreement between the local police and the local treatment facilities, the addict tends not to be criminalized for addiction alone but is held fully responsible for crimes against persons or property. With free treatment readily available, the addict has no excuse for trafficking in drugs or for other criminal activities.

The details of treatment are left to the clinic physician and the addicted patient to work out. Treatment, as in the United States, comprises a large umbrella, including psychiatric services, practical assistance in job training and job finding, marital counseling, advice about AIDS prevention, and help in settling problems with law enforcement, among other services. Detoxification may be a part of this treatment (especially for young addicts), followed by a plan for abstinence through hospitalization, placement in a halfway house, peer group attendance on the 12-step model, or other approaches. Methadone maintenance is included among the options, but, as in the United States, there are too few clinics to meet the need. Especially for older people who have been heroin addicts for many years, it is recognized that abstinence may be an unrealistic goal. For such patients, the treatment plan may include drug maintenance—occasionally (even now, in some clinics) on intravenous heroin, but more typically on oral methadone. In response to the growing AIDS epidemic among intravenous drug users, a deliberate change of emphasis has been recommended at the highest levels of drug policy making. The aim of keeping addicts in treatment with a view to preventing the spread of HIV is now perceived as having higher priority than just stopping the addictive behavior. Thus, confrontational approaches (such as pressing for detoxification and abstinence) are being modified in favor of more permissive ones.

The present position concerning the prescription of heroin as part of a treatment plan for heroin addicts is perhaps best summarized by Philip H. Connell, one of Britain's leading experts on addiction. He had been a leading figure in the clinics of the 1960s that had made heroin available to addicts as part of a treatment plan. In 1990 he was asked if now, in hindsight, he would still prescribe intravenous heroin. He replied that perhaps it was justified for "a very small proportion of very chaotic and disturbed addicts. ... But the last thing that I would recommend anybody should do is to say right, all you have to do is give heroin, give all the drugs you want to an addict, and everything will be fine. That would indeed, in my view, be a recipe for catastrophe."

GOING DUTCH: SOFT AND HARD DRUGS

Utrecht is an ancient university city in the center of the Netherlands, less than an hour from Amsterdam on those wonderful Dutch trains that run precisely on time. The old windmills are gone, but the city center is full of lovely seventeenth-century buildings on picturesque canals. My guide was a professor of social psychology with a special interest in drug policy. We entered a little coffee shop. On the counter was a surprising menu, featuring cannabis products. On one side were listed four brands of hashish, on the facing page five brands of marijuana leaf. A young man sitting at the counter was sipping coffee, and a sweet aroma made it obvious what he was smoking. The scene seemed very strange; but I had to admit, it didn't look like a den of iniquity.

The Dutch are proud of what they call their "pragmatic" policy on drugs, which differs significantly from both the American and the British approaches. "Drug use is neither favored nor encouraged," writes Eddy L. Engelsman, a key government official in the Ministry of Welfare, Health, and Cultural Affairs, "but if people take drugs, the least we can do is to limit the hazardous effects. ... We hold the view that drug use is not primarily a problem for police and the courts, but rather a matter of public health and social well-being." An official government document states that "criminal law plays only a minor part in preventing individual drug abuse. Although the risks to society must, of course, be taken into account, every possible effort must be made to ensure that drug users are not caused more harm by criminal proceedings than by the use of the drug itself."

I had heard and read many journalistic accounts about the supposed legalization of marijuana in the Netherlands, but what I learned on the spot was quite different from what I had expected. Beginning in 1976, a very sharp distinction was made between "hard drugs" (heroin, cocaine) and "soft drugs" (cannabis).* Alcohol and nicotine are not included in these classifications at all. The Dutch innovation was not to change the laws substantially, but to enforce them—with respect to cannabis—in a discretionary manner. Thus, on the one hand, importing, manufacturing, possessing for sale, and selling cocaine, amphetamines, heroin, and other opiates remains illegal and subject to heavy penalties. Possession of small amounts of these "hard" drugs for personal use is a felony, but subject to lighter penalties. Sale or possession of cannabis, on the other hand, is a mere misdemeanor, punishable by a fine. Here is where discretionary enforcement enters the picture. While I was studying the cannabis menu, a police officer entered, chatted a bit with the proprietor and the customer, and departed. I was puzzled, for the coffee-shop manager was selling marijuana and hashish in flagrant violation of the law. What was going on? My host explained the system, and the chief of police later verified what I had heard.

The Dutch argue that enforcing a strict prohibition on "soft drugs" would merely drive the users underground and bring them into con-

---

* I use the terms "hard drug" and "soft drug" for convenience, but they are not actually used officially in Netherlands government policy, which speaks of "drugs presenting an unacceptable risk," on the one hand, and "cannabis products" on the other.

tact with criminal elements trafficking in more dangerous drugs. The specially designated coffee shops are licensed to operate, but only under strict rules—no advertising, no sale to minors under age 16, no minors allowed on the premises, no "hard" drugs in or near the shop, and no breaches of decorum. In addition, these places are permitted only in certain specified areas of the city. As long as the rules are observed, the police do not enforce the law; but the moment they are broken, the proprietor not only can lose his license but also faces criminal charges.

Has this policy led to an expansion of the pool of cannabis users? As with so much data from real life, the answers are not clear. It all depends on how the sampling is done, on whether one believes self-reports, and on which trends in drug use are actually consequences of policy changes. Dutch government sources claim (and some independent surveys confirm) that there has not been any major increase in cannabis use. Even opponents of the policy have to admit that it has not led to a massive recruitment of young people to the use of marijuana and hashish. However, there is a long-term concern that is harder to counter—that legitimizing cannabis (even though it is not actually legalized) will eventually lead to wider use, that changes in social acceptance of a drug occur slowly, possibly requiring generations rather than a few years to come about.

I spent a most interesting half hour with Dr. Wiarda, Utrecht's Chief Commissioner of Police. He was an extraordinary man, with a doctoral degree in law and a humane attitude toward the drug problem. He epitomized, for me, a major difference in law-enforcement attitudes between the Netherlands and the United States. Of course, there are educated and humane police chiefs in the United States, too, but such qualities in the law-enforcement community are not always given adequate recognition. And the Dutch have nothing like our tradition of wild-west shootouts, rampant "macho" attitudes, disrespect for ethnic minorities, disdain for drug addicts, and—too often—corruption. These differences could well make it impossible to transplant Dutch drug policies, even if we regarded them as enlightened. Dr. Wiarda saw no problems in the practical workings of the cannabis policy. Toward heroin, cocaine, and amphetamines he was ambivalent. While enforcing those prohibitions strictly, he expressed the same frustrations heard from police in the United States concerning the apparent failure of prohibition to ameliorate the hard-drug situation. Perhaps, he mused, all drugs should be legalized.

I accompanied a couple of narcotics officers on their daily sweep of the large shopping mall next to the main railway station. This police action could just as well have taken place in any U.S. city; the main aim was to harass the intravenous drug users and alcoholics, most of them homeless derelicts. The storekeepers and their customers (often upright citizens from farming communities) considered the "junkies" to be a nuisance and wanted them removed. The merchants' association had even provided the police with a special fund to hire additional narcotics officers. As we made the rounds, the officer in charge, an energetic and intelligent young woman, would stop and question drug users, seeking information about a recent burglary. Probably because of stringent and effective enforcement, the cost of hard drugs throughout the Netherlands is very high, and many addicts engage in property crime as a livelihood. Unlike the drug scene in American cities, there is relatively little serious violence—no doubt reflecting the major difference in violent behavior and ownership of firearms in the two countries. In 1989, for example, the total number of homicides in Amsterdam—a city of 700,000—was 46!

The next day found me in Amsterdam, waiting on the stoop in front of Binninkant No. 46, one of those charming old three-story attached buildings that line the canals. Across the little street were houseboats tied up along the bank. A lovely old brick church on the other side had a clock tower, and the chimes were just striking half past the hour. The man I was waiting for was late, but my patience was soon rewarded. A group of young people strode up the street with a businesslike air. Their leader, Rene Mol, introduced himself, and I followed him up the steep steps into the building. I had come to find out what a "junkie union" was, an unimaginable concept in the United States.

Angelique van der Meer is a former heroin addict who had become a full-time employee of the union. A few others sat around a table with us and joined the discussion as she told me the history and purpose of the union. Actually called the Medical Social Service for Heroin Users, it had been organized fifteen years before by parents of heroin addicts. Its aim was to ameliorate conditions of life for "junkies." Now I learned, to my astonishment, that the city government provided a subsidy sufficient to pay the salaries of three staff members. The union, in turn, represented the interests of drug users to the appropriate municipal agencies. Currently, they were attempting to secure improved housing for prostitutes addicted to heroin. In the Netherlands, the welfare system provides a minimum stipend for anyone with a regular address. This creates a special problem for homeless addicts, a problem that the union was also trying to grapple with.

I was curious to find out the attitude of this union, so devoted to the welfare of intravenous drug users, to drug use itself. About hard drugs the answer was clear—they were absolutely opposed to their use, and sought to encourage addicts to become abstinent. At the same time, the union saw the addicts as victims whose rights and welfare required protection. Moreover, they believed that giving up hard drugs had to be a voluntary action, not something compelled by the government. Meanwhile—again the pragmatic approach—the union tried to promote harm-reduction policies. They carried out educational programs about AIDS prevention; the walls were covered with posters urging the use of condoms and clean needles. In these health-related matters, the union and the government reinforced each other's efforts.

A striking difference between Dutch and American policies was the openness of the AIDS prevention campaign. The United States is, at long last, catching up with European realism about how to prevent the spread of this epidemic. We know that intravenous drug users constitute a large pool of infection, which is spread both by needle sharing and by sexual activity. The addict group includes many prostitutes, who become a major channel for spread of the epidemic into the heterosexual population. Addicts, with their impulsive and compulsive drug-seeking and drug-using behavior, are not easily influenced to change their behavior; heroic efforts may be required.

Government policy in the Netherlands rests on intensive, explicit education—directed at the general public as well as at school children—on how AIDS is spread and how the spread can be prevented. For heroin users, in addition to well-disciplined methadone programs of the kind one sees in other countries, a few of the larger cities have established a system of "methadone buses"—an innovative solution to the "NIMBY" problem described in Chapter 16. These buses tour the city, stopping in the neighborhoods for an hour at a time and dispensing methadone to all addicts. There are no onerous requirements, no tedious paperwork, and no waiting lists. There are no urine tests, and continued heroin use is not cause for expulsion. Addicts drink their methadone on the spot; they are never given any to carry away with them. The harm-reduction principle behind the liberal dispensing policy is obvious—every dose of methadone an addict takes by mouth is better than a dose of heroin by vein. The bus also dispenses free sterile needles and syringes, as well as free condoms. Personnel on the bus offer counseling services and referral to definitive treatment facilities. Does it work in preventing AIDS? All we can look at is what fraction of intravenous drug users are HIV-positive. The Dutch claim this is remarkably low—only a few percent in Amsterdam—compared with over two-thirds in New York City.

In the Netherlands, marijuana is used in moderation, and without dreadful harm, by a few percent of young people, as it is in the United States. Could the pragmatic Dutch policy on cannabis be instituted in America, perhaps on a trial basis in one state? Alaska, Oregon, California, and eight other states began to move in that direction in the 1970s, adopting more lenient laws concerning possession of small amounts for personal use; but that trend was reversed by voters and legislatures before long-term results could be evaluated. However, in the few instances in which adequate data were obtained, there was clearly an increase in consumption during the few years of relaxed prohibition. Unfortunately, much that is attractive about the innovative approach to the drug problem in the Netherlands would probably not be applicable to the United States. The Netherlands is a small, heavily industrialized country, only the size of Vermont and New Hampshire, with a population of fifteen million. Although ethnic minorities (chiefly from Surinam and the East Indies) have immigrated in recent years, the country as a whole, historically and culturally, remains very homogeneous, in contrast to the United States. On the one hand, their policy of discretionary enforcement of drug prohibitions could not work in a society ridden with racism, as ours is; inner-city ethnic minorities would surely be targeted unfairly, while drug use by other segments of the population would be ignored. On the other hand, we could well adopt the humane feature of the Dutch attitude toward addicts, regarding them as victims of a disease, and providing treatment for all who desire it.

"NEEDLE PARK"

It is January, 1991. Switzerland is cold and raw. If you are not on the ski slopes, it is best to be indoors. But here I am, standing in a park in the middle of Zurich, a cold wind chilling my face, and the pervasive dampness numbing my feet.

The fame of this "needle park" had spread worldwide to all who despair over the epidemic of intravenous drug use. I had heard this novel Swiss experiment praised by journalists and politicians. I had heard it put forward as a model approach to dealing with drug addicts. I had to see it for myself, study its history, and learn how it really worked.

Around me, in the little park, are about a hundred young people, some still teenagers, some more mature, huddled together against the cold. I watch the scene intently. Money is changing hands in exchange for drugs. A little kiosk, once a public lavatory, houses a first-aid station, with a young doctor in attendance. At a window of the kiosk, brand-new syringes and needles, as well as condoms, are being dispensed, free.

I watch as a shabbily dressed young woman nearby rolls up the sleeve of her overcoat. Holding a filled syringe between her teeth in order to free both hands, she improvises a tourniquet by hanging a shopping bag over her arm, spinning it to twist the rope handle tightly. She tries impatiently to find a vein with the needle, poking herself again and again until she can draw blood back into the syringe. I judge by her ineptness that she is still a novice. When she finds the vein, she lets the shopping bag spin free, releasing the tourniquet, and with a deep sigh of satisfaction she injects the heroin. A few minutes later she is overcome by nausea, and walking onto the nearby grass, she bends over double, retching and vomiting—a textbook example of heroin's effect on the novice user, an unpleasant side-effect that wears off with repeated use.

A couple of police officers in uniform stroll by, casually surveying the scene. The young doctor, assigned to the first-aid station by the Department of Social Welfare of the municipality, tells me how he resuscitates one or two overdose victims every day. As in some surrealistic film, while addicts buy, sell, and self-inject all around us, we hold a professional discussion about the use of naloxone in heroin overdose. Here is an example, he explains, of a situation in which this opiate antagonist is inappropriate because of its short duration of action. Naloxone can certainly revive people with lethal doses of heroin in their systems; but then a victim, who feels quite normal, may go off and die somewhere else when the naloxone wears off before the heroin is eliminated from the body. So the doctor uses naloxone only in the most extreme cases, usually depending instead on conservative methods—artificial respiration, sensory stimulation, exercise, and close observation for long enough to make sure that recovery is complete. He is nearly at the end of a six-month rotation in this job. Eager to return to the practice of medicine in a more favorable clinical environment, he expresses frustration and irritation at what he sees as a mere pretense of providing needed clinical services to these unfortunates.

A few paces away is a group of tables under a quaint rotunda that had once served as an open-air bandstand. The ground is littered with paper syringe wrappers. Here entrepeneurs are selling drugs openly—chiefly heroin and cocaine. Also for sale is the traditional equipment, such as bent spoons and spirit lamps for dissolving the powdered drugs. One man is extracting cocaine with a solvent to make free-base crack suitable for smoking; crack, I learn from the doctor, is not yet on the market here as a regular commodity. As I take in this strange scene, the same two police officers walk over and have a friendly discussion with one of the dealers. I learned later that although the police are under orders not to interfere with drug sales or drug use, they are permitted to seek information in the course of investigating personal or property crimes. Earlier that day, a commissioner of police had showed me a map of Zurich with a red dot for each property crime committed in the past year. Right in the center of the cloud of red dots was—you guessed it—"needle park."

An ancient green school bus stands nearby, and I follow some of the addicts inside. Here a potbelly stove radiates warmth, hot tea and coffee and cookies are available, and two social workers are in attendance. Operated by the Department of Social Welfare, the bus provides shelter from the cold, but the crude facilities and lack of privacy are hardly conducive to serious counseling. Around a long table, near the stove, sit a couple of dozen addicts, many of them "nodding off" under the influence of heroin, some just sitting quietly and sipping a hot drink.

I wanted to know how this remarkable place had come into being. So the next day found me sitting with Emilie Lieberherr, an economist and politician, a member of the City Council, and director of the Department of Social Welfare. Dr. Lieberherr was primarily responsible for the park's establishment. She viewed it as the embodiment of a harm-reduction policy. Intravenous drug use goes on anyway, she argued, and law enforcement is ineffective in stopping it, so why not recognize it and give it a safe place to operate? Distributing syringes and needles and condoms was meant to help reduce the spread of AIDS, the green bus was a statement to addicts that someone cared about them, the social workers available for counseling might help with some urgent problems such as homelessness, and the presence of a physician could save lives.

The humanitarian motive was certainly there. But a more pragmatic (and misanthropic) motive could not escape one's notice. Concentrating illicit drug use in "needle park" cleared addicts out of the rest of the city—the shopping malls, railroad stations, and other public facilities—where merchants and other upright citizens had objected strongly to their presence. The leniency of the police in "needle park" contrasted sharply with their energetic hounding of addicts out of the "respectable" parts of the city.

Later that day I spoke at length with Gonzague Kistler, Surgeon General of the canton of Zurich. He was vituperative in his opposition to "needle park." Centralizing intravenous drug use was exactly the wrong policy, he argued; it should be decentralized by sending addicts back to their home towns and villages, where they were known, where they had family, where they could get individual help, where they could be hospitalized if necessary, where someone cared about them. In addition, he argued, "needle park" acted as a magnet, attracting addicts from elsewhere in Europe, especially from Germany, where drug prohibitions are rigorously enforced. Worst of all, in Dr. Kistler's opinion, the park served to attract unstable young people to the drug scene, and thus to recruit new addicts from among the most vulnerable youths. Finally, he argued, the existence of open and visible drug trafficking and self-injection, under the auspices of the city government and under the eyes of the police, conferred an undesirable cloak of legitimacy on intravenous drug use itself.

As my Boeing 747 climbed away over the city, I could look down on the little park, situated on a tiny island between two streams, right in the center of the city. From this remote vantage point in the sky it seemed a lovely spot. Who would imagine the human misery concentrated down there? It seemed to me that the needle park was a wrong way to deal with the problem of intravenous drug use. I mused over the fact that an economist-politician had advocated and actually managed to establish it, while expert medical opinion opposed it. In much the same way, in the United States, the chief advocacy for legalizing the presently illicit drugs comes from people without medical training, who are uninformed about the actual dangers of the drugs and of drug addiction.

Humane treatment, it seemed to me, could be offered to those addicts who desire it, even while the prohibitions on dangerous drugs remain in effect and are strongly enforced. It seems to me that the citizens of Zurich (or of any city) have a right not to be confronted with addicts using drugs in their streets and public places; but then they also have an obligation to provide humane services to those who are victimized by the addictive drugs. Perhaps there might even be properly equipped and comfortable clinic facilities, where, for a limited time, addicts might actually inject pure drugs under medical supervision. I actually proposed such a scheme years ago (see Suggestions for Further Reading) as a first step in a sequential and comprehensive treatment program; but it has never been tried.

A year after my visit, "needle park" was closed. According to the newspaper reports, it had gotten "completely out of hand." Addicts from all over Europe had poured into the city, crime had soared. The noble (if naive) experiment had failed. But how could it have succeeded? Surely no addicts could have been cured in this park. And now, unfortunately, instead of adopting a more humane approach, stressing treatment, the city officials appear to have gone right back to the punitive police policy of hounding the addicts and driving them underground or to jail or to some other city.

In this chapter an attempt has been made to draw some lessons from addiction policies in three European countries—Great Britain, the Netherlands, and Switzerland. Much of the chapter is based on my own study visits in January 1991. What seems to work well are pragmatic harm-reduction policies based on the disease concept of drug addiction. There is no indication that relaxing prohibitions on the most dangerous addictive drugs (and therefore making them more available) would be useful. The Dutch policy of distinguishing between soft and hard drugs (and the quasi-legalization of cannabis) seems to work there, but it is unclear how effective it would be in America. Finally, the short-lived "needle park" experience in Zurich suggests that simply adopting a laissez-faire attitude toward use of all the presently illicit addictive drugs would not solve any drug addiction problems—least of all the problems that afflict the addicts themselves.

CHAPTER 18

The Legalization Debate

T here has been a lot of talk in recent years about legalizing drugs that are presently illicit. But what, exactly, is meant by legalization? Is cocaine to be sold to minors in supermarkets? Except for the most extreme libertarians, even those advocating "legalization" agree that there have to be some legal restrictions on addictive drugs after all. So we must ask, Which drugs, what restrictions? This chapter examines the dual strategy of supply reduction and demand reduction, considers how corruption undercuts attempts to control supply, draws lessons from the history of alcohol prohibition in the United States, and addresses directly some of the arguments for legalization.

SUPPLY REDUCTION, DEMAND REDUCTION

Obviously, there are two ways to wage a "war on drugs." Most forceful, most visible, and therefore most appealing politically, is to attempt to cut off illicit drugs at the source and at every level of the distribution chain. All such activities are described as *supply reduction*. The other and less dramatic way is by *demand reduction*, comprising all the methods of reducing people's wish to obtain addictive drugs—prevention education, targeting especially vulnerable groups, ameliorating conditions of life that lead to drug-seeking behavior, providing treatment and social rehabilitation services. Certain functions of the law-enforcement system also contribute to reducing demand—for example, incarceration of addicts and the close monitoring of their abstinence while under supervision on probation (an alternative to jail) or parole (following early release).

Supply reduction and demand reduction are not mutually exclusive alternatives. Both strategies have the same goal, to reduce the total consumption of addictive drugs. Supply reduction seeks to accomplish this by reducing the availability of the drugs to the would-be consumer. With ideal success of a supply-reduction strategy, the drug would no longer be available at all. However, this goal is only occasionally and partially attained in one locale or another, and probably can never be achieved universally. The way the supply-reduction strategy actually works is to raise the price of drugs on the street through classic market forces. It should be kept in mind, however, that price can be a confusing measure because pure drugs are rarely sold as such, but are "cut" with inert substances like milk sugar. So the true price has to be expressed per unit weight of pure drug. The street price of what is sold can seem to remain constant, but lower percent purity means higher actual price to the consumer. Drug demand is clearly elastic enough to respond to price changes, so that successful supply reduction can, in principle, reduce demand.

The demand-reduction strategy produces results more slowly—often much more slowly. With respect to prevention, as we saw in Chapter 15, this frustrating pace is illustrated by the nicotine experience. The educational campaign to spread the news about the health hazards of smoking has now been in effect for more than a generation, since the mid-1960s. And it has, indeed, produced a substantial change in smoking behavior. This change is pervasive, it cuts through the whole society, and it is being reinforced year after year by new statutory regulations at the federal, state, and local levels. Nevertheless, there remains a very large group of hard-core nicotine addicts who are unwilling or unable to alter their behavior. More discouraging, the impact on recruitment of new youngsters to this addiction, especially in the past five years, has not been as great as one might have hoped.

With illicit drugs we must expect a similar slow change. First, the uncommitted occasional users will get the educational message, then little by little the more heavily addicted will follow suit, leaving a hard-core group untouched. How easily educational messages will affect the recruiting of youngsters to the use of cannabis, heroin, cocaine, amphetamines, and other illicit drugs is uncertain. Many who are addicted to them—in contrast to cigarette smokers—are alienated from mainstream society, lead chaotic lives, and are not reached easily by educational messages.

Demand reduction by offering treatment is most effective for the hard-core addict group. Every addict reaches a point where life is so out of control (or rather, so controlled by a drug) that some remedy is sought. Often dosage has escalated to an unbearable point, so that obtaining sufficient drug is simply beyond the addict's means. Sometimes a serious adverse effect provokes a decision to seek treatment—a toxic reaction, a near-lethal overdose, a serious infection requiring hospitalization. Sometimes a religious conversion changes the addict's whole outlook on life, and drugs are rejected. As discussed in previous chapters, demand is effectively reduced during treatment, but the big unsolved problem is how to sustain that demand reduction and prevent relapse after treatment.

CORRUPTION

The drug business is, of course, no mom-and-pop affair. In 1990 its volume, internationally, amounted to more than 100 billion dollars. It is run by huge cartels, with resources adequate to ensure the flow of goods to the market and the flow of cash back into their own pockets through an organized system of "money laundering." It is big business, run on a colossal scale. In effect, the cartels have their own armies and their own means of transport by land, sea, and air. Banks under their control, in sheltered spots around the world, manage their huge finances. In countries like Colombia, where much of the cocaine is produced, they openly challenge the government, conducting their operations by a combination of bribery and terror. The brazen way the drug lords of Medellín assassinated judges, prosecutors, and elected officials startled the world a few years ago. And that same kind of outlaw shadow-government operates, to some extent, in other drug-producing countries around the world, such as Peru, Afghanistan, and Thailand. When it comes to interfering with the operations of the drug cartels, "war on drugs" is no longer a metaphor but a reality; the situation calls for actual military force.

The foreign policy of the United States is at least partially responsible for the current situation. During all the years of the Cold War, support of anticommunist forces throughout the world had top priority. The CIA's covert operations were sheltered from scrutiny and often made use of whatever "assets" could be found. For rebels against a government that was under Soviet influence, it was a perfect opportunity to be supported militarily by the United States, while at the same time engaging in the lucrative business of exporting or transshipping drugs. The policy goes back to World War II, when the Office of Strategic Services (the predecessor of the CIA) obtained the help of the Mafia kingpin Charles "Lucky" Luciano in preparing the way for the Allied landing in Sicily. The quid pro quo (whether or not intended) was that the United States turned a blind eye to certain of Luciano's illicit activities, including heroin trafficking. During the Vietnam War, the United States obtained the support of Laos tribesmen by permitting export of their heroin. (These policies are documented in great detail by A. W. McCoy in *The Politics of Heroin*, listed in Suggestions for Further Reading.)

The Kerry Committee of the U.S. Senate brought to light a similar state of affairs concerning the Nicaraguan rebels (the "Contras"). As revealed also in part during the Iran-Contra investigation, the covert nature of U.S. military aid made it easier for the recipients to conduct drug operations than would have been the case in a normal operation open to public scrutiny. Thus, the same aircraft (often operated by CIA dummy companies) that carried arms illegally to Contra bases were used to carry cocaine or marijuana back to the United States. Many citizens—and I was one of them—found it hard to believe that our own government was secretly permitting this drug trafficking at the very time we were professing to conduct a war against drugs. But the Kerry Committee report and other well-documented research findings force an open-minded person to face the facts. CIA officials have always admitted—without confirming the specifics—that covert foreign policy objectives often mean dealing with unsavory characters. For example, if you want to assassinate a Lumumba in the Congo, an Allende in Chile, or a Castro in Cuba (that attempt failed), criminal elements will be on your payroll, and no surprise if some of them are in the drug business! The end of the Cold War may now provide an opportunity to deal more forcefully and more effectively—ideally through the United Nations—with the production and export of addictive drugs in all countries.

To reduce corruption in drug law enforcement within the United States is also not an easy task. All one has to do is read the newspapers to see how frequently agents of the Drug Enforcement Administration or of local police drug squads are arrested, charged, and convicted of either accepting bribes or of actually participating in the drug distribution network. At the lowest level of enforcement—the cop on the beat—newspaper photos of drug markets conducted openly, with police standing by, tell us that something is radically wrong. When money is the carrot and coercion—including the real threat of death—by traffickers is the stick, it is difficult for police officers, bureaucrats in the law-enforcement system, or customs inspectors to resist. And when nothing seems to make a serious dent in drug availability, despite all the rhetoric of politicians, it is little wonder that law-enforcement agents can become cynical. It is not a very big step from cynicism to "Whatever I could do wouldn't have any lasting effect, so I may as well double my salary—I'm underpaid anyway!"

The situation I describe here—locally, nationally, and internationally—powerfully fuels the arguments in favor of legalizing all addictive drugs. According to these arguments, if the presently illicit drugs were legal, the market price would drop drastically, drug quality controls could be implemented, tax revenues could be collected, gun battles for market share would cease, respect for the law would be restored, and corruption would be ended. No doubt many, though probably not all, of these desirable things would happen, but at what cost to the public health? The central issue is the effect of increased availability on the number of first users and consequently on the number who become addicted.

WAS PROHIBITION A FAILURE?

The main premise of the argument in favor of strict legal controls is that they actually reduce the consumption of addictive drugs. If that were not so, all drug regulations would be foolish. The Chinese experience is relevant. Opium addiction was widespread in China in the first half of this century and there were many millions of addicts. Although opium was nominally prohibited, enforcement was lax, corruption was rife, and government officials as well as warlords benefited from the opium traffic. The Communist government, when it came to power in 1949, made eradication of opium addiction a major and well-advertised national goal. Although at that time the methods were not publicized abroad, it is clear now that they were truly Draconian. Evidently, traffickers were summarily executed by the thousands. Addicts were sent to the countryside for rehabilitation through hard labor and re-education after undergoing "cold-turkey" withdrawal. Subsequently their state of abstinence was closely monitored. Experts visiting China after the Cultural Revolution (in the eighties) reported with astonishment that neither drug addicts nor addictive drugs could be found anywhere.

That harsh policy was not an aberration of the early days of the revolutionary regime. While I was teaching a course at Beijing Medical University in 1991, I was told that after a drug-free quarter century, opiate addiction was reappearing because of importation of heroin across the southern border. The government's reaction had not softened with the passage of time. I read a newspaper account and personally watched the TV coverage of a public hanging of 52 alleged heroin traffickers in a public square. Thousands watched, and the governor of the province gave a rousing speech, saying, "This is how we deal with drug traffickers!" Such methods are incompatible with our concepts of personal liberty, and I abhor them. My point here is simply that harsh methods can, without doubt, be effective in reducing the incidence of drug addiction.

Another example comes from Japan. Immediately after World War II, a large supply of amphetamines, which had been stocked by the military, found its way onto the civilian market. A serious epidemic of amphetamine addiction ensued. The government stepped in with strong, unambiguous, and well-publicized law-enforcement measures. Supplies were seized, traffickers and users were jailed. In short order the epidemic was terminated, and amphetamine addiction has not been a serious problem since then in Japan.

Drastic measures are most effective when they command public support. That was true in China, where revolutionary fervor created consensus for the many policies instituted to build the new society. It was true in Japan, where the national will was being mobilized to build a new nation on the ashes of defeat. It is true today in Saudi Arabia and other Moslem countries dominated by Islamic law, where the prohibition of alcohol is enforced with severe penalties.

American history is relevant, too—our national prohibition of alcohol. The temperance movement at the turn of the century led first to state-by-state prohibition laws. By 1916 alcohol was effectively illegal in most states, and this status was codified in federal law by the Eighteenth Amendment and the Volstead Act in the years just after World War I. Everyone knows that Prohibition engendered serious problems. There was widespread bootlegging, new criminal gangs got a foothold, and spectacular violence sometimes erupted as rival traffickers fought for market share. Furthermore, many ordinary citizens violated the law, so that disrespect for law in general was fostered. Those consequences weigh in heavily on the cost side of the ledger. But on the benefit side, it is clear that Prohibition did result in a major reduction in the consumption of alcohol and a concomitant major decrease in the harm caused by alcohol. To say that Prohibition failed is simply wrong without close examination of its effects on alcohol consumption.

Figure 18.1 is a historical record of U.S. deaths from alcoholic liver cirrhosis and from all other causes combined, over a time span of more than 50 years. A continuous slow decline of the general death rate is evident, with a brief upswing during the 1918 influenza epidemic. In contrast, deaths from alcoholic cirrhosis dropped very sharply soon after the institution of Prohibition, remained at a low level throughout that period, and climbed again after repeal in 1933. An important virtue of liver cirrhosis as an indicator is that it is due almost exclusively to alcohol, and that it is a serious enough illness to bring its victims

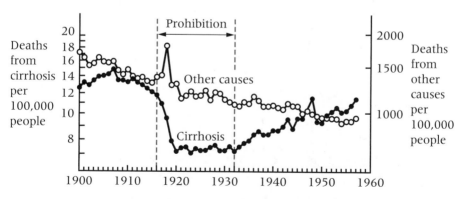

FIGURE 18.1 Death rates from alcoholic liver cirrhosis and all other causes, United States. Vertical scales are logarithmic. [From H. Kalant and O. J. Kalant, *Drugs, Society and Personal Choice*, Addiction Research Foundation, Toronto, 1971, Fig. 5.]

to a hospital; thus it is an objective measure of heavy drinking, which can not easily be concealed. Accurate consumption figures are, of course, impossible to obtain for the period when alcohol was illegal, but research has demonstrated that cirrhosis is a good indicator of total consumption of alcohol by a population. Those who drink most heavily are in the "tail of the distribution curve" (in statistical terms). When everyone drinks more, there are more people in that tail of the curve; when everyone drinks less, there are also fewer heavy drinkers. Interestingly, one might have guessed that even when the population as a whole reduces its consumption, alcoholic addicts do not—that their demand for alcohol is inflexible. The data, however, refute that idea; the response to reduced availability is across the board.

Figure 18.2 presents a similar picture, even more dramatic, for the death rate from cirrhosis in Paris. Deaths from all other causes declined slowly over the 30 years covered by the graph, with a brief increase during the years of World War II. Deaths from cirrhosis were fairly stable until the war came to French soil, when alcohol rationing was instituted: the cirrhosis death rate then fell precipitously. When rationing was abolished, the rate rose promptly again to pre-war levels.

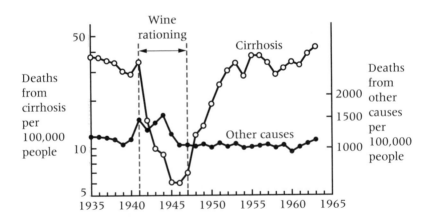

FIGURE 18.2 Death rates from alcoholic liver cirrhosis and all other causes, Paris, France. Vertical scales are logarithmic. [From H. Kalant and O. J. Kalant, *Drugs, Society and Personal Choice*, Addiction Research Foundation, Toronto, 1971, Fig. 6.]

A remarkable experiment was carried out by P. Kuusi in 1951–1953 in several villages of rural Finland that had been "dry" for many years. The farmers residing in these villages could obtain alcohol legally only by travelling some 15-30 miles to a large town with a government monopoly liquor store. Beer and wine stores were opened in selected experimental villages while no change was made in matched control villages. Careful interviewing yielded baseline information about consumption of the various alcoholic beverages before the experiment began. Then the same subjects were interviewed a year or two later. The experiment showed that beer and wine consumption rose dramatically in the villages where the new beer and wine stores were opened. Significantly, these increases were not accompanied by a corresponding decrease in the drinking of legal or illegal hard liquor. So making it easier to get beer and wine resulted in a substantial increase in total alcohol consumption. At the same time there was little or no change in the control villages.

In summary, the consumption of addictive drugs is responsive to availability, and availability is affected by legal status. These are not absolutes, of course. Even when an addictive drug is prohibited—as alcohol was from about 1916 to 1933, or as cannabis, heroin, cocaine, and amphetamines are today—some people break the law and obtain it anyway. But it is easy to appreciate that during Prohibition a person could not walk into the nearest store and buy liquor, nor drop into the corner bar, nor have a couple of martinis at a business lunch, nor partake of beer at an athletic event, nor have a drink or two on an airplane, nor drink wine or champagne openly at a public reception, nor be influenced by liquor advertisements on billboards and in magazines or beer advertisements on television and radio. Yes, some folks did drop into a speakeasy once in a while, and some laid in stocks of bootleg liquor. But all in all, it was much less of a drinking culture than we live in today.

"THE DRUGS I USE ARE NONE OF YOUR BUSINESS"

Among the many definitions of legalization is one that is based on the principle that government has no right to limit people's freedom to do what they wish to their own bodies, and therefore to use whatever drugs they wish. This point of view is easy to understand, and its total consistency makes it attractive. It is usually called libertarian, but I would characterize it as selfishly anarchistic. It is important to recognize its full implications.

Modern societies, especially those with representative governments, try, by means of appropriate laws, to protect their citizens against harm. In our technically advanced civilization, there are many sources of potential harm that the ordinary person is not equipped to understand and recognize or is powerless to avoid. Familiar examples are air and water pollution, toxicity due to lead in gasoline or paint, radioactive waste, inadequately treated sewage, electric shock problems in household appliances, and fire hazards in public accommodations. An example that touches the drug problem concerns toxic substances in foods or cosmetics, and dangerous drugs prescribed by physicians or sold over the counter. Protecting consumers against these various hazards is the function of several federal agencies, such as the Environmental Protection Agency and the Food and Drug Administration, as well as agencies of state, county, and municipal governments.

A somewhat different kind of harm prevention concerns hazards that are obvious, against which prudent people protect themselves. Here risk-taking behavior by some is deemed to be a proper concern of society because the adverse consequences may harm others or because the harm the risk takers do to themselves will place an additional burden on the rest of us. Classic examples of the latter rationale are laws mandating seat belts and motorcycle helmets. The truth is—and fortunately so—we are, on the whole, a compassionate society. Imagine coming upon a motorcycle accident in which the rider lies by the side of the road with severe head injuries. Seeing no helmet, do you ignore the victim and drive away, saying, "Rider, it's your problem, not mine; after all you failed to take sensible precautions"? It seems to me that, like it or not, we are, and ought to be, concerned about our fellow human beings. If that is true, we have a vested interest in risk avoidance by others. No person is an island, and there are few if any truly "victimless" crimes.

As it is a universally accepted principle that the law should protect one person from being harmed by another, we should be especially concerned about the effect of maternal drug use on fetal health and the future development of the child. Every civilized society takes collective responsibility for the educational development of its new citizens, a commitment that is expressed in the fact that we support universal education through taxation, even if we have no children. And there is a growing consensus today that universal access to health care is a right of every citizen and therefore is a burden on every taxpayer. The tragedy of a child born malformed or mentally retarded as a result of unknown causes has always been accepted as a responsibility that a humane society willingly accepts. But what if that tragedy results predictably from maternal drug use? Is not the drug-using behavior of the pregnant woman a legitimate concern for everyone?

If we deny the right of government to be concerned about any of these matters, it will follow, of course, that government has no right to be in the business of regulating addictive drugs. However, if we accept any role of government in harm prevention and harm reduction, we will have to drop the philosophical generalizations and come to grips with details. What degree of regulation is appropriate for which addictive drugs, and for what reason?

The propensity of experimental animals to self-inject heroin or cocaine, and to become truly addicted, is universal. However, it can be modified by environmental factors, so it is not permissible to conclude by analogy that all humans would become addicts if there were no legal controls. We do have to infer, however, that if all addictive drugs were easily available to everyone, and if there were no social pressures of any kind to discourage their use, a very large number of people would become addicted, probably many times the current number. Alcohol and nicotine give us some insight into what can happen when addictive drugs are freely available—there are at least 50 million nicotine addicts and 15 million alcohol addicts in the United States. Since heroin, cocaine, and amphetamines are no less powerfully addictive than alcohol, free availability might well bring us many times more than the few million cocaine and heroin addicts we have now. Is that a price we are willing to pay?

"GIVE THEM THE DRUGS THEY WANT"

Do not make the presently illicit drugs available to everyone—young and old—without restriction, some argue, but do provide the drugs to bona fide confirmed addicts. The argument is that they are already using anyway, and that they are the main source of society's drug problems. The hope is that we might thereby undercut the black market and eliminate drug-related crime. In addition, it is argued, furnishing addicts with pure drugs of reliable quality would improve their health in view of their present use of impure street drugs of uncertain strength. These and similar proposals have been urged repeatedly for some 25 years during the recurrent "war on drugs." Some politicians, fed up with urban crime, believe that if we give the addicts heroin and cocaine and whatever other drugs they want, they will stop stealing and stop shooting each other and innocent passersby. Until one considers the practical details, it seems an ideal way to solve the problem of illicit drugs. However, as noted in Chapter 17, one of the things commented upon by most British experts about the period when heroin was furnished to London addicts at very low cost was the failure of that policy to wean them away from criminal activities. Frequently, illicit drug use and criminality are not cause and effect but parallel forms of antisocial behavior.

Let us consider a few of the practical difficulties in implementing a policy of making the presently illicit drugs available to addicts. Obviously, we would first have to decide who qualifies as an addict. That is not so simple. We could test for dependence on heroin, for example, and then make the drug available only to those who pass the test. But what about the 18-year-old who uses heroin occasionally but has not yet become dependent? When we refuse that person heroin, would we not be saying, Go out and use more, and when you become dependent and can pass our test, we'll give you the heroin you want?

Perhaps dependence is a poor criterion. We might instead say, very simply, that anyone who is already using an illicit drug should be able to get it. We could test a sample of urine and know with certainty if a person has used an opiate or cocaine or amphetamine or marijuana in the previous few days. But what about youngsters who have smoked crack once or twice and liked it, but are not using enough of it (or using it frequently enough) to test positive? Perhaps the price was limiting their use. In order to qualify for legal and cheap supplies of crack, they would first have to use it more heavily on the street.

If people are going to use a black-market drug anyway, it is argued, far better that they use a pure, sterile drug obtained from a clinic. But that word "anyway" is troublesome. The prevalence of addiction is related to the availability and social acceptability of each drug, as well as to how intolerable and oppressive are the conditions under which people live. The easier we make it to obtain a drug, and the more socially acceptable, the more people will use it, especially if nothing has been done to change their conditions of life. The experience of U.S. troops in Vietnam showed clearly, at least for heroin, how drug availability affects drug consumption. There, where heroin was pure, cheap, and readily available, many thousands of American young men became addicted who would never have even experimented with heroin at home. Moreover, when they returned home, the great majority of them never used heroin again.

There would presumably have to be some ceiling on dosage dispensed. We can predict with fair confidence, on the basis of studies at the Lexington facility of the National Institute on Drug Abuse and elsewhere, that heroin and cocaine addicts will escalate their dosage to that ceiling. When their demands for more are rejected, they are likely to look to the street (this happened in Britain), and thus to sustain an illicit market after all. Ironically, the addict would then have to spend even more for the illicit drugs because tolerance to the increased dosage would greatly increase the amount of supplemental drug needed to produce the desired psychotropic effect.

Finally, a complex set of deterrents—not least the illicit status—is presently stopping all but a few children and adolescents from trying heroin. To some degree, the existence of clinics or dispensaries where cocaine and heroin are distributed will provoke the thought, "It can't be all that bad if a government clinic dispenses it. Maybe I can find some and try it—just once, of course." All addicts used their drug "just once" the first time.

Many prominent politicians and thoughtful people from other walks of life who are fed up with crime in the streets think that abolishing drug prohibitions entirely—or at least giving addicts their drugs of choice on demand—will solve the drug problem. But they define the drug problem as crime in the streets rather than as drug addiction itself. According to the medical and public-health perspective presented here, neither the extreme course of legalizing the drugs for everyone nor the more limited one of giving drugs to the addicts would solve any problem—not for society and certainly not for the addicts—but would have predictable adverse consequences. Some problems have no perfect solutions, but some "solutions" can be worse than the problems they are meant to solve.

Drug policy should aim to reduce the prevalence of drug addiction and the recruitment of new addicts. Every policy has its costs, both monetary and human. Prohibitions cause harm, but this harm has to be weighed against the damage that is caused by the drug being prohibited. Chapter 19 proposes concrete policies based on what we know about each family of addictive drugs. The general aim is to achieve an optimal degree of harm reduction by means of a reasonable degree of regulation—as little as necessary—for each addictive drug.

CHAPTER 19

New Strategies for the War on Drugs

What is the purpose of government policy on addictive drugs? What should we be trying to accomplish, and why? It is certainly in the interest of society as a whole to reduce the amount of damage done by drug addiction. This means preventing youngsters from being drawn into using addictive drugs in the first place. It means cutting down the amount of drug use by people already addicted, improving their physical and mental health, and trying to free them of their addiction. It also means reducing the harm caused to others as a result of drug use by addicts. At the same time, we have to take care that implementing drug policy does not cause more harm to individuals and society than do the drugs themselves. To strike the right balance requires careful, thoughtful analysis with a recognition that changes come slowly, that there are no quick fixes.

In the discussion that follows, I first propose general policies that apply to all the addictive drugs and to the drug addiction problem as a whole. Then, since each drug calls for a different approach according to the specific dangers it presents to the individual and to society, I suggest detailed drug-by-drug policies.*

GENERAL POLICIES

1. Consider drug addiction to be primarily a public-health problem. Drug policies have too often been driven by public panic and media hysteria, to which politicians respond by whatever actions they think will be reassuring in the immediate crisis. This pattern does not address the real need. It is time to return the drug problem to the domain of medicine and public health, where it belongs. For many reasons, it is logical to approach drug addiction as if it were an infectious disease (see Chapter 1)—such concepts as incidence, prevalence, relative immunity, and genetic and environmental influence on susceptibility can be applied by analogy to both. Also analogous—and important for preventing the spread of drug addiction—is the fact that it is primarily new users who transmit the behavior to their peers.

Similarly, attempts at eradication, education, treatment, and disease containment are comparable—quarantine, for instance, has sometimes been used, especially in severe and life-threatening epidemics. Quarantine can be an effective tool (particularly for diseases that are transmitted readily by casual contact), but it always raises ethical and legal issues concerning the degree to which it is permissible to restrict the personal liberties of those who are infected in order to protect those who are not.

The argument that the analogy of addiction to infectious disease is false because people are passive victims of infectious disease but actively seek out addictive drugs was discussed at length in Chapter 1. There it was pointed out that in both cases human behavior is responsible, at least in part. The person who gets AIDS through promiscuous unprotected sex and the person who gets lung cancer through addictive smoking are equally responsible for the public-health burden they place on society.

---

* Many of the proposals offered herein are borrowed from a lengthy scholarly article co-authored with my Canadian colleague Dr. Harold Kalant and published in the 28 September 1990 issue of the journal *Science* (volume 249, pp. 1513–1521).

The public-health approach rests on a philosophy of *harm reduction*. This is an attitude, a way of approaching difficult and sometimes intractable problems, which is commonplace in public-health and medical practice. It is the very opposite of rigid, judgmental attitudes based on concepts of morality. Earlier chapters presented examples of how countries like the Netherlands and the United Kingdom have implemented harm-reduction policies in the field of addiction. The reorientation of thinking that is proposed here would counter the kind of simplistic "drug war" mentality that has been so unproductive in the past. The slogan "war on drugs," however, has much to recommend it. It is appropriate in the same way that we might speak of a war on AIDS or a war on poverty. The metaphor implies—correctly, in the case of drug addiction—that there is a serious threat to the people, that national resources need to be mobilized, that a united nation can best accomplish what is called for, that large investments of money and energy will be required, that the effort commands a high priority, that the best minds need to be tapped for solutions, that "business as usual" will not do.

Harm reduction should be a central strategy in the war on drugs. Physicians recognize that some diseases can neither be eradicated nor cured. They simply do the best they can to reduce the harm, acknowledging and accepting that not every problem has a totally satisfactory solution. Illustrative is the physician's approach to a chronic disabling disease like rheumatoid arthritis. No cure is yet known, but the pain and disability can be managed moderately well with appropriate medications. The condition is subject to relapses, even after long periods of remission—a noteworthy similarity to the drug addictions.

The key to treating such conditions is to avoid unrealistic expectations and to accept small victories gratefully. Then it is important not to regard relapse as failure, but rather as a challenge to reinstitute and improve the treatment. Although it would be lovely if by some magical means we could wipe out all drug addictions, that is just not going to happen. Once we recognize and accept that reality, we can go forward to craft realistic policies for reducing the harm done by each addictive drug to the addicts and to society.

A *President's Advisory Committee on Drug Addiction (PACDA)* should be established, in recognition of the importance of the problem to the nation's health. This would be analogous to the existing President's Council of Advisers on Science and Technology (PCAST), a nonpartisan group of experts who advise at the highest level concerning all aspects of science policy. Most of the members ought to be drawn from outside the government—drug addiction experts in the fields of medicine, public health, education, and the law. Represented also should be the Secretaries of the Departments of Health and Human Services, Education, Justice, and Defense. The public-health model must be the stated basis on which PACDA is convened. Its mission will be to draw up specific recommendations for legislative, executive, and judicial actions at federal, state, and local levels of government in order to implement rational and consistent harm-reduction policies. Most important, the mission of PACDA must include all the addictive drugs, not only the illicit ones.

2. Consider crime—whether or not drug-related—to be primarily a law-enforcement problem. Chapter 18 examined some of the arguments for legalizing the presently illicit drugs in the hope of reducing drug-related crime. I noted there that any gains in crime reduction would be more than offset by costs to society due to expanded drug use. Furthermore, the actual reduction in crime would be far less than hoped for by those who believe that most street crimes are direct consequences of drug prohibitions. No doubt a part of the deadly violence in our inner cities is due to battles over market share in the drug business, but no knowledgeable sociologist would deny that the root causes of the violence go much deeper. It is true that criminality is often associated with addiction to the illicit drugs. But criminal actions such as large-scale trafficking, gun battles over turf, burglary, robbery, and shop-lifting should be dealt with on their own terms and not be allowed to detract from the public-health approach to the majority of addicts. Violent crime and property crime, whatever their causes, must be dealt with so that innocent citizens can enjoy the right to live in a safe neighborhood, to go about their peaceful pursuits without fear. In short, we should deal with drug-related crime as we deal with any criminal activity.

Only rarely, in a public-health model, need law enforcement enter the picture in dealing with the majority of the addicts. A constructive policy will distinguish between the victims and the predators, between the addicts and the traffickers, who are the real criminals. And the law can distinguish easily between the health problems of addicts and the serious criminal actions associated with addictive drugs. There is a precedent in the way we handle a legally available drug, alcohol. Numerous control measures are directed principally at the traffickers— the manufacturers, advertisers, and distributors. For example, those who manufacture alcohol illicitly, who distribute it without paying the taxes, or who sell it to minors, are subject to criminal sanctions. But users are affected by the law only to the extent that their drug use results in rowdy behavior, drunk driving, assault, or other violations of the rights of others—behaviors that are in themselves criminal.

The objection is often raised that on the street it is impossible to make a clear distinction between users and traffickers because so many users of illicit drugs are also sellers. I find this a specious argument. The major traffickers deal in such large quantities that their status is unambiguous. The fact is, however, that major traffickers are difficult to apprehend; instead, it is much more attractive to expend police efforts on street addicts, who typically divide and sell some of their own heroin, cocaine, or marijuana. Admittedly, going after the "big fish" is easier said than done, and to do it effectively will require tackling the pervasive problem of corruption at all levels of the law-enforcement system.

The laws on possession of illicit drugs ought to be modified so that we stop filling the jails and prisons with hapless users, as in our present revolving-door system. In this regard, one of the unfortunate consequences of the panic-driven policies of recent years has been the establishment of mandatory minimum sentences for drug offenders. This misguided approach has deprived judges of the discretionary power to distinguish, in the case of illicit drugs, between major and minor crimes, between significant and trivial offenses. Judge Robert W. Sweet of the U.S. District Court in New York has been an especially strong voice for restoring judicial discretion in sentencing, and other judges have supported his position. In short, the principle of letting the punishment fit the crime needs to be reestablished in the field of drug offenses.

A rational and cost-effective policy would also relieve the present overburdening of the courts and jails with minor offenses by addicts and would concentrate almost entirely on interrupting the distribution chain at higher levels. Totally eliminating the supply of illicit drugs is an illusory hope so long as demand remains strong and the funds available for purchases are sufficient to support the international cartels and to corrupt the law-enforcement system. Nevertheless, there is certainly value—even symbolic value can be important—in continuing to make arrests of major traffickers and in seizing large drug shipments at our borders. However, present allocations in the 12 billion dollar annual federal budget for the U.S. "war on drugs"—70% for supply reduction, 30% for demand reduction—seem to be badly out of balance. At the very least, these proportions ought to be reversed. That

such a drastic change would not have a disastrous effect can be sur-
mised from the Canadian experience, where 30% for supply reduction
and 70% for demand reduction has been the rule for years.

3. Make demand reduction the primary strategy. Throughout
history societies have attempted to eliminate one addictive drug or
another (whichever was most abhorrent to the dominant culture) by
harsh punitive measures, including even capital punishment for the
users. Sometimes such measures have been effective, as was noted in
Chapter 18. But whether truly Draconian policies might work is really
an academic question for Americans. American society is built on respect for human rights, as enshrined in the U.S. Constitution's Bill of
Rights. To sacrifice those principles for the sake of reducing or even
eliminating (if it were possible) drug addiction would—I hope and
trust—not be acceptable to the majority of citizens.

Therefore, without infringing on constitutional liberties, the best
hope of making a significant impact on the drug problem is to reduce
demand, and to do so patiently and systematically, by a two-part approach.

One part is to expand prevention education. Continue and ac-
celerate the current trend toward honest, health-based, elementary
and secondary education about all addictive drugs. Get rid of the misleading terms "alcohol and drugs" and "nicotine and drugs," which
imply that alcohol and nicotine are not drugs, whereas they are actually the ones that cause the greatest harm to public health. Moreover,
they are the gateway drugs, the ones that children and adolescents use
first, after which some of them progress to marijuana, cocaine, and
heroin.

Educate in an even-handed manner about the effects of all the
addictive drugs. "Just say no!" is useful and necessary, but by no means
sufficient. Teach why saying no is a wise policy. Teach that children
should not use any addictive drugs because—whatever their legal
status—they are harmful to health and can lead to uncontrolled use
and all the consequences of the addicted state. Concerning those drugs
that are illicit, every child, at the appropriate grade level, should be
taught respect for the law in a context of learning the history and basis
of the drug laws and the mechanisms that a democratic society makes
available for debating and changing them.

The other part of the approach is to make treatment readily and
universally available. This is one of the most reliable and cost-effective

ways of reducing demand for drugs. As noted earlier, the number of funded treatment "slots" presently falls far short of meeting the demand. Every day an addict spends in treatment is a day of reduced drug use and of reduced crime (to the extent that criminal activity was motivated by the need to support the addiction). As discussed in preceding chapters, this socially beneficial effect of treatment on drug-related crime has been well demonstrated. In addition, since the addict's motivation to enter treatment is often weak, finding a treatment facility and being admitted rapidly to treatment must be made easy. We have much to learn from the Netherlands about how to do this, as explained in Chapter 17.

4. Enact and implement laws that support social norms. Advocates of drug legalization commonly argue as though legal restrictions and education were mutually exclusive. They point to the salutory progress in the United States in reducing the prevalence of nicotine addiction. "See," they argue, "the harmful use of an addictive drug is best reduced through education, through health consciousness, in short, through voluntary actions *rather than* through governmental intrusions." But "rather than" implies a false dichotomy, which distorts what actually happened with tobacco smoking.

What is really interesting about the historic decline in smoking over the last 25 years is that it illustrates how laws and education complement each other. Which leads which? is a question that can be argued endlessly for each drug. In the case of smoking, it is clear that biomedical science led the way in providing irrefutable evidence of the health hazards—evidence summarized in the 1964 Surgeon General's Report. Then, as education made people more aware of the health hazards and made nonsmokers more aware of their rights, people became more accepting of increased regulation. As an example, the ban on smoking in commercial air travel was instituted on flights of two hours or less, then later extended to all domestic flights. Regulation of smoking in restaurants began with establishment of smoking and nonsmoking sections, but now, in many places, it is giving way to a total prohibition. As awareness grew, and with more nonsmokers and former smokers in the population, tougher regulations became acceptable, such as prohibition of smoking in all public facilities and in the workplace. A nice example of a symbolic action with wide educational impact is the recently instituted ban on smoking in the White House. Increased taxation as a means of reducing consumption is also becoming more acceptable. Much more needs to be done, as proposed below, but we see here a working model of how regulations can promote attitudinal change, and how attitudinal change can make ever tougher regulations more acceptable. These examples also illustrate how regulations short of complete prohibition can sometimes be effective without significantly criminalizing an addictive behavior. At the same time, educational efforts concerning harm reduction should be directed to those hard-core addicts who continue to resist total abstinence.

5. Address the spread of AIDS by intravenous drug users. We need—urgently—to deal, head-on, with the role of intravenous drug use (primarily of cocaine, amphetamines, and heroin) in the spread of AIDS. The AIDS virus (HIV) accidentally found a foothold in the community of gay men in the United States, but it soon spread, through bisexual contacts, to an increasing number of women. The spread of HIV among intravenous drug users, both gay and heterosexual, affects all of society, for the virus will not confine itself to the addict group any more than it has to the gay community. Prostitutes, especially, play a role in transmitting the virus; and prostitution is a common means of financial support for addicts. Providing sterile needles and condoms to all addicts is a policy already instituted in many communities, and it ought to be implemented everywhere. The data now show convincingly that providing sterile needles and syringes does not recruit new users to the pool of intravenous drug users.

It is true that there is no scientific proof that needle exchanges and condom distribution will stop the spread of HIV among intravenous drug users. However, the public-health approach to a death-dealing virus must be based on whatever partial evidence is already available, on common sense, and on the need to teach the facts about intravenous drug use and AIDS. Unfortunately, powerful forces are opposed to this simple public-health measure because of worry about "sending the wrong kind of message." It seems to me that the wrong kind of message would be "We don't care whether AIDS continues to spread or not." With respect to needle exchanges, as for some other aspects of drug policy, we have much to learn from countries like the United Kingdom and the Netherlands.

Even more important than needle exchanges in stemming the spread of the AIDS epidemic is the expansion of methadone maintenance programs to accommodate all heroin addicts who are willing to enroll. It is irrefutable that when addicts are stabilized on an adequate dosage of methadone in a well-run program with ancillary services, they drastically reduce or discontinue their intravenous drug use and thus their sharing of needles.

6. Address the problem of fetal damage caused by addictive drugs. The special problem of addictive drug use by pregnant women will need urgent and very careful consideration by PACDA. This issue is of major concern to society for both humanitarian and economic reasons. Drugs used by a pregnant woman affect in several ways how her fetus will develop and thus how much of a burden that child may ultimately be on society. First, there are the obvious congenital malformations, such as are seen in fetal alcohol syndrome. Second, evidence (though still inconclusive) from both animal and human studies suggests the possibility of permanent damage to the developing brain, resulting in mental retardation and behavioral abnormalities that may only be evident years later. Third, both because of drug effects and because the addicted woman is unlikely to maintain her own health during pregnancy, the infant is likely to be born prematurely and of low birth weight, causing an array of adverse health consequences. Fourth, the newborn baby is likely to be dependent on the addictive drug and require detoxification treatment.

What to do about this problem is a thorny question. The noncontroversial part of the answer is that pregnant addicts ought to be afforded free treatment for their drug addiction, coupled with free prenatal care; that is a good cost-effective investment for society. But should we do more? PACDA needs to consider whether a case can be made for compulsion—for allowing the interests of society to override the civil liberties of the individual. Long-acting injectable contraceptives, which have recently come onto the market, can be made available. Some argue that court-ordered compulsory contraception may be appropriate in some cases. Compulsory diagnostic procedures, which are virtually free of risk, could provide findings that would justify abortion of a severely damaged fetus. Public debate is needed about how to develop disincentives to pregnancy in untreated addicts, and about the degree to which the interest of society in healthy babies justifies government intervention. The birth of a drug-damaged child is not only a tragedy; it can also be considered a crime against humanity—provided, of course, that effective alternatives are made universally available to female addicts of child-bearing age.

7. Increase funding for basic and applied research. This recommendation may be discounted as self-serving, coming as it does from a researcher. History teaches us, however, that investment in biomedical research pays off handsomely. The more we know, the better we can apply our knowledge to solve problems. Basic research yields the understanding that permits us to fashion novel practical solutions, without which there would be only guesswork and superstition. Applied research teaches us how best to develop and implement the novel practical solutions.

Consider the development of methadone maintenance. Many years of basic research on the biologic actions of opiates were needed before—in Germany during World War II—methadone could be synthesized as a morphine substitute for pain relief. Since the chemical structure of methadone is not even close to that of morphine, it never would have been developed were it not for the deep understanding, generated over many years of basic research, of those structural properties of the morphine molecule that were responsible for its biologic effects. And the idea of using methadone for maintenance because of its long duration of action depended on much prior research concerning how drugs are metabolized and eliminated from the body. Finally, applied research was needed to demonstrate that methadone really works in heroin addicts, that it is both safe and efficacious.

Both basic and applied research deserve support as part of any coordinated government attack on drug addiction. PACDA should review the mechanisms of research funding to see if there is need for greater leadership at the federal level in ensuring that the most important problems in addiction are attacked as promptly as new knowledge and new technology permit. Numerous unsolved problems call for solutions. For example, we are desperately in need of treatment for cocaine addiction. Why is no satisfactory pharmacotherapy available? Because it is only recently that basic research has shown us where and how cocaine acts in the brain. With that knowledge in hand, it might now be possible to develop surrogate agonists analogous to methadone or antagonists analogous to naltrexone. If we understood more about the neurochemistry of craving, we might be able to develop anti-craving medications, and thus address the all-important relapse problem. We might discover how to prevent the paranoid psychosis that results from heavy binge use of cocaine or amphetamines. If we knew more about the brain damage caused by chronic use of these drugs, we might learn how to prevent or repair that damage. We might even learn how to prevent or reverse the destructive effects of alcohol or cocaine on brain development in the unborn child.

DRUG-BY-DRUG POLICIES

Each of the addictive drugs calls for a different degree and kind of regulation. The sensible policy for each one will lie somewhere between total legalization and total prohibition. Some of the drugs need tighter regulation than we have now, some need a relaxation of prohibitions, and some need no major policy change at all. My recommendations are not set in concrete; policies ought to be flexible enough to adapt to changing conditions. Therefore the drug-by-drug policies will have to be reexamined continuously by PACDA.

1. Nicotine. Here we have a powerfully addictive and dangerous drug that is too easily available at far too low a cost, and that consequently causes enormous harm to individuals and society. The public-health hazard of nicotine addiction consists in the chronic diseases and death caused by tobacco smoking, the damage to the fetus of pregnant, heavily addicted smokers, and the minor health effects of second-hand smoke. In an ideal world, tobacco products would be banned entirely, would not be manufactured, would not be sold. Possibly, had the health costs been recognized a century ago, total prohibition of nicotine products might have saved millions of lives. However, to institute prohibition now, when so many people are already addicted, would engender new and significant costs of many kinds. Nevertheless, many positive steps short of outright prohibition could be taken which would be effective from a harm-reduction standpoint. Specifically, I would propose several types of action, as outlined in the following paragraphs.

First of all, make it harder for minors to get cigarettes. Most states do have laws forbidding sales to minors, but they are not well enforced. Banning cigarette machines would have a beneficial impact. The most useful measure, in my opinion, would be to restrict the sale of tobacco products to liquor stores, where effective means of preventing sales to minors have long been in effect. At the same time, without denying any adults the right to purchase tobacco products, it would be less convenient for them than if they had merely to go to the local drug store or supermarket.

Second, regulate cigarette advertising more strictly and invest public funds in counter-advertising, as was mandated not long ago in

California by a voter initiative. As cigarette advertising is already banned from radio and television, there is precedent for attempting to ban it also from the print and billboard media. An interesting legal challenge for consumer advocates will be to discover how to prohibit incidental background advertising in motion pictures or television, such as showing a cigarette brand name in the background at a sports event, or emblazoned on the T-shirts of athletes. Ban blatant propaganda directed to children, such as the notorious "Joe Camel" advertisements; such advertising could also be challenged through class action law suits against the tobacco companies, brought by parents with support from the government. The claim (some would say spurious claim) of First Amendment rights raised by the tobacco companies should be pursued through the courts until a clarification of constitutional law is achieved. It may be noted in this connection that the First Amendment has not been construed to prevent FDA or other consumer protection agencies from prohibiting false product labeling and false advertising.

Third, increase taxes on tobacco products in order to reduce consumption, but without raising the price so high as to promote a significant black market. Earmark the tax revenues exclusively for prevention education (including anti-smoking advertisements), treatment of hard-core smokers, and research on nicotine addiction. Current policy, both at the federal and state levels, treats tobacco (and alcohol) taxes as general revenue. The proposed change would have only a small impact on total tax revenues—1% for the federal government, 2% on average for the states. The chief reasons for earmarking are to get rid of the present immoral arrangement in which the government profits from sales of this truly destructive substance and to avoid any ambivalence (however subconscious) on the part of government about the desirability of reducing tobacco consumption. In addition, substantial incremental sums (in 1988 about 5 billion dollars federally, another 5 billion in the states) would become available for prevention education, treatment, and research—sums that would decrease appropriately in proportion to decreased need as consumption decreases.

Fourth, continue to institute new restrictive regulations about where and when smoking is permitted. As the number of nicotine addicts declines—it is now down to 28% in the United States—such restrictions become more and more socially acceptable; indeed they are demanded by the majority. Ordinary citizens can play a constructive role by helping to create an anti-smoking climate in their own communities, withholding their patronage, if necessary, from businesses that promote, advertise, or glamorize smoking.

Finally, bring economic policies of the federal government with respect to tobacco into line with its status as a product which, when used as directed, causes illness and death. Enact legislation to prevent tobacco exports. An early step could be to abrogate the present government policy of actively promoting tobacco exports, especially to developing countries, where demand is very high and anti-smoking campaigns are only just being initiated. At the same time, abolish all domestic subsidies to tobacco growers, coupling this with active steps to promote alternative crops.

2. Alcohol and related drugs. Like nicotine, these dangerous addictive drugs, especially alcohol itself, are responsible for huge social costs. Alcohol is directly responsible for an enormous number of accidental deaths, homicides, and chronic illnesses with fatal outcome. From the public-health standpoint, alcohol is as dangerous to the addicted user as is nicotine, and it is clearly more dangerous to the fetus. Moreover, unlike nicotine, its direct effects on behavior are much more dangerous to society as a whole. The present degree of regulation varies greatly among the states. One example is the definition of the blood alcohol level considered to be presumptive evidence of "driving while intoxicated." Another example is the restriction of sales—only Canada and a few U.S. states now do this—to state-run liquor stores. Greater uniformity would be desirable to convey an unambiguous message to the public about the dangers of this addictive drug. (An analogy that comes to mind is the uniform national speed limit on the highways.)

Much could be done to discourage consumption without returning to outright prohibition, as suggested in the following paragraphs.

First, as with nicotine, increase taxation to a degree that would discourage consumption without unduly encouraging a black market. The optimum level could be found experimentally by keeping accurate records of sales and hiking the tax from time to time or from place to place over a long period. As proposed for tobacco, earmark the tax revenues for prevention education, treatment, and research. Continue and expand the policy of taxing weaker products like beer and wine less than distilled liquors as a means of trying to shift consumption from the stronger and more dangerous to the weaker and less dangerous product.

Second, remove alcohol, in all its forms, from supermarket shelves, and restrict its sale to licensed liquor stores. This recommendation is supported by the Canadian experience, which showed increased consumption when service by clerks was supplanted by self-service. Consider the further step of permitting only state-operated liquor stores, making it less convenient but still possible to purchase liquor, and at the same time removing commercial pressures on the public to buy. As noted for tobacco, this restriction to special liquor stores will also be effective in preventing sales to minors.

Third, find a legally acceptable formula for abolishing "happy hours" and all other reduced-price gimmicks that are intended to increase consumption of alcohol. Establish alcohol-free times and places; a working model already exists in the British policy of forcing pubs to close during certain hours of every day. Ban alcohol on college campuses and at sports events and other public entertainments and ceremonies, and make it unavailable under as many circumstances as possible—for example, in all forms of public transportation. Make all official federal, state, and local government social functions alcohol-free, thus setting a model for alcohol-free office parties and private receptions. Measures like these help, albeit slowly, to change the present societal acceptance of alcohol as a natural, virtually indispensable accompaniment of so many social activities.

Fourth, forbid all advertising of alcoholic beverages, including beer and wine, in all the media; and find a way also to restrict background advertising, as with tobacco products. Citizen pressure on the motion picture and television industries to eliminate favorable depictions of drinking (as of smoking) could be highly effective. PACDA, as well as private organizations, could promote and coordinate such public campaigns with respect to all the addictive drugs.

Fifth, continue the present trend toward tougher law enforcement on "driving while intoxicated." Establish the uniform low blood level of 0.05% in all the states as presumptive evidence of intoxication; this level may be attained after only one or two drinks, and research has established that it causes definite behavioral impairment. Make penalties for drunk driving more severe, as in countries like Sweden—for example, loss of driver's license for a year at the first offense, jail time for the second offense. Effective law enforcement does, indeed, alter behavior, as evidenced by the "designated driver" procedure that has long been in effect in Sweden and is becoming popular now in the United States. I favor random roadblocks with compulsory breathalyzer testing on the highways, despite the arguments of civil libertarians. As long as the stops are truly random and the highway police are not permitted to use the occasion for irrelevant searches, it seems to me that protection of the public from dangerous drivers far out-weighs the inconvenience and alleged "invasion of privacy."

Finally, PACDA in consultation with the medical profession should study the controversy over the prescribing of benzodiazepines. These drugs are much like alcohol in their neurochemical, behavioral, and addictive properties; and they are therefore classified with alcohol in this book. Reckless overprescribing of benzodiazepines (such as Valium) has, in some cases, produced a significant addiction problem. Although these drugs are intended to allay anxiety and promote sleep, their effects tend to dissipate on regular long-term use, and dependence (especially on high dosages) then makes discontinuance difficult. In 1990 New York state instituted a system of triplicate prescriptions with centralized record keeping. The number of prescriptions fell dramatically. More impressive, the street price of illicit benzodiazepines rose, indicating that there had been significant diversion under the old and less tightly controlled system. Critics claim, however, that psychiatrists and other physicians are now more reluctant to prescribe these drugs even when their patients would be benefited. Moreover, more dangerous anti-anxiety and sleep-promoting drugs are sometimes being prescribed instead. The question—which requires more solid data before it can be answered—is whether benzodiazepines should be more tightly regulated on a national basis.

3. Opiates. Retain the present total prohibition on heroin (which is not needed in medical practice) and the present restriction of other opiates to medical use; I see no compelling reason to modify their current legal status. The immediate need is for expansion of methadone treatment so that all who wish treatment can obtain it easily. This is especially important as an effective means of preventing the transmission of HIV by needle sharing. The Dutch system of "low-threshold" treatment programs has much to recommend it, based on the reality that when motivation to seek treatment is weak, it is in society's best interest to "go the extra mile" to bring addicts into treatment. "Going the extra mile" may even be taken literally, with methadone dispensed from a mobile van to registered addicts in their own neighborhoods—an approach that might circumvent the interference of local zoning regulations with establishing methadone clinics.

Expedite FDA approval of alternative surrogate opiates such as LAAM and buprenorphine (and new medications as they are developed) so as to give physicians a full range of pharmacologic options for treatment. The historic record clearly shows that heroin addiction is a serious life-threatening disease, that the life expectancy of heroin addicts is radically shortened because of suicide, violence, infections (now including AIDS), associated alcoholism, and overdoses. This poor prognosis places heroin addiction in the same category as certain cancers and other lethal diseases like AIDS, which have required FDA to reconsider its caution over the possible toxicity of proposed medications in view of the urgent need for treatment. The rigorous scientific criteria for proof of safety and efficacy, appropriate in most contexts, may have to be relaxed somewhat in recognition of the known high probability of a fatal outcome in heroin addiction.

Proper medical practice entails determining, by an appropriate diagnostic test, that an applicant for treatment is a bona fide confirmed opiate addict, as described in Chapter 10. Therefore, make diagnosis and treatment of opiate addiction the exclusive business of physicians and health workers, without bureaucratic interference by state and federal governments. Establish medical (not governmental) criteria for admission to treatment, for dosage, and for duration of treatment. The legitimate role of government is to ensure that methadone and similar surrogate opiates, which are lethally dangerous to nontolerant people, are administered under strictest supervision. Allow patients to take the medication at home only after they have demonstrated by their behavior and by urine testing that they have stopped using illicit drugs and are responsible enough to exercise due caution. Finally, with treatment universally available, hold to account for their crimes any addicts who continue to engage in criminal activities, just as if they were not drug addicts.

4. Cocaine and amphetamines. Because of the dangerous behaviors induced by these drugs—more disruptive to the user and more threatening to society than the effects of opiates—and because of the intensity of the addiction, leave in place the present prohibitions.

More research is needed, both basic and applied, that could lead to effective pharmacotherapy for this addiction. Research is also urgently needed, both in animals and in humans, to establish conclusively if, under what conditions, and to what extent cocaine and amphetamines are harmful to fetal development, especially as regards the intellectual development of a child born to an addicted mother. The potential consequences are so serious that the present lack of solid information about this question seems truly absurd. Addiction to cocaine (especially to crack), although far from our most important problem in terms of numbers of people affected, is certainly, together with alcohol, the most serious in terms of disruptive effects on society.

5. Cannabis. Although this drug can not be described as harmless, the present degree of regulation seems excessive (cannabis is legally almost indistinguishable from opiates or cocaine in this respect). The key question is whether relaxing the prohibition on marijuana would lead to a major increase in the number of users. The Dutch experiment suggests that this might not happen. There may, indeed, be advantages (as the Dutch argue) in making cannabis available through mechanisms that do not bring users into contact with traffickers in the "hard" drugs (heroin and cocaine). On the principle that weak forms of an addictive drug are safer than concentrated forms, any experimental modification of the present prohibition should apply only to marijuana leaf, not to hashish.

I suggest that PACDA study this issue with a view to implementing a few controlled experiments in penalty reductions or in discretionary enforcement of the laws. The key phrase here is "controlled experiments." First, before making any change in the legal status of cannabis, ensure that data systems are in place for following the outcome systematically. Second, allow the modified regulations to operate for long enough to establish clearly what happens. As social changes occur only slowly, "long enough" could mean many years, even decades. Finally, by appropriate use of pardons or parole, rectify the injustices being suffered right now by some unfortunates who posed no threat to society but are nevertheless serving prison terms for mere possession of modest amounts of marijuana for personal use. Let the punishment fit the crime!

On the other hand, stricter enforcement is required, with adequate testing, to ensure that cannabis is not used in sensitive professions (for example, transportation) where public safety is at stake. Likewise, when technology permits, the public deserves to be protected from impaired motorists "driving while stoned"—just as it can now be protected from those "driving while intoxicated"—for example by random stops for marijuana testing on the highway.

More animal research is urgently needed to clarify whether irreversible brain damage can be caused by heavy chronic use of cannabis. A few research reports have indicated truly alarming toxic effects on the brain; but remarkably, no government agencies have taken the lead to ensure that adequate replications of the critical experiments would be carried out.

Finally, prevention education has an especially important role in blocking the progression, in young people, from the gateway drugs, nicotine and alcohol, to cannabis. The sustained downward trend in cannabis use among high school students is encouraging, but more data are needed on dropouts—the very ones who are most likely to become users of cannabis. PACDA should focus major attention on the cost-effectiveness of prevention education techniques, so that what works and can be afforded is quickly implemented nationally. And equally important, what does not work, or works only marginally, or is absurdly expensive, should be eliminated. When social scientists make a heavy investment of research funds and energy and emotion in a particular education project, it is easy to understand their bias in its favor. But research on prevention education, because such large numbers of students have to be studied over such a long time, is necessarily very, very expensive, and therefore requires stringent, objective evaluation in the public interest.

6. Caffeine.   Certainly caffeine is the least harmful of the addictive drugs, yet it is also the most widely used; and there is increasing concern that it may not be entirely harmless after all. Medical experts worry about the large amounts of caffeine taken freely by children in the form of soft drinks. An educational campaign to reduce caffeine consumption would be in order, complemented by the commercial manufacturers' production of caffeine-free products to cater to an expanding market. Indeed, the consumption of decaffeinated coffee and caffeine-free herb tea has been increasing steadily. Could caffeine be removed entirely as a food additive, and retained only in natural products like coffee and tea? The Food and Drug Administration can mandate this and other measures, such as requiring a warning label or discouraging sales to children. These are policies that should be studied by PACDA. Although there would surely be no harm in promoting a caffeine-free diet for children, I do not think sufficient evidence is yet in hand to make a firm recommendation for government action.

7. Hallucinogens.   The hallucinogenic drugs constitute a vanishingly small part of the total drug addiction problem. Nevertheless, their unpredictable (and sometimes truly dangerous) effects on behavior justify the present prohibition on their use. The popularity of hallucinogens waxes and wanes, and with the passage of time one or another comes into and goes out of fashion. As they appeal primarily to youngsters looking for new sensations, intensive education is desirable to warn of the true hazards. Illustrative of the problem is the recent epidemic use of "ecstasy" (see Chapter 14) on college campuses before the possible risk of brain damage became known. There seems to be a widespread lack of understanding of the danger—in principle— of exposing the brain to any substance that grossly alters its function. This carelessness about chemical maltreatment of the brain is probably in large measure a consequence of the inadequate teaching of biologic science at all levels of our educational system.

A specific issue that requires PACDA study and recommendation is the legal status of peyote, as used in the religious services of the Native American Church (see Chapter 14). Although federal laws and those of 23 states exempt this practice from the prohibitions on hallucinogens, the Supreme Court in 1990 ruled that the states are not required to do so, despite the religious freedom clause of the First Amendment.

WHAT NEXT?

In this book I have taken you on a long journey through familiar and unfamiliar territory. The rationale for writing it was my conviction that by learning more about drug addiction, in all its complexity, the intelligent citizen of a democracy would be better equipped to understand and evaluate the way society now deals with the drugs and the addicts.

Part One explored similarities and differences among the seven families of addictive drugs—their actions in the brain, their addictiveness, and the way they induce tolerance and dependence. The basis was laid for considering drug addiction to be primarily a public-health problem. An important goal of future research will be to work out all the chemical steps between the binding of an addictive drug to its receptor and the ultimate effect of the drug on reward systems and behavior. Another research aim is to learn about genetic predisposition to addiction in order to clarify why it is that only a fraction of all the people who try an addictive drug find it attractive enough to use repeatedly and thus to become addicts. Research accomplishments will inevitably lead to novel methods of prevention and treatment, as they always have in the field of biomedicine.

Part Two expanded on the theme—drug by drug—that addicts are victims of a disease. For each of the seven drug families we saw how the disease typically develops and how it can be treated. These chapters laid the basis for the later discussions of what degree of regulation is appropriate for each drug. Future research will focus on establishing, in rigorous trials, what present treatments are best for each addiction, and what better treatments can be developed.

Part Three examined some major societal issues concerning prevention education, treatment, and relapse. We noted that although criminality is associated with addiction to the illicit drugs, blaming the criminal behavior wholly on the addiction is entirely too simplistic. The major role of intravenous drug use in the epidemic spread of AIDS was analyzed. British, Dutch, and Swiss approaches to the addictive drugs were considered to see what lessons might be learned for U.S. drug policy. The debate over legalizing addictive drugs was analyzed, recognizing that most people do agree that drugs need some degree of regulation. I have suggested that the degree of regulation ought to be different for each drug, tailored to the danger posed by that drug to individual and societal health and well-being. In the present chapter, therefore, I have offered general and specific recommendations for drug policy consistent with our present scientific and medical knowledge. The central theme here again was that drug addiction should be regarded as primarily a public-health problem, and addressed accordingly at all levels of government.

Government actions are important in addressing the drug addiction problem, but they are not enough. In a democratic society, public involvement is also essential—to help bring about the needed statutory and regulatory changes through the political process, to create an environment supportive of those changes, and to promote the attitude that drug addiction is primarily a public-health problem. I hope that concerned citizens, better informed after reading this book, may contribute in one way or another to making the "war on drugs" more effective by urging their elected officials to adopt more rational drug policies. A few illustrative examples:

- Support organizations like Mothers Against Drunk Driving, which are influential in promoting the necessary tougher regulations on alcohol.

- Make known to the media and the advertisers your outrage about the glamorization of alcoholic beverages, cigarettes, and other addictive drugs in the motion pictures, television, radio, and print media.

- Exert political pressure on Congress and the White House to reverse the absurd 70:30 funding ratio of supply reduction to demand reduction in the "war on drugs," to abolish all forms of tobacco subsidy, and to stop the cynical export of our tobacco products to third-world countries.

■ Demand that treatment be made readily available for all addicts who seek it.

If you find merit in my recommendations, make yourself a crusader for change. Very likely, drug addictions will always be with us, but eventually the harm they cause can be reduced considerably. The key strategy is—through education as well as through laws that reinforce the social norm—to change public attitudes, and thus to reduce demand. Addictive drugs affect us all, and we can all help to create a new climate of awareness and understanding.

Suggestions for Further Reading

This annotated list contains a selection of books and articles that either expand on some of the topics in the book or provide further historic background. Besides the readings that are listed under General Sources, materials relevant to particular chapters will be found under chapter headings. (References are organized in chronologic order within each subdivision).

The following simple key will help guide the reader in choosing among the readings:

A. Nontechnical, easy reading for the nonexpert; or written for the expert but understandable without too much difficulty by the nonexpert.

B. Technical, written for scientists; includes references to the scientific literature concerning experiments described in the text.

A/B. A mix of both; or difficult material but not wholly inaccessible to nonexperts.

GENERAL SOURCES

A. H. Kalant, O. J. Kalant: *Drugs, Society and Personal Choice*. (Paper Jacks, General Publishing Co., Ontario, 1971.)

Despite its early publication date, this little gem, directed primarily toward the intelligent lay reader, is still instructive and worthwhile.

A. E. M. Brecher: *Licit and Illicit Drugs*. (Little, Brown, Boston, 1972.)

This book, commissioned by Consumers Union, was a landmark first attempt to treat all addictive drugs in an even-handed manner. Although strongly biased in favor of decriminalizing possession of all drugs, it nevertheless remains an important source of information. Several of the specific recommendations for changes in drug policy are similar to those proposed here in Chapter 19.

A. D. R. Gerstein, H. J. Harwood, Eds.: *Treating Drug Problems*, Vol. 1. (Institute of Medicine, National Academy Press, Washington, DC, 1990.)

An analysis by an expert committee of the multiplicity of health and social problems associated with drug addiction in the United States.

B. A. G. Gilman, T. W. Rall, A. S. Niles, P. Taylor, Eds.: *Goodman and Gilman's The Pharmacological Basis of Therapeutics*, 8th ed. (Pergamon, New York, 1990.)

The definitive textbook of pharmacology. It includes major chapters on addictive drugs and on general aspects of drug metabolism.

B. W. B. Pratt, P. Taylor, Eds.: *Principles of Drug Action—The Basis of Pharmacology*, 3d ed. (Churchill Livingstone, New York, 1990.)

Detailed technical treatment of many pharmacologic principles that are applicable to the addictive drugs. This is the standard textbook for graduate students in pharmacology.

B. C. P. O'Brien, J. H. Jaffe, Eds.: *Addictive States*. (Volume 70, Research Publications, Association for Research in Nervous and Mental Disease, Raven Press, New York, 1992.)

This multi-author collection, of varying degrees of technical difficulty, is extremely informative and up-to-date, covering biology, toxicology, behavior, epidemiology, and treatment.

A/B. National Institute on Drug Abuse (NIDA) Research Monograph Series, U.S. Department of Health and Human Services (DHHS), Rockville, MD, available from U.S. Government Printing Office, Washington, DC 20402.

A monograph series devoted exclusively to addictive drugs and drug addiction. More than 100 volumes (and more are added every year), each a collection of articles of varying degrees of technical sophistication on important and timely aspects of drug addiction.

A/B. Biomedical journals devoted exclusively to addictive drugs and drug addiction:

Addiction Research
Addictive Diseases
Advances in Alcohol and Substance Abuse
Alcohol
Alcohol and Alcoholism
Alcohol and Drug Research
Alcoholism: Clinical and Experimental Research
American Journal of Drug and Alcohol Abuse
British Journal of Addiction
Chemical Dependencies
Drug and Alcohol Dependence
International Journal of the Addictions
Journal of Addictive Diseases
Journal of Drug Issues
Journal of Psychoactive Drugs
Journal of Studies on Alcohol
Journal of Substance Abuse Treatment
Recent Developments in Alcoholism

CHAPTER 1: INTRODUCTION

B. E. C. Senay: "Drug Abuse and Public Health—A Global Perspective." (*Drug Safety* 6, Supplement 1: 1–65, 1991.)

A comprehensive worldwide survey, with several hundred references and detailed tables, documenting the case that addictive drugs present public-health problems (often, at present, of increasing severity) in all countries.

A/B. National Household Survey on Drug Abuse. (U.S. Department of Health and Human Services, Public Health Service, Alcohol, Drug Abuse, and Mental Health Administration, DHHS Publication No. [ADM] 92-1887, Washington, DC, 1992.)

Statistical source material for the prevalence data in Chapter 1 and Figure 1.1.

B. *Diagnostic and Statistical Manual of Mental Disorders, Third Edition Revised (DSM-III-R).* (American Psychiatric Association, Washington, DC, 1987.) Also: *Classification of Mental and Behavioural Disorders (ICD-10): Clinical Descriptions and Diagnostic Guidelines.* (World Health Organization, Geneva, 1992.)

These two manuals contain the official diagnostic terminology and descriptions of the psychoactive substance use disorders.

PART ONE: ADDICTIVE DRUGS AND THE BRAIN

CHAPTER 2: THE BRAIN'S OWN DRUGS

For opioid peptides and morphine in the brain see readings under Chapter 10, especially the *Opioids* compendium edited by A. Herz.

A. L. A. Stevens: *Explorers of the Brain.* (Knopf, New York, 1971.)

An easy-to-read, lively account of the history of discoveries concerning the anatomy, physiology, and chemistry of the brain.

A/B. J. C. Eccles: *The Understanding of the Brain.* (McGraw-Hill, New York, 1977.)

A straightforward description and explanation of neurons, synaptic transmission, pathways, and brain function, written by one of the great modern neurophysiologists.

A. R. Restak: *The Brain.* (Bantam, New York, 1984.)

The text for a widely praised TV series, with many outstanding figures in color.

A. R. Bergland: *The Fabric of Mind.* (Viking Penguin, New York, 1985.)

Historical insights into brain research, developing the theme that the brain is a hormonal organ with many of the same hormones as found in other parts of the body.

B. A. Goldstein, Ed.: *Molecular and Cellular Aspects of the Drug Addictions.* (Springer-Verlag, New York/Berlin/Heidelberg, 1989.)

The proceedings of a 1988 symposium, this volume contains eight technical contributions presenting recent basic research findings on the neurobiology of the drug addictions.

A. K. Klivington: *The Science of Mind.* (MIT Press, Cambridge, 1989.)

An attractive book of coffee-table size, assembled with the help of a group of distinguished scientific advisors who also contribute a short special chapter here and there. The book covers the anatomy, chemistry, and function of the brain in a very up-to-date fashion.

A/B. N. R. Carlson: *Physiology of Behavior.* (Allyn and Bacon, Boston, 1991.)

A large and well-illustrated standard undergraduate textbook with very complete coverage of basic neurobiologic principles and of speech, memory, addictions, and mental disorders.

B. J. R. Cooper, F. E. Bloom, R. H. Roth: *The Biochemical Basis of Neuropharmacology*, 6th ed. (Oxford University Press, New York, 1991.)

A well-illustrated standard textbook on the chemistry of the brain, the neurotransmitters, the receptors, and the effects of psychotropic drugs.

A. *Mind and Brain*: A special issue of *Scientific American*, Vol. 267, No. 3, September 1992.

Articles bringing the reader up to date on various aspects of brain research, not specifically related to drug addictions.

CHAPTER 3: LOCKS FOR THE ADDICTIVE KEYS

For opioid receptors see Chapter 10 readings, especially the *Opioids* compendium edited by A. Herz.

B. L. Stryer: *Biochemistry*, 3d ed. (W. H. Freeman, New York, 1988.)

Beautifully presented, this is a widely used textbook of biochemistry, which covers in great detail receptors, gene action, membranes, enzymes, and other fundamental mechanisms that underlie the actions of addictive drugs.

A. H. N. Wagner, Jr.: "Sosman Lecture—Drugs, Behavior, and Brain Chemistry." (*American Journal of Roentgenology* 155: 925–931, 1990.)

An easy-to-read description of ligand PET scanning, especially of dopamine and opioid receptors in brain.

A. M. Holloway: "Rx for Addiction." (*Scientific American* 264: 94, March 1991.)

An account of the PET scanning technique applied to some addictive drugs.

B. J. Frascella, R. M. Brown, Eds.: *Neurobiological Approaches to Brain-Behavior Interaction*. (NIDA Research Monograph 124, DHHS Publication ADM92-1846, Rockville, MD, 1992.)

Technical articles with emphasis on modern techniques for studying reward pathways, self-administration, and mapping of sites in brain by PET scanning, microdialysis, and other techniques.

B. T. N. H. Lee, Ed.: *Molecular Approaches to Drug Abuse Research*, Vol. II: *Structure, Function, and Expression*. (NIDA Research Monograph 126, DHHS Publication ADM92-1846, Rockville, MD, 1992.)

Up-to-date technical articles on receptors, neurotransmitters, and regulation of systems affected by addictive drugs.

B. M. E. Linder, A. G. Gilman: "G proteins." (*Scientific American* 257: 56, July 1992.)

> A clearly written account of these important molecules, which mediate the effects of several addictive drugs.

Chapter 4: Addictive Behavior

B. R. A. Wise: "The Neurobiology of Craving—Implications for the Understanding and Treatment of Addiction. (*Journal of Abnormal Psychology* 97: 118–132, 1988.)

> Contains references to literature on the method of conditioned place preference and reviews the evidence for a dopaminergic reward system that underlies craving produced by opiates and cocaine.

A/B. R. A. Glennon, T. U. C. Jarbe, J. Frankenheim, Eds.: *Drug Discrimination—Applications to Drug Abuse Research.* (NIDA Research Monograph 116, DHHS Publication ADM92-1878, Rockville, MD, 1992.)

> These articles elaborate on the drug discrimination technique described in the text.

B. G. F. Koob: "Drugs of Abuse—Anatomy, Pharmacology and Function of Reward Pathways." (*Trends in Pharmacological Research* 13: 177–184, 1992.)

> A description of the reward systems on which addictive drugs act, with emphasis on their anatomic distribution in the brain.

Chapter 5: Pain and Pleasure

A. A. Goldstein: "Thrills in Response to Music and Other Stimuli." (*Physiological Psychology* 8: 126–129, 1980.)

> The full description of the music experiment described in the text.

A/B. B. Stimmel: *Pain, Analgesia, and Addiction—The Pharmacologic Treatment of Pain.* (Raven Press, New York, 1983.)

> Good general treatments of basic pain pathways, roles of neurotransmitters, relationship to emotions, pain-relieving actions of various drugs, and principles of pain management. Although written for clinicians, and by now somewhat out of date, some parts of this book may be of interest to the nonexpert.

B. X. H. Chen, J. S. Han: "All Three Types of Opioid Receptors in the Spinal Cord Are Important for 2/15 Hz Electroacupuncture Analgesia." (*European Journal of Pharmacology* 211: 203–210, 1992.)

A technical paper with the most recent information on the basic science of acupuncture, with references to earlier studies.

A/B. *PAIN—The Journal of the International Association for the Study of Pain.* (Published monthly by Elsevier, Amsterdam.)

Regular reviews and technical articles—some readable by the nonexpert—on the basic and clinical aspects of pain and its treatment.

CHAPTER 6: TOLERANCE AND DEPENDENCE

B. A. Goldstein, P. Sheehan: "Tolerance to Opioid Narcotics. I. Tolerance to the 'Running Fit' Caused by Levorphanol in the Mouse." (*Journal of Pharmacology and Experimental Therapeutics* 169: 175–184, 1969.)

Experiments to determine the critical interval for development of tolerance.

B. D. L. Cheney, A. Goldstein: "Tolerance to Opioid Narcotics. III. Time Course and Reversibility of Physical Dependence in Mice." (*Nature* 232: 477–478, 1971.)

An experiment to determine the critical interval for development of dependence. A partial description appears in the text.

B. S. M. Johnson, W. W. Fleming: "Mechanisms of Cellular Adaptive Sensitivity Changes—Applications to Opioid Tolerance and Dependence." (*Pharmacological Reviews* 41: 435–488, 1989.)

Difficult reading for the nonexpert, but very comprehensive, with a large number of references to earlier studies.

B. K. A. Trujillo, H. Akil: "Opiate Tolerance and Dependence—Recent Findings and Synthesis." (*New Biologist* 3: 915–923, 1991.)

A concise summary of the most recent findings pointing toward a coherent view of how brain mechanisms are altered by long-term exposure to opiates.

CHAPTER 7: ARE ADDICTS BORN OR MADE?

A/B. R. W. Pickens, D. S. Svikis, Eds.: *Biological Vulnerability to Drug Abuse.* (NIDA Research Monograph 89, DHHS Publication ADM88-1590, Rockville, MD, 1988.)

Analysis of evidence for genetic predisposition to addiction.

A/B. C. R. Cloninger, H. Begleiter, Eds.: *Genetics and Biology of Alcoholism.* (Banbury Report 33, Cold Spring Harbor Laboratory Press, 1990.)

A collection of 22 papers from a conference, including contributions by the leading investigators of genetic predisposition to alcohol addiction, with interesting discussions after each paper.

B. C. R. Cloninger: "D2 Dopamine Receptor Gene Is Associated but Not Linked with Alcoholism." (*Journal of the American Medical Association [JAMA]* 266: 1833–1834, 1991.)

A review of several attempts, with mixed success, to replicate the original finding by RFLP analysis of a gene for predisposition to alcohol addiction.

PART TWO: THE DRUGS AND THE ADDICTS

CHAPTER 8: ADDICTIVE SUICIDE NICOTINE

A. *Smoking and Health, Surgeon General's Report.* (U.S. Department of Health, Education, and Welfare, PHS Publication No. 1103, U.S. Government Printing Office, Washington, DC 20402, 1964.)

The original report documenting tobacco smoke as a health hazard. Further reports followed every few years (not listed here) on special aspects of smoking and health.

A. D. G. Zaridze, R. Peto, Eds.: *Tobacco—A Major International Health Hazard.* (International Agency for Research on Cancer, IARC Scientific Publications No. 74, Lyon, 1986.)

Worldwide epidemiology and history, with special discussion of low-tar and low-nicotine cigarettes.

A. *The Health Consequences of Smoking: Nicotine Addiction. A Report of the Surgeon General, 1988.* (U.S. Department of Health and Human Services, Rockville, MD 20857; U.S. Government Printing Office, Washington, DC 20402, 1988.)

Summary of the definitive information documenting the addictive properties of nicotine.

A. A. Goldstein: *Learn More Smoke Less.* (Published by the author, 1988. Available from New Leaf Distributing Co., 5425 Tulane Drive SW, Atlanta GA 30336-2323, 800-326-2665.)

A practical harm-reduction day-by-day guide to reducing cigarette consumption. For the intelligent, highly-motivated, hard-core nicotine addict who has quit and relapsed repeatedly, without being able to sustain abstinence.

A. J. Slade: "The Tobacco Epidemic—Lessons from History." (*Journal of Psychoactive Drugs* 21: 281–291, 1989.)

A history of the tobacco industry and of the growth of cigarette smoking in the United States and other countries.

B. J. R. Hughes: "Combined Psychological and Nicotine Gum Treatment for Smoking—A Critical Review." (*Journal of Substance Abuse* 3: 337–350, 1991.)

A technical review by a leading researcher on smoking cessation.

B. M. M. Kilbey, K. Asghar, Eds.: *Methodological Issues in Controlled Studies on Effects of Prenatal Exposure to Drug Abuse.* (NIDA Research Monograph 114, DHHS Publication ADM91-1837, Rockville, MD, 1991.)

The articles in this collection discuss the difficulties—alluded to in Chapter 8 and elsewhere—of proving conclusively that a certain drug affects human fetal development adversely.

CHAPTER 9: DRINK AND BE MERRY? ALCOHOL AND RELATED DRUGS

For genetics of alcohol addiction see also suggested readings for Chapter 7.

B. P. Kuusi: *Alcohol Sales Experiment in Rural Finland.* (The Finnish Foundation for Alcohol Studies, Helsinki, 1957.)

An unusual controlled prospective study of the effects of opening beer and wine stores in randomly chosen, previously "dry" rural areas.

A. *Alcoholics Anonymous.* (Alcoholics Anonymous World Series, Inc., New York, 1976.)

The official account of the principles and ideals on which the movement is based, with description of the first 12-step programs.

A. D. B. Goldstein: *Pharmacology of Alcohol.* (Oxford University Press, New York/Oxford, 1983.)

Although directed primarily toward health professionals and medical students, this short but comprehensive account by an alcohol researcher is not too difficult for the lay reader.

B. C. R. Cloninger, S. Sigvardsson, M. Bohman: "Childhood Personality Predicts Alcohol Abuse in Young Adults." (*Alcoholism, Clinical and Experimental Research* 12: 494-505, 1988.)

A very unusual study, in which personality traits of children were related to their drinking habits 16 years later.

B. F. E. Bloom: "Neurobiology of Alcohol Action and Alcoholism." (*Annual Review of Psychiatry* 8: 347–360, 1989.)

A technical review by one of the authors of the elementary textbook of neuropharmacology listed in readings for Chapter 2.

B. R. A. Harris, A. M. Allan: "Alcohol Intoxication—Ion Channels and Genetics." (*FASEB Journal* 3: 1689–1695, 1989.)

Molecular biology of the ion channels in the brain that are affected by alcohol.

B. N. K. Mello, J. H. Mendelson, S. K. Teoh: "Neuroendocrine Consequences of Alcohol Abuse in Women." (*Annals of the New York Academy of Sciences* 562: 211–240, 1989.

A review of the medical literature concerning disturbance of hormonal systems (especially female sex hormones) by alcohol.

A. J. M. Moskowitz: "The Primary Prevention of Alcohol Problems—A Critical Review of the Research Literature." (*Journal of Studies on Alcohol* 50: 54–88, 1989.)

A critical view of what prevention education has (and has not) accomplished, with extensive references to articles on prevention research.

A. R. Baggott: *Alcohol, Politics and Social Policy*. (Avebury, Gower Publishing Company, Aldershot, 1990.)

A detailed history and analysis of government efforts in the United Kingdom to control alcohol consumption by means of taxation policies and other legislation.

B. P. J. Little, M. L. Adams, T. J. Cicero: "Effects of Alcohol on the Hypothalamic-Pituitary-Gonadal Axis in the Developing Male Rat." (*Journal of Pharmacology and Experimental Therapeutics* 263: 1056–1061, 1992.)

A technical review of experiments in animals and humans, with information about the mechanisms whereby alcohol depresses male sex hormone levels.

B. J. R. Volpicelli et al.: "Naltrexone in the Treatment of Alcohol Dependence." (*Archives of General Psychiatry* 49: 876–880, 1992.)

A technical account of the surprising finding that this opioid antagonist is useful in treating alcohol addicts.

CHAPTER 10: ADDICTIVE TRANQUILITY THE OPIATES

A. I. Chein, D. L. Gerard, R. S. Lee, E. Rosenfeld: *The Road to H—Narcotics, Delinquency, and Social Policy*. (Basic Books, New York/London, 1964.)

A classic sociologic study of heroin addiction and heroin addicts.

A. D. F. Musto: *The American Disease—The Origins of Narcotics Control*.

(Yale University Press, New Haven, 1973.) By the same author: "Opium, Cocaine and Marijuana in American History." (*Scientific American* 265: 40, July 1991.)

> A history of societal attitudes toward the addictive drugs that are now illicit in the United States.

A. H. F. Judson: *Heroin Addiction in Britain—What Americans Can Learn from the English Experience.* (Harcourt Brace Jovanovich, New York and London, 1974.)

> A readable account of the "British system" in its early phases, when heroin addiction seemed still to be under control.

B. R. E. Meyer, S. M. Mirin: *The Heroin Stimulus—Implications for a Theory of Addiction.* (Plenum Medical Book Co., New York/London, 1979.)

> Contains reports of controlled experiments with volunteers in a closed ward that were devoted to studying the behavioral effects of heroin in humans.

A. V. P. Dole: "Addictive Behavior." (*Scientific American* 243: 138–140, 142, 144, December 1980.) Also: "Implications of Methadone Maintenance for Theories of Narcotic Addiction." (*Journal of the American Medical Association* 260: 3025–3029, 1988.)

> Explanations and speculations by the inventor of methadone maintenance.

A. D. Latimer, J. Goldberg: *Flowers in the Blood—The Story of Opium.* (Franklin Watts, New York, 1981.)

> A delightful and thorough history of the opiates.

A. J. Kaplan: *The Hardest Drug—Heroin and Public Policy.* (University of Chicago Press, Chicago/London, 1983.)

> Analysis of the heroin problem in the United States by a well-known legal scholar.

A. J. Davis: *Endorphins—New Waves in Brain Chemistry.* (Dial Press/ Doubleday, Garden City, NY, 1984.)

> A popularized account of the discoveries of the past 15 years, enlivened by accounts of the personal lives and working habits of some of the scientists.

A. J. Goldberg: *Anatomy of a Scientific Discovery.* (Bantam, New York, 1988.)

> A popularized account of the discovery of endogenous opioid peptides.

B. J. E. Zweben, J. T. Payte, Eds.: "Opioid Dependence and Methadone Maintenance Treatment." (*Journal of Psychoactive Drugs* 23, No. 2, 1991.)

A collection of articles updating the status of methadone maintenance. It includes reprints of two classic articles from 1966 and 1973.

B. A. Herz, Ed.: *Opioids I and II.* (*Handbook of Experimental Pharmacology*, Vol. 104 I/II, Springer-Verlag, Berlin/Heidelberg/New York, 1993.)

A definitive and detailed technical account of the biology, chemistry, and behavioral aspects of the opioids. Nearly 1,700 pages in all, these two volumes will be the definitive source of information about opioids for years to come.

CHAPTER 11: THE WILD ADDICTIONS COCAINE AND AMPHETAMINES

A. C. Van Dyke, R. Byck: "Cocaine." (*Scientific American* 246: 128–141, March 1982.)

A history and pharmacology of coca and cocaine. Out-of-date biochemistry but interesting history. As the article was written early in the current epidemic of cocaine use, the authors tend to underrate the health hazards and addictiveness of this drug.

A. A. M. Washton, M. S. Gold, Eds.: *Cocaine—A Clinician's Handbook.* (Guilford Press, New York, 1987.)

A multi-author text covering the basic biomedical aspects of cocaine addiction treatment, and miscellaneous topics such as testing and effects on pregnancy.

A. G. Nahas: *Cocaine—The Great White Plague.* (Paul S. Eriksson, Middlebury VT, 1989.)

A history of cocaine addiction, enlivened by personal accounts of this pharmacologist-physician's observations. The author's extreme antipathy toward the use of all the illicit psychoactive drugs is expressed throughout this book.

B. F. H. Gawin: "Cocaine Addiction—Psychology and Neurophysiology." (*Science* 251: 1580–1586, 1991.)

A technical review of the behavioral short-term and long-term effects and toxicity of cocaine.

B. S. Schober, C. Schade, Eds.: *The Epidemiology of Cocaine Use and Abuse.* (NIDA Research Monograph 110, DHHS Publication ADM-91-1787, Rockville, MD, 1991.)

A collection of technical papers with graphs and tables.

A. P. Kalix: "Chewing Khat, an Old Drug Habit that Is New in Europe." (*International Journal of Risk and Safety in Medicine* 3: 143–156, 1992.)

A fascinating account of Nature's own amphetamine and the ancient custom of chewing the leaves to obtain the stimulant effect.

B. W. L. Woolverton: "Cocaine Self-Administration—Pharmacology and Behavior." (*In* NIDA Research Monograph 124, DHHS Publication ADM92-1846, Rockville, MD, 1992.)

A summary of recent and previous animal studies.

B. *Cocaine—Scientific and Social Dimensions.* (Ciba Foundation Symposium 166, John Wiley & Sons, New York, 1992.)

A timely collection of presentations, with lively discussion.

CHAPTER 12: HIGHS AND LOWS OF GETTING STONED Cannabis

A. G. Le Dain et al.: *Cannabis—A Report of the Commission of Inquiry into the Non-Medical Use of Drugs.* (Information Canada, Ottawa, 1972.)

The widely quoted Canadian government examination of the problems associated with marijuana and hashish, and what to do about them. The commission's report led to changes in Canadian government policy, and the arguments for and against various recommendations make interesting reading even 20 years later.

A. *Marijuana and Health.* (Institute of Medicine, National Academy Press, 1982.)

Concise summaries of marijuana's effects on the various organ systems, with focus on the many gaps in our knowledge that call for further research. Contains a strong recommendation for increased federal research funding to a level commensurate with the widespread use of cannabis.

B. L. E. Hollister: "Cannabis—1988." (*Acta Psychiatrica Scandinavica*, Supplement 345: 108–118, 1988.)

A review of the basic and clinical pharmacology by a leading clinical investigator of the addictive drugs.

A. J. C. Negrete: "What's Happened to the Cannabis Debate?" (*British Journal of Addiction* 83: 359–372, 1988.)

This article notes the declining interest in marijuana research in recent years—a reflection of diminished public concern about this drug—and warns about the dangers of this trend.

A. M. S. Gold: *Marijuana.* (Plenum, New York, 1989.)

History, pharmacology, psychiatric complications, treatment. Contains a useful section with questions and answers on topics of general interest to the public.

A. M. A. R. Kleiman: *Marijuana—Costs of Abuse, Costs of Control.* (Greenwood Press, New York, 1989.)

> An interesting and well-balanced discussion of the effects of enforcement on supply and demand and on criminality, with policy recommendations reminiscent of the Dutch policies described in Chapter 17.

A. E. W. Single: "The Impact of Marijuana Decriminalization—An Update." (*Journal of Public Health Policy* 10: 456–466, 1989.)

> An examination of the effects of decriminalizing cannabis use in various U.S. states during the 1970s, with emphasis on the few controlled studies that were carried out at the time.

A. T. M. Beardsley: "Cannabis Comprehended—The 'Assassin of Youth' Points to a New Pharmacology." (*Scientific American* 263: 38, October 1990.)

> Modern developments in basic biomedical research on cannabis.

B. M. Herkenham et al.: "Cannabinoid Receptor Localization in Brain." (*Proceedings of the National Academy of Sciences USA* 87: 1932–1936, 1990.)

> Specific sites in the brain that bind a radiolabeled cannabinoid ligand.

B. R. Seth, S. Sinha: "Chemistry and Pharmacology of Cannabis." (*Progress in Drug Research* 36: 71–115, 1991.)

> A comprehensive technical review.

B. W. A. Devane et al.: "Isolation and Structure of a Brain Constituent that Binds to the Cannabinoid Receptor." (*Science* 258: 1946–1949, 1992.)

> Technical evidence that a natural brain lipid may be the endogenous ligand of the same receptor that responds to THC, the active principle of marijuana and hashish.

CHAPTER 13: THE GENTLE STIMULANT CAFFEINE

A. H. E. Jacob: *Coffee—The Epic of a Commodity.* (Viking Press, New York, 1935.)

> Although somewhat fictionalized to capture reader interest, this book is a thorough history of coffee, coffee houses, and coffee plantations, with emphasis on the economics of the international coffee trade.

A. A. Ellis: *The Penny Universities—A History of the Coffee-Houses.* (Secker & Warburg, London, 1956.)

> A scholarly treatise describing the coffee-house phenomenon in England in the seventeenth and eighteenth centuries.

A. R. S. Hattox: *Coffee and Coffeehouses—The Origins of a Social Beverage in the Medieval Near East.* (University of Washington Press, Seattle, 1985.)

A lively scholarly account of the origins of coffee in Ethiopia and Yemen, and its sixteenth-century spread through the institution of coffee houses in Cairo, Damascus, and Constantinople.

B. N. L. Benowitz: "Clinical Pharmacology of Caffeine." (*Annual Review of Medicine* 41: 277–288, 1990.)

A brief but thorough review of recent research on the health effects and addictive potential of this most widely used drug.

B. B. Stavric: "An Update on Research with Coffee/Caffeine." (*Food and Chemical Toxicology* 30: 533–555, 1992.)

A summary of very recent studies on the possible adverse effects of coffee drinking on health.

CHAPTER 14: CHEMICAL FANTASIES THE HALLUCINOGENS

A. R. E. Schultes, A. Hofmann: *Plants of the Gods.* (McGraw-Hill, New York, 1979.)

Co-authored by a leading botanist and the psychopharmacologist who discovered LSD, this book is lavishly illustrated with photos and sketches of the hallucinogenic plants and of the circumstances in which they are used in native religious rituals.

A. R. G. Wasson: *The Wondrous Mushroom: Mycolatry in Mesoamerica.* (McGraw-Hill, New York, 1980.)

A fascinating account of the history and religious use of hallucinogenic mushrooms in indigenous societies of Central America by the leading researcher of this topic.

A. M. D. de Rios: *Hallucinogens—Cross-Cultural Perspectives.* (University of New Mexico Press, Albuquerque, 1984.)

A study of 11 cultures worldwide—from Australia to Siberia, from Peru to Equatorial Africa—in which hallucinogens are used in religious rituals under the guidance of shamans.

A/B. D. F. Aberle: *The Peyote Religion Among the Navaho*, 2nd ed. (University of Oklahoma Press, Norman, OK, 1990.)

A scholarly text by a leading anthropologist, with descriptions and photographs of the peyote ceremonies, as well as a historical perspective on the role of the peyote cult in Navaho society.

B. M. E. Carroll: "PCP and Hallucinogens." (*Advances in Alcohol and Substance Abuse* 9: 167–190, 1990.)

> A review of research on the pharmacology, epidemiology, and addictive potential of the hallucinogens as a group, with emphasis on PCP.

A/B. E. J. M. Langdon, G. Baer: *Portals of Power—Shamanism in South America.* (University of New Mexico Press, Albuquerque, 1992.)

> A collection of scholarly accounts of the religious use of various hallucinogens in several indigenous cultures.

Part Three: Drugs and Society

Chapter 15: Just Say No?

B. J. Stewart, H. de Wit, R. Eikelboom: "Role of Unconditioned and Conditioned Drug Effects in the Self-Administration of Opiates and Stimulants." (*Psychological Review* 91: 251–268, 1984.)

> A technical review summarizing the evidence for the "priming effect" and for the role of conditioned stimuli in initiating relapse to drug use in experimental animals and ex-addicts.

A. *Understanding Drug Treatment.* (An Office of National Drug Control Policy White Paper, U.S. Government Printing Office, Washington, DC 20402, 1990.)

> A useful overview, which stresses the importance of research to establish what treatments are effective.

A. L. D. Johnston, P. M. O'Malley, J. G. Bachman: *Smoking, Drinking, and Illicit Drug Use among American Secondary Students, College Students, and Young Adults, 1975–1991,* Vols. I and II. (National Institute on Drug Abuse, Publication No. 93-3480, Washington, DC, 1992.)

> Statistical source material for the drug use data in Figures 15.1 and 15.2.

B. C. G. Leukefeld, W. J. Bukoski, Eds.: *Drug Abuse Prevention Intervention Research—Methodological Issues.* (NIDA Research Monograph 107, DHHS Publication ADM-91-1761, Rockville, MD, 1991.)

> Analysis of methods of conducting prospective controlled studies in the schools, expanding on the material presented in the text, including the Kansas City experiment.

Chapter 16: Lessons from the Street

B. M. D. Anglin, Y. I. Hser: "Treatment of Drug Abuse." (*In* M. Tonry, J.

Q. Wilson, Eds.: *Drugs and Crime*, pp. 393–460, University of Chicago Press, Chicago, 1990.)

> Analysis of the effects of voluntary and compulsory treatment on criminal activity by addicts.

B. C. G. Leukefeld, R. J. Battjes, Z. Amsel, Eds.: *AIDS and Intravenous Drug Use—Future Directions for Community-Based Prevention Research.* (NIDA Research Monograph 93, DHHS Publication ADM-90-1627, Rockville, MD, 1990.)

> Some estimates of the extent of further HIV transmission to be expected among intravenous drug users, and research on possible methods of stopping the spread.

A. *America—Living With AIDS.* (Report of the National Commission on AIDS, U.S. Government Printing Office, Washington, DC 20402, 1991.)

> Analysis and recommendations, including removal of legal barriers to purchase and possession of injection equipment, expanded access to health care, and aggressive development of new therapies.

CHAPTER 17: LESSONS FROM ABROAD

A. A. Goldstein: "Heroin Addiction—Sequential Treatment Employing Pharmacologic Supports." (*Archives of General Psychiatry* 33: 353, 1976.)

> A proposal by the author to bring heroin addicts into treatment by offering sterile pure heroin injections in a clinic, followed by obligatory progression to surrogate opiates, then to antagonists and eventually to a drug-free state.

B. *Single Convention on Narcotic Drugs, 1961, as Amended by the 1972 Protocol.* (United Nations, New York, 1977.)

> Text of the international agreement covering opiates, coca, and cannabis.

A. E. Single, P. Morgan, J. de Lint, Eds.: *Alcohol, Society, and the State.* (Addiction Research Foundation, Toronto, 1981.)

> Includes a historical survey of drug control policies (primarily alcohol) in several countries, with analysis of consequences.

A. G. Edwards: "What Drives British Drug Policies?" (*British Journal of Addiction* 84: 219–226, 1989.)

> An overview of historical developments that led to the present British policies on addictive drugs, by the "guru" of drug addiction research and policy in Britain.

A. G. F. van de Wijngaart: "The Dutch Approach—Normalization of Drug Problems." (*Journal of Drug Issues* 20: 667–678, 1990.)

A clear exposition of the similarities and differences between drug policies in the Netherlands and in other countries, by a leading participant in their development.

A. *UK Action on Drug Misuse—The Government's Strategy.* (Home Office, UK, Central Office of Information, London, 1990.)

A summary of activities of the British government in relation to addictive drugs. Contains a list of 18 agencies, including the Standing Conference on Drug Abuse (SCODA, 1-4 Hatton Place, Hatton Garden, London EC1N 8ND), which is the national coordinating body for nongovernmental agencies in the field of drug abuse. Statistical bulletins may be obtained from Statistical Department, Home Office, Lunar House, Croydon, Surrey CR0 9YD.

Chapter 18: THE LEGALIZATION DEBATE

A. A. Goldstein: "Heroin Maintenance—A Medical View. A Conversation Between a Physician and a Politician." (*Journal of Drug Issues* 9: 341–347, 1979.)

A response to proposals made about 25 years ago that heroin should be legalized to solve the heroin addiction problem at that time. Of historical interest, reflecting how little the problems or the proposed solutions have changed over the years.

A. D. T. Courtwright: "Charles Terry, the Opium Problem, and American Narcotic Policy." (*Journal of Drug Issues* 16: 421–434, 1986.)

A historian looks at the development of attitudes and policies toward narcotics in the early years of the twentieth century.

A. L. Cockburn: *Out of Control—The Story of the Reagan Administration's Secret War in Nicaragua, the Illegal Arms Pipeline, and the Contra Drug Connection.* (Atlantic Monthly Press, New York, 1987.)

A well-documented account of how U.S. foreign policy affected the drug trade. Further revelations are found in the Kerry Committee Report, immediately below.

A. Senate Committee on Foreign Relations, Subcommittee on Terrorism, Narcotics and International Operations: *Drugs, Law Enforcement and Foreign Policy* (Kerry Committee Report, U.S. Government Printing Office, Washington, DC 20402, 1989.)

An official report on how some aspects of U.S. foreign policy resulted in increased importation of illicit addictive drugs.

A. M. B. Krauss, E. P. Lazear, Eds.: *Searching for Alternatives—Drug-Con-*

trol Policy in the United States. (Hoover Institution Press, Stanford, CA 94305, 1991.)

> Multi-author proceedings of a conference held in 1990, with emphasis on policy issues and good representation of the various positions in the legalization debate. Note especially the contributions of E. L. Engelsman and D. Turner on Dutch and British drug policies, respectively.

A. A. W. McCoy: *The Politics of Heroin—CIA Complicity in the Global Drug Trade*. (Lawrence Hill Books, Brooklyn, NY, 1991.)

> A revised and updated version of his classic, *The Politics of Heroin in Southeast Asia* (1972), documenting the role of U.S. foreign policy in the illicit drug traffic during the Cold War. Includes references to findings of Senator John Kerry's subcommittee in the 1980s.

A. E. A. Nadelmann: "Thinking Seriously about Alternatives to Drug Prohibition." (*Daedalus* 121: 85–132, 1992.) Also: "Drug Prohibition in the United States—Costs, Consequences, and Alternatives." (*Science* 245: 939–946, 1989.)

> Arguments by a political scientist who is a leading advocate of legalizing the presently illicit drugs.

CHAPTER 19: NEW STRATEGIES FOR THE WAR ON DRUGS

A. G. Le Dain et al.: *Final Report of the Commission of Inquiry into the Non-Medical Use of Drugs*. (Information Canada, Ottawa, 1973.)

> An exhaustive compilation (1,148 pages) of research summaries and policy recommendations for Canada, relevant also for the United States. A separate report devoted exclusively to cannabis is listed above under readings for Chapter 12.

A. A. Goldstein, H. Kalant: "Drug Policy—Striking the Right Balance." (*Science* 249: 1513–1521, 1990.)

> A detailed analysis of policy issues and a more comprehensive version of much of the material covered in this chapter.

A. *National Drug Control Strategy—A Nation Responds to Drug Use*. (The White House, U.S. Government Printing Office, Washington, DC 20402, 1992.)

> The official program of the U.S. "war on drugs" under the Bush administration.

A. *Drug Abuse Research—Federal Funding and Future Needs*. (United States General Accounting Office, GAO/PEMD-92-5, 1992.)

A report to the Chairman, Committee on Government Operations, House of Representatives, analyzing the federal investment in research on causes, prevention, and treatment of drug abuse.

A. M. Falco: *The Making of a Drug-Free America—Programs That Work.* (Random House, New York, 1993.)

A recipe for new drug policies, much along the lines laid out in this book, placing emphasis on reducing demand by expanding prevention and treatment programs. The author analyses the features of programs she judges to be effective.

A. M. A. R. Kleiman: *Against Excess—Drug Policy for Results.* (Basic Books, New York, 1993.)

At the present writing, this book was not yet available for review. However, the author's reputation and previous writings suggest it will contain well-considered proposals for changes in our drug policies.

Index

Boldface page number indicates location of definition for indexed term.